HARDPRESS.NET
HOME OF HARD-TO-FIND BOOKS

The Poetical Works of Horace Smith and James Smith ...

by Horace Smith

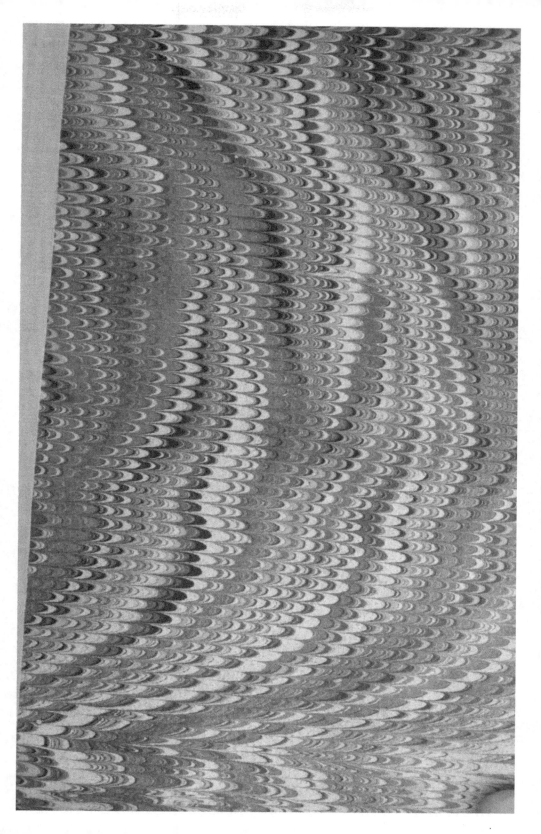

Horatio Smith.   James Smith

THE

POETICAL WORKS

OF

HORACE SMITH AND JAMES SMITH,

AUTHORS OF THE "REJECTED ADDRESSES."

WITH

PORTRAITS AND A BIOGRAPHICAL SKETCH.

EDITED BY

EPES SARGENT.

NEW YORK:
MASON BROTHERS,
108 & 110 DUANE STREET.
1857.

LECTROTYPED BY
THOMAS B. SMITH,
82 & 84 Beekman St.

PRINTED BY
C. A. ALVORD,
15 Vandewater-St. N. Y.

PREFACE.

THE present is the first American edition of the collected poems of HORACE SMITH. Many of them have been printed in our newspapers and magazines, and not a few are favorites familiar to all true lovers of poetry. No one can read them without admitting the just claim of their author to a high place among the sons of song. His humorous pieces, too, are neat and lively versifications of anecdotes that usually carry with them a point if not a moral.

While as a poet HORACE SMITH was incomparably superior to his brother, the latter, in his *vers de societé*, may claim perhaps equal merit. SPENCER and PRAED were not more felicitous in their poetry of fashion than JAMES SMITH. The topics show the man and his associations, and his poems are so many finished daguerreotypes of London society in the first half of the nineteenth century. In this light they will always be interesting and amusing—and may be admitted into collections of British poetry, from which similar sketches by Swift and Prior, of a grosser period, ought to be excluded. It is no small virtue of the popular writers whose poems are contained in our present volume, that, though wits and satirists, they are always gentlemen.

It is to the *Rejected Addresses* that these ingenious brothers are mainly indebted for their celebrity ; and this work still retains its popularity undiminished. It is admitted to be in all respects *unique*, and perfect after its fashion.   Indeed, it well deserves the high praise bestowed on it by the most fastidious, if not the most able critic of his day— the critic who had sat in judgment on nearly all the authors imitated in this remarkable volume.   The literary world had never before witnessed such an exhibition of the peculiar talent, which could be paralleled only by the marvellous execution of the mocking-bird.   Our reprint of this work is from the twenty-third London edition, and the notes inclosed in brackets are from the pen, we believe, of Mr. Peter Cunningham.

The prefatory memoir is compiled from a variety of sources, and claims no credit beyond that of judicious condensation and arrangement of materials.   For so much of it as relates to JAMES SMITH we have relied generally upon the biographical sketch prefixed to his collected miscellanies.   A series of papers in the *New Monthly Magazine* have also been freely used without special acknowledgment.   They are entitled *A Greybeard's Gossip*, and are reminiscences of his literary contemporaries, by HORACE SMITH.   Other sources of information are mentioned in the text.

TABLE OF CONTENTS.

Poems by Horace Smith.

MISCELLANEOUS.

CONTENTS.

HUMOROUS.

Poems by James Smith.

LONDON LYRICS.

MISCELLANEOUS.

Rejected Addresses.

BIOGRAPHICAL MEMOIR.

THE subjects of the following Memoir were the sons of Robert Smith, an eminent legal practitioner of London, who held for many years the office of Solicitor to the Ordnance. JAMES SMITH was born on the 10th of February, 1775; and HORACE SMITH on the 31st of December, 1779. The elder son was educated by the Reverend Mr. Burford at Chigwell, in Essex, was articled to his father on leaving school, and finally succeeded to his professional business and his appointment of Solicitor to the Ordnance. Horace received the same education as his brother, became a member of the Stock Exchange in London, acquired a fortune, and retired with his family to Brighton. For nearly half a century they were both distinguished in London society for their social accomplishments, and their clever contributions to the literature of the period.

Horace Smith entered active life as a clerk in a merchant's counting-house, where he was more attentive to light literature and the drama than to bills of exchange, invoices, and charter-parties. His first literary effort was a short poem lamenting the decay of public taste in theatrical exhibitions, and the encouragement given to dumb shows, to the neglect of such sterling productions as the *West-Indian* and *The Jew;* to the author of which comedies he dedicated his effusion, and forwarded it to him by the post, with his own name and address. The communication brought to the counting-house an old gentleman of distinguished appearance, whose large and profusely powdered head was flanked with cannon curls, and endorsed with a substantial pig-tail; his corbeau-colored suit was of antique cut, and he bore a golden-headed cane. This apparition inquired for Mr. Smith. "We have two of that name," replied the nearest clerk, "which of them do you want?" "I want Mr. Smith, *the poet.*" The clerk was astounded at such a demand, and the grave master petulantly exclaimed, "We have no *poet* here, sir"—and resumed his writing. The poor culprit, unable to deny his identity, jumped from his tall stool, and hurried into the ante-room the unwelcome visitor, who announced himself as Mr. Cumberland.

Such was the introduction of Horace Smith to the celebrated dramatist. It led to an acquaintance and intimacy with the two brothers. The first literary work in which the young poets assisted with their veteran friend, was the *Pic Nic* newspaper, established in 1802 by Colonel Greville, for the double purpose of vindicating certain amateur theatricals which he had given in conjunction with M. Texier, and of checking the scandalous personalities with which some of the newspapers were assailing the aristocracy. The other principal contributors were Sir James Bland Burgess, Monsieur Peltier, Mr. Croker, Mr. J. C. Herries, Mr. Bedford, and Mr. Combe; all of them writing gratuitously except the last-named gentleman, who was the editor, and who had long been living in the rules of the King's Bench. Of the party thus engaged in the conduct of an obscure and short-lived periodical, several became afterwards eminent. Herries, then a clerk in the Treasury, rose to be Chancellor of the Exchequer. Mr. Croker, after attaining the important post of Secretary of the Admiralty, was a clever contributor to the *Quarterly Review*. Peltier was made notorious by his trial for a libel on the First Consul Bonaparte, in which Mackintosh gained his early forensic laurels.

Colonel Greville was a gay and fashionable man, a modification of Sir Harry Wildair, and it may well be supposed that the *Pic Nic*, with gratuitous contributors, and an editor within the rules, struggled with a sickly and precarious existence. So the colonel dismissed the whole corps editorial at one of their weekly meetings, with the announcement that he had engaged a young Irishman of surpassing talent, who would undertake for a sum equal to Combe's *honorarium*, to get up and edit the whole paper. Saying this, he left the room, and returned with Mr. John Wilson Croker, who, being thus "trotted out," was bent upon showing his paces to the best advantage. His conversational powers were even then of a very high order, and he exhibited them with all the ardor and copiousness of an aspiring Hibernian. Cumberland, buttoning up his coat, preserved a sullen silence until he had left the room. "Well," said Greville, "what do you think of my new friend? He talks a good deal, I must confess, but he talks well." "*Half* of that is true," replied the dramatist, and departed in dudgeon.

The young Irishman did not revive the *Pic Nic*, and it was soon merged in the *Cabinet*, to which Rogers and Sir Thomas Lawrence were occasional contributors, with the old corps of the *Pic Nic* reinstated. But the *Cabinet* disappeared in 1803, and in 1809 was published the first number of the *London Review*, "conducted by Richard Cumberland." In this work the names of the authors were prefixed to their articles, a novelty that did not take with the public. The brothers Smith lent their aid to their friend, but his journal survived only to the second number.

At the instance of its projector, they also wrote several of the prefaces to a new edition of *Bell's British Theatre*, published about this time under the sanction of Mr. Cumberland's name. The distinguished editor, who honoured both parties with his friendship, was pleased in having them for his coadjutors; and they were naturally flattered in being thought worthy of his preference.

Mr. Cumberland died in 1811, and when Horace Smith last saw him he was much altered and attenuated, his white hair hanging over his ears in thin flakes, his figure stooping, his countenance haggard. It was during the early period of his acquaintance with Cumberland that Horace first tried his hand at a romance, producing one, according to the taste of the times, full of monks, monsters, trap-doors, and spectres. This he submitted to his friend, and it was returned with an unfavourable verdict. The author immediately burned it. "You showed talent, my dear boy," said the dramatist, "in writing that work, but you have evinced much more in committing it to the flames."

From the year 1807 to 1810, James Smith was a constant contributor to the *Monthly Mirror*, then the property of Thomas Hill, Esq., at whose cottage, at Sydenham, himself and his brother were frequent guests. This was a favourite resort of the poets, wits, artists, and actors of the time; and their merry-makings brought together many whose names will live long in the literature of England. A *symposium* at Hill's was quite as memorable an affair as a breakfast at Rogers's, though an entirely different style of entertainment.

At the Sydenham gatherings the brothers Smith used to recite a dialogue written by themselves, a farrago of nonsense, abounding in solecisms and absurdities, yet so far approximating to a sensible discourse as to mislead a careless or obtuse listener. As it was gravely delivered, the interlocutors appeared to be deeply interested, and at times excited; and as "true no-meaning puzzles more than wit," it became difficult to discover that the whole was a piece of solemn Tom-foolery. Hill's habitual guests were too sharp-witted to be themselves entrapped, but the hoax was reserved for the embarrassment or amusement of the occasional visitors.

In the *Monthly Mirror* originally appeared the poetical imitations entitled *Horace in London*, which were subsequently published in a single volume by Mr. Miller, who purchased half the copyright of the *Rejected Addresses*. Both brothers contributed to those parodies of the Roman bard; but the larger portion, distinguished by the letter J., was from the pen of James. Possessing but a fugitive interest, though sometimes the Latin text was ingeniously adapted to the characters and occurrences of the passing hour, these papers, in their collected form, had but a limited sale. They were re-published in this country on their original appearance, but the allusions in them have become obscure, and their merit would hardly justify their reproduction with the notes necessary to make them generally understood.

Most of the particulars connected with the first appearance of the *Rejected Addresses* will be found in the preface to the eighteenth edition. This little volume appeared on the re-opening of the Drury Lane Theatre, in October, 1812, the idea having been casually started by Mr. Ward, secretary to the theatre, exactly six weeks before the first night of performance. Eagerly adopting the suggestion, James and his brother lost not a moment in carrying it into execution. It was arranged what authors they should respectively imitate. Horace left London on a visit to Cheltenham, executed his portion of the task, and returned to town a few days before the opening, when each submitted his papers to the other, for any omissions or improvements that might appear requisite. These, however, seldom exceeded verbal alterations, or the addition of a few lines. James furnished the imitations of Wordsworth, Southey, Coleridge, Crabbe, Cobbett, and numbers 14, 16, 18, 19, and 20. He supplied also the first stanza to No. 4, *Cui Bono?* *By Lord B.* Of all the rest of the original work Horace was the author. Of the eighteenth edition (Murray's) James wrote the notes, and his brother the preface. The copyright, which had been originally offered to Mr. Murray for twenty pounds, was purchased by that gentleman, in 1819, after the sixteenth edition, for £131. Several editions have been since published in England and the United States. Its success has induced numerous imitations on both sides of the water—which only serve to show the great difficulty of the work of the brothers Smith, and the rareness of the peculiar talent necessary to its accomplishment.

Soon after the appearance of the *Rejected Addresses*, the authors were invited to meet a large dinner-party at the house of Sir Humphrey and Lady Davy. During a momentary silence, a deaf old lady who had not caught the names, or did not recognize *the* Smiths among their numerous family, called out to the hostess from the further end of the table, "Lady Davy! I'm told the writers of the *Rejected Addresses* have brought out a new work called *Horace in London*, which is uncommonly stupid."

The company immediately began to talk very loudly and merrily to drown this ill-timed sally, while the hostess leaned forward to James Smith, and exclaimed, "Poor old lady! I hope you'll excuse her. I have no doubt she was told that the work in question was uncommonly *clever*, not stupid. But her ears are always playing at cross purposes." "Yes, yes, I understand it all," was the reply. "She hears upon the same principle as the Irish echo, which, if you shout 'How d'ye do, Pat?' replies 'Indeed, I'm mighty bad.' And so is our *Horace in London,*—mighty bad indeed. Your friend's informant was quite correct in saying it is uncommonly stupid; but there's nothing new in the remark, for we ourselves have always maintained the same opinion, and I'm glad to find we have got the public with us."

When Anstey, author of the *New Bath Guide*, was presented to Bishop Warburton, the veteran said, "Young man, I will give you a piece of advice: you have written a highly successful work;—never put pen to paper again." James Smith used to cite this authority for the resolution to which he inflexibly adhered, not to compromise the reputation he had acquired by any future, less successful undertaking.

He wrote anonymously, as an amusement and relief—and

scattered about his *vers de societé* in manuscript and in the magazines, but having won a welcome wherever he went, and a desirable position in society as a man of talent and wit, he wanted all motive for more serious exertion.

James Smith's contributions to Mr. Mathews's Entertainments were thrown off with marvellous facility. " Smith is the only man," Mathews used to say, " who can write clever nonsense," —and of all humourists of his time Mathews was the best calculated to give full effect to it; though his powers, when the occasion required it, could take a much higher range. They have received a worthy tribute in the beautiful poem by which Horace Smith has honoured the memory of his friend. The combined humour of Mathews and James Smith was first displayed in the *Country Cousins*, which appeared in 1820, at the English Opera, and for many nights convulsed the town with laughter.

In the two succeeding years, and with the same prosperous result, the *Trip to France*, and the *Trip to America*, were produced.

For these latter works Mr. Mathews paid him a thousand pounds—a sum to which the receiver seldom made allusion without shrugging his shoulders, and ejaculating, " A thousand pounds for nonsense!" At other times he would contrast this large amount with the miserable fifteen pounds given to Milton for his *Paradise Lost;* reconciling himself, however, to the disproportion by quoting from the well-known couplet, that the real value of a thing " is as much money as 'twill bring;"—and adding, that his scrimble-scramble stuff always filled the theatre, and replenished the treasury.

At a later period he was still better paid for a more trifling exertion of his muse; for having met at a dinner-party the late Mr. Strahan, the King's printer, then suffering from gout and old age, though his intellectual faculties remained unimpaired, he sent him next morning the following *jeu d' esprit :—*

" Your lower limbs seem'd far from stout,
When last I saw you walk :
The cause I presently found out,
When you began to talk.

" The power that props the body's length
In due proportion spread,
In you mounts upwards, and the strength
All settles in the head."

This compliment proved so highly acceptable to the old gentleman, that he made an immediate codicil to his will, by which he bequeathed to the writer the sum of three hundred pounds!

As one of his earliest recollections, James Smith would relate that he had once been patted on the head by Lord Mansfield, as he stopped for a minute to converse with the narrator's father in Highgate church-yard. The imposition of this judicial hand, however, did not inspire him with any ardent love of the profession for which he was destined. The passion, which in him mastered all others, was a fervent devotion to the drama. For many years he was never absent from either of the principal theatres on the first performance of a new piece; and during the greater portion of his life his favourite lounge was in the boxes or the green-room, where, above all places, his appearance, manners, and wit, secured him a welcome and flattering reception.

Though James Smith only amused himself with letters, and threw off his "copies of verses" with great facility, for his lady friends, the Lyrics and Miscellaneous Poems that he permitted to be printed, almost merit the praise bestowed on them by a naturally partial critic. "His poetry," says his brother Horace, "in which the sportive sallies of his fancy and the corruscations of his wit seem to find a more congenial element for their display, is ever terse, buoyant, racy, and delightful. Modulated by a fine, almost a fastidious ear, you seldom meet an inharmonious line, a forced inversion, or an inaccurate rhyme; a merit the more difficult of attainment, because his proneness to antithesis, brevity, and epigram, led him to sharpen almost every stanza into a point.

"In double rhymes, the paucity of which in our language presents an almost insurmountable barrier to their extensive use, he took such especial delight, that it may be questioned whether any writer can compete with him in the frequency and the happiness of their introduction. His facility, however, did not betray him into slovenliness; his 'easy writing' was never 'hard reading;' and if—because his works are not more bulky—he is finally to be enrolled among the 'mob of gentlemen,' who gleam

"'Like twinkling stars the miscellanies o'er,'

he will undoubtedly shine with no inferior or unconspicuous light in that poetical galaxy."

But James Smith owed his social position to other than his literary claims. He possessed fine colloquial powers, was always genial and good-natured, set off his great personal attractions by scrupulous attention to dress, and was in all respects a thorough gentleman. "It was difficult," wrote one who was intimately acquainted with him in his latter years, " to pass an evening in his company without feeling in better humour with the world; such was the influence of his inexhaustible fund of amusement and information, his lightness, liveliness, and good sense. No man ever excelled him in starting a pleasant topic of conversation, and sustaining it; nor was it well possible for a party of moderate dimensions, when he was of it, to be dull. The droll anecdote, the apt illustration, the shrewd remark, a trait of humour from Fielding, a scrap of a song from the Beggar's Opera, a knock-down retort of Johnson's, a couplet from Pope or Dryden,—all seemed to come as they were wanted; and as he was always just as ready to listen as to talk, they acted, each in turn, as a sort of challenge to the company to bring forth their budgets, and contribute towards the feast. As he disliked argument, and never lost his temper, or willingly gave offence, it would have been no easy matter for others to lose theirs, or to offend him."

In the wide circle of his London acquaintance, one of the houses at which he most delighted to visit was that of Lady Blessington, whose conversational powers he highly admired, and to whose *Book of Beauty* he became a contributor. To this lady he was in the habit of sending occasional epigrams, and complimentary or punning notes.

When not otherwise engaged, he would take his plain dinner at the Athenæum, the Union, or the Garrick Club, always restricting himself to a half-pint of sherry, from the fear of his old enemy the gout. The late Sir William Aylett, a grumbling member of the Union, and a two-bottle man, observing him to be thus frugally furnished, eyed his cruet with contempt, and exclaimed, "So, I see *you* have got one of these cursed life-preservers."

Although few persons had been more constantly exposed to the temptation of convivial parties, James Smith, at every period, was a strictly temperate man; an abstemiousness which could not, however, ward off the attacks of gout. These began to assail him in middle life, increasing in their frequency and severity, until, gradually losing the use and very form of his limbs, he sank at times into a state of utter and helpless decrepitude, which he bore with an undeviating and unexampled patience.

His last illness was not of long continuance nor was it attended with suffering, either mental or corporeal. To death itself he had ever expressed a perfect indifference, though he was anxious to be spared a painful or protracted exit; a wish in which he was fortunately gratified. He died in his house in Craven-street, on the 24th December, 1839, in the sixty-fifth year of his age, and was buried under the vaults of St. Martin's church.

Allusion has been made in this memoir to Tom Hill's cottage at Sydenham, and the guests who visited there. It is famous in the kind report of many men of note. It was much frequented by Campbell during his residence at Sydenham, and it was there that the Smiths habitually met Mathews and sometimes his fellow-comedian Liston; Theodore Hook; Edward Dubois, afterwards author of *My Pocket Book*, a *jeu d'esprit*, written in ridicule of Sir John Carr's *Travels;* Leigh Hunt and his brother John; John Taylor, editor of the *Sun* newspaper; Horace Twiss; Barron Field; and T. Barnes, who was afterwards distinguished as the " thunderer" of the *Times.* To this circle, Mathews with his mimicry, his rich flow of anecdote, and his irresistible comic songs, was a constant source of amusement; but Hook is said to have been its more genuine and natural Momus. Horace Smith, in the early part of Hook's career, expressed a total disbelief in his alleged improvisation. One of his good-natured friends repeated the remark. " Oh, the unbelieving dog!" exclaimed the vocalist, " tell him if I am called upon again, he himself shall dictate the subject and the tune, which of course involves the metre; but it must be some common popular air." All this took place, and Hook produced one of his most brilliant songs. " I made a very humble palinode for my mistrust!"—said the doubter long afterwards,—" and expressed the astonishment and delight with which his truly wonderful performance had electrified me. Not without difficulty, however, had I been enabled to believe my own ears, and several days elapsed before I had completely recovered from my bewilderment, for, as an occasional rhymester, I could well appreciate the difficulty of the achievement." Hook repaid the hospitality of his

Sydenham Amphitryon by depicting him as the *Hull* of *Gilbert Gurney.* Hill also sat for Paul Pry, and was familiarly pointed out in London as its original. He lived to an advanced age, and, though he met with pecuniary reverses, retained his freshness of appearance, and cheerfulness of disposition, to the last.

In the year 1813 Horace Smith wrote a comedy in five acts, entitled *First Impressions, or, Trade in the West;* the authorship of which he had concealed from all but his friend Barron Field, at whose chamber, in the Temple, he had agreed to dine on the night of the first representation, that they might proceed to the theatre together. Mr. Langsdorff, an attaché of some German embassy, was present, and joined the party for Drury Lane, where they took their places in the pit. All went on smoothly until the delivery of a speech by one of the actors, to the effect that the money raised in England for a single charity often exceeded the revenue of a whole German principality. "Vot is dat?" whispered Langsdorff to the *incog.* author; "does he laff at de Jairmans? den I shall damn his blay." Thereupon he set up a low hiss, which he renewed with increased vigour on every reappearance of a certain character, till he succeeded in establishing a decided opposition. As the clamour waxed louder the author joined in it, loudly vociferating, "off! off!!" A fortunate change, however, took place in the humour of the audience, and they finally put down the playwright and his German friend, and the piece was successful, being acted subsequently twenty nights. A farce of his, entitled *The Absent Apothecary*, was less fortunate, and was incontinently damned on its first night.

With Horace Smith, literature and his city business went hand in hand. Before he relinquished his counting room a friend met him posting westward one day about three o'clock. "Where are you going so fast, Smith?" "Who would not go fast to Paradise (Paradise row, Fulham)? I am going to sin like our first parents." "How? there are no apples to pluck at Fulham, yet." "No; but there is ink to spill, though—a worse sin, perhaps. I have promised L—— something, I cannot tell what. Who the deuce can hit upon any thing new, when half the world is racking its brains to do the same?"

"This," adds the reminiscent, who wrote a few months after the death of Horace,—"this is thirty years ago, and now the utterer of that remark is within the precincts of the tomb; while the intervening time saw no diminution of his regard for intellectual pleasures, nor, with much to flatter his talents in the way of his literary labours, any decrease of that modest feeling in regard to his own writings, which is one of the strongest attestations of merit. In this respect he differed from his brother, who had, or always impressed the minds of others that he had, a full sense of the merit of his own compositions."

The success of Horace Smith in the *Rejected Addresses* attached him to a life of letters, and as soon as he had acquired a competency he abandoned the vocation of a money-changer. In spite of the reproaches of his city friends he seized the moment for retiring while independence was within his grasp. " The hope of future gain"—he remarked—" might lead him to risk what he had secured." This was about the year 1820. When the crash of 1825 occurred, he was able to turn the tables on those who had reproached him. " Where are those now who called me a fool for retiring, when I had the independence that satisfied my wishes ? Who was right ? I pity them !"

During a residence in France that followed his retirement from active business, in conjunction with one or two friends, he projected the establishment of an English newspaper in Paris. They could never procure the consent of the French government, however, nor its refusal, to the undertaking, and it was abandoned. During his residence abroad, and on his return to England, he was a constant contributor to the *New Monthly Magazine*, then edited by his friend, the poet Campbell. He sometimes wrote also for the *London Magazine*, conducted by John Scott, a man of uncommon ability in his profession, who fell in a duel that followed his indignant and bitter invectives against Lockhart, and his associates in *Blackwood's Magazine*. He had been previously connected with Scott in editing the *Champion* newspaper, to which John Hamilton Reynolds and T. Barnes, afterwards of the *Times*, were also contributors. About the year 1825, however, he gave up writing for periodicals, and commenced his career as a novel writer by the publication of *Brambletye House*, his first and best historical novel. This was followed by *Tor Hill, Reuben Apsley, Jane Lomax, The New Forest, Walter Colyton, The Moneyed Man, Adam Brown*, and *Arthur Arundel ;* all of which were published, we believe, by Mr. Colburn.

Horace Smith was the author of more than fifty volumes,

besides those which he edited. Many of these were published anonymously, and perhaps have never been acknowledged. They exhibit not only great industry, but also great tact and versatility in the writer.

"It was about 1826," says a writer in the *New Monthly Magazine*, "that he published his first novel. He had some time before taken up his abode at Tunbridge Wells, quitting London and his lodgings at 142 Regent-street, of which he declared himself heartily sick. Even at this distance of time, we remember a dinner he gave there before he started—the last, it is probable, that he ever gave in London—and the hilarity of the guests, among whom were some of the celebrated wits of the time, most of whom are now no more. At Tunbridge Wells we soon paid him a visit, while residing in Mount Edgecombe Cottage. He was, as usual, kind, entertaining, and hospitable. We think of that time with melancholy pleasure. His qualities were the most amiable, the most gentle, in those days, that can be conceived. Surely, if integrity, sincerity, and real friendliness deserve happiness, they must be his. There we met an old friend of his whom we have not seen for years—a clever and ingenious man; the author of a novel not enough known." A pilgrimage to Penshurst, the old seat of the Sidneys, suggested on this occasion, was the origin of *Brambletye House*. Smith remarked that such buildings were the best foundation scenes for novels; and it was no wonder that they had been so often chosen. It was about this time that some one recommended the female name of *Zillah* as one peculiarly pleasing. "To me," said Horace, "it would of course be doubly interesting. She was a lady of the very earliest descent; the mother of Tubal Cain, the first of the Smiths, and of course the founder of my family."

"Both brothers," continues the writer we have last quoted, "were clever men and piquant writers, but Horace Smith was something beyond this. He possessed talents of a wider scope than James; his views were more extended; he was more intellectually accomplished; had seen much more of the world, and thought deeper. James was a wit, an agreeable companion, possessed of a fine vein of humour, but circumscribed in the extent of his information, and, as a natural consequence, more concentrated in himself. James selected his subjects, for the most part, within the circle in which he moved, and continued to move through life. A happy point, well made, it was his delight to repeat at the dinner-table or in the evening party. His jokes—and excellent they were—thrown off among convivial friends—in short, society, cheerfulness, and its accompaniments—constituted the *summum* of his life's pleasures. His frame was not active; his bachelor habits and dinings-out rendered him a subject for the gout, to which disorder he ultimately fell a victim. From his office in Austin Friars to his residence in the Strand constituted the major part of his journeyings. Horace, on the contrary, was of an active make. A year or two after we first knew him, he visited Italy; and returning, for some time made France his residence. We first saw James at his office in Austin Friars, nearly thirty years ago. He looked as serious as the parchment and papers surrounding him. He seemed in this situation as little of a wit as can well be imagined. A joke took place on this visit often subsequently repeated. There were two Smiths on the same side of the court, and we had very naturally knocked at the door of the first we came to. On entering his office, we mentioned our mistake. 'Ay,' said James Smith, 'I am James the first; he must abdicate.'

"It is difficult to say which of the two was the most witty in the social hour. Both brothers may be characterized rather as possessors of a high talent for humour, than of that sparkling wit which characterized Hook. Sometimes, with all his wonderful readiness, it was hit or miss with Hook, who aimed at notoriety no matter how acquired. The Smiths were both graver men, and would have thought to run a joke too near to a failure was akin to one. We have known Horace Smith indignant at Hook's jesting, not only ill, but out of place, in his wild manner.

"James Smith wanted the cordial spirit of his brother; there was, we fancied, little warmth of heart about him. He seemed to mingle somewhat of his professional character in social intercourse. On this account we surmise that James will be much sooner forgotten by his friends than Horace. Both brothers were delightful companions. Many an hour of mental depression have we felt relieved by their society. The humour and gladiatorial displays of wit that occurred in their company, were always gentlemanly, generous in temper, unimpeachably moral, and never the splenetic outpouring of ill-feeling. Horace, or Horatio, as he always subscribed himself, was not only the most accomplished, but the most genial spirit of the two. He was as much attracted to the society of literary men who made no pretension to be wits, and to solid and serious reading as to the gay and light."

Leigh Hunt, in his expressive use of odd epithets, says that Horace Smith was "delicious." He never met with a finer nature in man, except in the single instance of Shelley, who himself entertained the highest regard for Horace Smith, as may be seen by the following verses, the initials in which the reader may fill up with his name :—

> " Wit and sense,
> Virtue and human knowledge, all that might
> Make this dull world a business of delight,
> Are all combined in H. S."

Shelley once said to Leigh Hunt—"I know not what Horace Smith must take me for sometimes : I am afraid he must think me a strange fellow : but is it not odd that the only truly generous person I ever knew, who had money to be generous with, should be a stock-broker! and he writes poetry too"—continued Shelley, his voice rising in a fervour of astonishment; "he writes poetry and pastoral dramas, and yet knows how to make money, and does make it, and is still generous." The pastoral drama alluded to was probably *The Nympholept*, published anonymously in 1821. Whatever may have been its merit, its circulation was limited, and it is no longer remembered.

"I believe," said Shelley on another occasion, "that I have only to say to Horace Smith that I want a hundred pounds or two, and he would send it to me without any eye to its being returned; such faith has he that I have something within me beyond what the world supposes, and that I could only ask his money for a good purpose." What Shelley says that Smith *would* have done for him, he was known more than once to have done for others with a delicacy that enhanced the generosity of the act.

Horace Smith took leave of the public in the preface to *Love and Mesmerism*, published in 1845, announced as his last work of fiction. He kept his resolution in this regard, but his pen could not remain idle. He subsequently wrote a series of entertaining papers for the *New Monthly Magazine*. He died at Tunbridge Wells, on the 12th of July, 1849, in his seventieth year.

The novels of Horace Smith were well received at the time of their appearance, and several of them are still republished. We find the names of three, not generally esteemed the best, still reprinted in the United States, in the select library of novels of the Brothers Harper.   As a poet, his productions were usually suggested by the events passing around him, and were printed in the monthly magazines of his friends, Campbell and John Scott. From these journals they were transferred to newspapers, readers, and class-books, till they became familiar to the public before their appearance in a collected form.   They deserve their popularity.   They are written in a philosophic, no less than a poetical spirit.   They exhibit no ordinary grace of expression, and the versification is always harmonious and skillful.   There is nothing of the obscure or spasmodic about them, but they are simple and effective.   The lines on the *Funeral of Campbell* are worthy of the great poet whom they commemorate.   The stanzas on Southey and Scott are full of solemnity and pathos.   The *Address to the Mummy* is picturesque and animated; and the *Sicilian Arethusa* not only seems a veritable fragment of ancient literature, but is as musical and melodious as any verse in the language.

The personal appearance of Horace Smith, according to Leigh Hunt, was highly indicative of his character.   His figure was good and manly, inclining to the robust; and his countenance extremely frank and cordial; sweet without weakness.   His character is succinctly and beautifully described, in the paragraph in which the London *Examiner* announced his decease, and paid a tribute to his memory.   " He was a man of correct taste and the most generous sympathies, a delightful writer both in prose and verse, a cheerful and wise companion and a fast friend.   No man had a wider range of admirable and genial qualities; and far beyond that private circle of which he was the great charm and ornament, his loss will be deeply felt."   If it would be difficult to find words to convey more graceful and emphatic praise, it would be equally so to find a man who, from all report, more fully deserves it than HORACE SMITH.

THE

POETICAL WORKS

OF

HORACE SMITH.

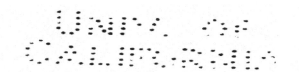

PREFATORY STANZAS.

TALK not to me of Necromantic wights,
    And dread magicians,
Who, by their potent spells, could conjure sprites,
    Ghosts, apparitions,
And raise the dead from the forgotten past,
Each in the perfect mould of pre-existence cast.

I, though no conjuror, have far outdone
    Such Archimages,
For, as I culled and pondered, one by one,
    These scattered pages,
From the dark past, and memory's eclipse,
Up rose in vision clear my life's Apocalypse.

Mutely each re-creative lay outpoured
    Its own revealings ;
Youth, manhood, age, were momently restored,
    With all their feelings.
Friends long deceased were summoned from the tomb ;
Forgotten scenes regained their vividness and bloom

Again did I recline in copses green,
    Gazing from under
Some oak's thwart boughs upon the sky serene,
    In reverent wonder ;
Or starting from the sward with ear acute,
To hear the cuckoo sound its soft two-noted flute.

Association ! thy transcendant power
    What art can rival ?
Muse-haunted strolls by river, field, or bower,
    At thy revival,
Return once more, and in their second birth
Bring back each former scent and sound of air and earth.

In social joys where song and music's zest
    Made beauty fairer,
In festive scenes with all their mirth and jest,
    Once more a sharer,
I see the smiles, and hear the laughter loud,
Of many a friend, alas ! now mouldering in his shroud.

So, when the hands are dust that now entwine
 These prompting pages,
Some future reader, as a jest or line
 His thought engages,
Feeling old memories from their grave arise,
May thus, in pensive mood, perchance soliloquise :

" I knew the bardling; 'twas his nature's bent,
 His creed's chief feature,
To hold that a benign Creator meant
 To bless the creature,
And giving man a boon denied to brute,
Loved him to exercise his laughing attribute.

" He felt that cheerfulness, when unalloyed
 With aught immoral,
Was piety, on earth, in heaven enjoyed ;
 And wished his laurel
To be a Misletoe, whose grace should make
The mirth-devoted year one hallowed Christmas wake.

" In mystic transcendental clouds to soar
 Was not his mission,
Yet could he mould at times the solid ore
 Of admonition ;
Offenceless, grave or gay, at least *that* praise
May grace his name, and speed his unpretending lays."

If such thy welcome, little Book! discard
   Fears of thine ordeal ;
Go forth, and tell thy readers that the Bard,
   With fervent, cordial
Feelings of gratitude and hope combined,
Bids them all hail, and wafts them every feeling kind.

HYMN TO THE FLOWERS.

DAY-STARS! that ope your frownless eyes to twinkle
  From rainbow galaxies of earth's creation,
And dew-drops on her lonely altars sprinkle
      As a libation.

Ye matin worshippers! who bending lowly
  Before the uprisen Sun, God's lidless eye,
Throw from your chalices a sweet and holy
      Incense on high.

Ye bright Mosaics! that with storied beauty,
  The floor of Nature's temple tesselate,
What numerous emblems of instructive duty
      Your forms create!

'Neath cloistered boughs, each floral bell that swingeth
  And tolls its perfume on the passing air,
Makes sabbath in the fields, and ever ringeth
      A call to prayer.

Not to the domes where crumbling arch and column
  Attest the feebleness of mortal hand,
But to that fane, most catholic and solemn,
      Which God hath planned;

To that cathedral, boundless as our wonder,
   Whose quenchless lamps the sun and moon supply;
Its choir the winds and waves—its organ thunder—
      Its dome the sky.

There, as in solitude and shade I wander
   Through the green aisles, or stretched upon the sod,
Awed by the silence, reverently ponder
      The ways of God,

Your voiceless lips, O Flowers! are living preachers,
   Each cup a pulpit, every leaf a book,
Supplying to my fancy numerous teachers
      From loneliest nook.

Floral Apostles! that in dewy splendour
   " Weep without woe, and blush without a crime,"
O may I deeply learn, and ne'er surrender
      Your lore sublime!

" Thou wert not, Solomon! in all thy glory,
   Arrayed," the lilies cry—" in robes like ours;
How vain your grandeur! ah, how transitory
      Are human flowers!"

In the sweet-scented pictures, heavenly artist!
   With which thou paintest nature's wide-spread hall,
What a delightful lesson thou impartest
      Of love to all!

Not useless are ye, Flowers! though made for pleasure:
   Blooming o'er field and wave, by day and night,
From every source your sanction bids me treasure
      Harmless delight.

Ephemeral sages! what instructors hoary
   For such a world of thought could furnish scope?
Each fading calyx a *memento mori*,
     Yet fount of hope.

Posthumous glories! angel-like collection!
   Upraised from seed or bulb interred in earth,
Ye are to me a type of resurrection,
     And second birth.

Were I in churchless solitudes remaining,
   Far from all voice of teachers and divines,
My soul would find, in flowers of God's ordaining,
     Priests, sermons, shrines!

ADDRESS TO A MUMMY.

AND thou hast walked about (how strange a story!)
   In Thebes's streets three thousand years ago,
When the Memnonium was in all its glory,
   And time had not begun to overthrow
Those temples, palaces, and piles stupendous,
Of which the very ruins are tremendous.

Speak! for thou long enough hast acted Dummy.
   Thou hast a tongue—come—let us hear its tune;
Thou'rt standing on thy legs, above-ground, Mummy!
   Revisiting the glimpses of the moon,
Not like thin ghosts or disembodied creatures,
But with thy bones and flesh, and limbs and features.

1 *

Tell us—for doubtless thou canst recollect,
    To whom should we assign the Sphinx's fame?
Was Cheops or Cephrenes architect
    Of either pyramid that bears his name?
Is Pompey's Pillar really a misnomer?
Had Thebes a hundred gates, as sung by Homer?

Perhaps thou wert a Mason, and forbidden
    By oath to tell the secrets of thy trade—
Then say what secret melody was hidden
    In Memnon's statue which at sunrise played?
Perhaps thou wert a Priest—if so, my struggles
Are vain, for priestcraft never owns its juggles.

Perchance that very hand, now pinioned flat,
    Has hob-a-nobbed with Pharaoh, glass to glass;
Or dropped a half-penny in Homer's hat,
    Or doffed thine own to let Queen Dido pass;
Or held, by Solomon's own invitation,
A torch at the great Temple's dedication.

I need not ask thee if that hand, when armed,
    Has any Roman soldier mauled and knuckled,
For thou wert dead, and buried, and embalmed,
    Ere Romulus and Remus had been suckled:
Antiquity appears to have begun
Long after thy primeval race was run.

Thou couldst develop, if that withered tongue
    Might tell us what those sightless orbs have seen,
How the world looked when it was fresh and young,
    And the great Deluge still had left it green—
Or was it then so old that History's pages
Contained no record of its early ages?

Still silent ! incommunicative elf !
   Art sworn to secrecy ? then keep thy vows ;
But prythee tell us something of thyself—
   Reveal the secrets of thy prison-house ;
Since in the world of spirits thou hast slumbered,
What hast thou seen—what strange adventures numbered ?

Since first thy form was in this box extended,
   We have, above-ground, seen some strange mutations.
The Roman empire has begun and ended,
   New worlds have risen—we have lost old nations,
And countless Kings have into dust been humbled,
While not a fragment of thy flesh has crumbled.

Didst thou not hear the pother o'er thy head,
   When the great Persian conqueror, Cambyses,
Marched armies o'er thy tomb with thundering tread,
   O'erthrew Osiris, Orus, Apis, Isis,
And shook the Pyramids with fear and wonder,
When the gigantic Memnon fell asunder ?

If the tomb's secrets may not be confessed,
   The nature of thy private life unfold :
A heart has throbbed beneath that leathern breast,
   And tears adown that dusty cheek have rolled :—
Have children climbed those knees, and kissed that face ?
What was thy name and station, age and race ?

Statue of flesh—Immortal of the dead !
   Imperishable type of evanescence !
Posthumous man, who quitt'st thy narrow bed,
   And standest undecayed within our presence,
Thou wilt hear nothing till the Judgment morning,
When the great Trump shall thrill thee with its warning.

Why should this worthless tegument endure,
    If its undying guest be lost for ever?
Oh! let us keep the soul embalmed and pure
    In living virtue, that when both must sever,
Although corruption may our frame consume,
The immortal spirit in the skies may bloom!

ADDRESS TO THE ORANGE-TREE AT VERSAILLES,

CALLED THE GREAT BOURBON, WHICH IS ABOVE FOUR HUNDRED YEARS OLD.

WHEN France with civil wars was torn,
And heads, as well as crowns were shorn
     From royal shoulders,
One Bourbon, in unaltered plight,
Hath still maintained its legal right,
And held its court—a goodly sight
     To all beholders.

Thou, leafy monarch, thou alone,
Hast sat uninjured on thy throne,
     Seeing the war range;
And when the great Nassaus were sent
Crownless away (a sad event!)
Thou didst uphold and represent
     The House of Orange.

To tell what changes thou hast seen,
Each grand monarque, and king and queen,
     Of French extraction,
Might puzzle those who don't conceive
French history, so I believe
Comparing thee with ours will give
     More satisfaction.

Westminster Hall,* whose oaken roof
The papers say (but that's no proof),
    Is nearly rotten,
Existed but in stones and trees,
When thou wert waving in the breeze,
And blossoms (what a treat for bees !)
    By scores hadst gotten.

Chaucer, so old a bard that time
Has antiquated every chime,
And from his tomb outworn each rhyme
    Within the Abbey ;
And Gower, an older poet whom
The Borough Church enshrines (his tomb,
Though once restored, has lost its bloom,
    And got quite shabby),

Lived in thy time—the first perchance
Was beating monks† when thou in France
    By monks wert beaten,
Who shook beneath this very tree
Their reverend beards, with glutton glee,
As each down-falling luxury
    Was caught and eaten.

Perchance when Henry gained the fight
Of Agincourt, some Gaulish knight
(His bleeding steed in woful plight,
    With smoking haunches),
Laid down his helmet at thy root,
And, as he plucked the grateful fruit,
Suffered his poor exhausted brute
    To crop thy branches.

* Rebuilt 1399.
† There is a tradition (though not authenticated) that Chaucer was
fined for beating a monk in Fleet-street.

THE ORANGE-TREE AT VERSAILLES.

Thou wert of portly size and look,
When first the Turks besieged and took
      Constantinople;
And eagles in thy boughs might perch,
When, leaving Bullen in the lurch,
Another Henry changed his church,
      And used the Pope ill.

What numerous namesakes hast thou seen
Lounging beneath thy shady green,
      With monks as lazy;
Louis Quatorze has pressed that ground,
With his six mistresses around—
A sample of the old and sound
      Legitimacy.

And when despotic freaks and vices
Brought on the inevitable crisis
      Of revolution,
Thou heard'st the mob's infuriate shriek,
Who came their victim Queen to seek,
On guiltless heads the wrath to wreak
      Of retribution.

Oh! of what follies, vice, and crime,
Hast thou, in thine eventful time,
      Been made beholder!
What wars, what feuds — the thoughts appal!
Each against each, and all with all,
Till races upon races fall,
      In earth to moulder.

Whilst thou, serene, unaltered, calm
(Such are the constant gifts and balm
      Bestowed by Nature!)

Hast year by year renewed thy flowers,
And perfumed the surrounding bowers,
And poured down grateful fruit by showers,
And proffered shade in summer hours
    To man and creature.

Thou green and venerable tree!
Whate'er the future doom may be,
    By fortune given,
Remember that a rhymester brought
From foreign shores thine umbrage sought,
Recalled the blessings thou hadst wrought,
And, as he thanked thee, raised his thought
    To heaven!

SICILIAN ARETHUSA.

Sicilian Arethusa! thou, whose arms
Of azure round the Thymbrian meadows wind,
Still are thy margins lined
With the same flowers Proserpina was weaving
In Enna's field, beside Pergusa's lake,
When swarthy Dis, upheaving,
Saw her, and, stung to madness by her charms,
Down snatched her, shrieking, to his Stygian couch.
Thy waves, Sicilian Arethusa, flow
In cadence to the shepherd's flageolet
As tunefully as when they wont to crouch
Beneath the banks to catch the pipings low
Of old Theocritus, and hear him trill
Bucolic songs, and Amoebæan lays.
And still, Sicilian Arethusa, still,

Though Etna dry thee up, or frosts enchain,
Thy music shall be heard, for poets high
Have dipped their wreaths in thee, and by their praise
Made thee immortal as themselves.   Thy flowers,
Transplanted, an eternal bloom retain,
Rooted in words that cannot fade or die.
Thy liquid gush and gurgling melody
Have left undying echoes in the bowers
Of tuneful poesy.   Thy very name,
Sicilian Arethusa, had been drowned
In deep oblivion, but that the buoyant breath
Of bards uplifted it, and bade it swim
Adown the eternal lapse, assured of fame,
Till all things shall be swallowed up in death.
Where, Immortality ! where canst thou found
Thy throne unperishing, but in the hymn
Of the true bard, whose breath encrusts his theme
Like to a petrifaction, which the stream
Of time will only make more durable?

THE SHRIEK OF PROMETHEUS.

SUGGESTED BY A PASSAGE IN THE SECOND BOOK OF APOLLONIUS RHODIUS.

FRESH was the breeze and the rowers plied
    Their oars with simultaneous motion,
When the Argo sailed in her stately pride
    By the laurelled shores of the Pontic Ocean.

The island of Mars with its palmy coves,
    The Sacred Mount, and Aretia's strands,
And Philyra's Isle with its linden groves,
    And Ophir's flood with its shelly sands,

Swiftly they passed—till, stretching far,
  On their right Bechirja's coast appears,
Where painted Sapirians, fierce in war,
  Bristle the beach with bows and spears.

At distance they saw the sunbeams quiver
  Where the long-sought towers of Colchis stood,
And marked the foam of the Phasis river,
  As it flung from its rocky mouth the flood.

The Argonauts gaze with hungry eyes
  On the land enriched by the Golden Fleece,
Already in fancy they grasp the prize,
  And hear the shouts of applauding Greece.

Jason looked out with a proud delight,
  Castor and Pollux stood hand in hand,
Showing each other the welcome sight;
  While fierce Meleager unsheathed his brand.

Laocoon bade the rowers check
  Their oars, as the sun to the water slanted,
For Orpheus sate with his harp on the deck,
  And sweetly the hymn of evening chanted,

While the heroes around, at each pause of sound,
  Stretched their right hands to the god of day,
  And fervently joined in the choral lay.

THE HYMN OF ORPHEUS.

Twin-born with Dian in the Delos isle,
  Which after the Ogygian deluge thou
Didst first illume with renovating smile,
  Apollo! deign to hear our evening vow.

CHORUS.

When thou'rt dim, our harp and hymn
  Thy downward course shall follow :
Hail to thee !—hail to thee !
  Hail to thee, Apollo !

God of the art that heals the shattered frame,
  And poetry that soothes the wounded mind,
Ten thousand temples, honoured with thy name,
  Attest thy ceaseless blessings to mankind.

CHORUS.

When thou'rt dim, our harp and hymn
  Thy downward course shall follow :
Hail to thee !—hail to thee !
  Hail to thee, Apollo !

Thy golden bow emits a gushing strain
  Of music when the Pythian serpent dies :
His eyes flash fire—his writhings plough the plain :
  Hissing he leaps aloft—then lifeless lies.

CHORUS.

When thou'rt dim, our harp and hymn
  Thy downward course shall follow :
Hail to thee !—hail to thee !
  Hail to thee, Apollo !

Pan of his pipe and rural science proud,
  Dreamt that his music might with thine aspire ;
The mountain Tmolus was the judge—and bowed
  His nodding woods in homage to thy lyre.

THE SHRIEK OF PROMETHEUS.

CHORUS.

When thou'rt dim, with harp and hymn
    Thy downward course we follow :
Hail to thee !——hail to thee !
    Hail to thee, Apollo !

From bowers of Daphne on Parnassus' Mount,
    While Delphic girls their Io Pæans sing,
The gifted Muses by Castalia's Fount
    With choral symphonies salute their king.

CHORUS.

When thou't dim, with harp and hymn
    Thy downward course we follow :
Hail to thee !——hail to thee !
    Hail to thee Apollo !

God of the golden lyre and laurel wreath,
    To thee each poet turns with yearning heart
And thoughtful eyes, invoking thee to breathe
    Thine inspiration——

                  With a start
The minstrel ceased—for over all the bark
    A baleful shadow on a sudden spread !
The Argonauts looked up, and saw a dark
    And monstrous eagle hovering o'er their head ;
So vast and fearful, that transfixed and pale
    They stood, with wild amaze o'ertaken :—
The vessel trembles, and the shivering sail
    Flaps as if with terror shaken.
Entranced they gazed—and silent till
    Philas, the son of Bacchus, seized his bow,
    And would have aimed it at the feathered foe,
But Mopsus, gifted with an augur's skill,

Gently held back his arm, and bade him wait
This dread portent—pronounce no word,
Nor dare to challenge Jove's own bird,
   The minister of unrelenting fate.

Extending now his oar-like wings,
Twice round the ship the monster swings,
   As if prepared to pounce upon his prey;
His eyes from forth his sable shroud
Shot fire, like lightning from a cloud ;
   But with a sudden dart he rushed away,
And clove the northward distance, where
   The heights of Caucasus their barrier throw,
Where crag on crag, chaotic giants bare
Their granite foreheads to the sky, and sit
   In desolate state beneath their crowns of snow.
Within these topmost peaks, there is a pit—
   A dizzy, gaunt, precipitous ravine,
Upon whose rocky floor environed round
   With walls of ice—by every eye unseen,
With adamantine chains Prometheus lies bound.

Thither the ravenous wonder winged his flight—
They saw him clear the intervening height,
   And sink behind it :—every eye
Is fixed upon the spot, and every heart
   Throbs with expectant agony.—
But naught is seen—no sounds impart
   The secret of that dread abyss :—
   Still do they gaze half-willing to dismiss
Their fears and hopes, for over plain and hill,
And smiling ocean—all is hushed and still.

Gracious God, what a shriek !
The monster with his beak

Is tearing out his victim's heart !
Lo! as that desolating cry
Echoes from the mountains high,
    And throws its fear afar, a start
Of horror seems to darken nature's face.——
    Athwart the quaking deep,
    Revolting shudders creep,
Earth trembles to her very base—
Air seems to swoon—the sky to frown—
The sun with ghastly glare sinks faster down.——
    Hark ! what a furious clash of chains !
Victim ! thou never canst unlock
The brazen bolts that root thee to the rock ;
    Vain are thy struggles and convulsive strains.
Ah me ! what dreadful groans are those
    Wrung from the very depths of agonies ;——
Now weaker moanings rise, till, worn with woes,
    The fainting wretch exhausted lies,
And all again is grim repose.

But still with throbbing breasts and steadfast eyes
    The heroes gazed upon the mountain's peak,
Till gorged with gore they saw the monster rise
    With blood-stained claws, and breast, and beak :
And as above them he resumed his flight,
    The arrested vessel shakes,
    The flapping main-sail quakes,
And all seemed turned to statues at the sight,
All but the son of Bacchus, who
    With flashing eyes and visage red,
Again upreared his bow and drew
    His longest arrow to the head—
When from the eagle's beak a drop of gore,
    (The heart's blood of Prometheus) fell

Warm on his hand ! upon the vessel's floor
  Down falls his bow ;—with shuddering yell,
And haggard eyes still staring on the drop,
He staggers back, clasping the mast to prop
His fainting limbs. Upon the pilot's forehead
  The dews of terror stood,
  And all in awe-struck mood
Pondered in silence on that omen horrid.

The sun went down, and far into the gloom
  The monster shot away—but none
Of the bewildered Argonauts resume
  The vessel's guidance as her way she won.—
None spake—none moved—all sate in blank dismay,
  Revolving in their minds this dread portent ;
And thus, abandoned to the sway
  Of the blind wind and watery element,
Through the whole night the Argo bore
Those throbbing hearts along the Pontic shore.

THE BIRTH OF THE INVISIBLE.

O SCENE of enchantment ! O vision of bliss !
What Paradisaical glory is this !
A garden ! a garden ! O rapturous sight !
More stately in beauty, more rich in delight,
Than any the Muse, in her leafiest hour,
Has fabled of golden Hesperian bower,
Or Fortunate Islands, or fields where the blest
In Elysium's sylvan beatitudes rest.
Lovely or rare, none can compare
With this heaven on earth so surpassingly fair !

Well, well, may its flowerets thus brightly expand,
For they feel the fresh touch of the Deity's hand;
And the trees that are rustling their branches on high,
Are raising their arms and their voice to the sky,
To give thanks to the Lord, at whose fiat sublime
They sprung from the earth in maturity's prime;
And the newly-born river that flows at their feet,
Is lisping an anthem its Maker to greet.
Lovely or rare, none can compare
With this heaven on earth so surpassingly fair!

What odorous incense upsprings from the sod,
Which has lately been pressed by the foot of its God!
What fragrance Sabæan the zephyrs exhale,
Where celestial breath has been left on the gale!
Behold! how the fruits deeply blush, where the sun
Has stamped his first kiss upon every one!
And hark! how the birds in sweet choral accord,
Send their voices' first offerings up to the Lord!
Lovely or rare, none can compare
With this heaven on earth so surpassingly fair!

No solace is wanting, no charms that dispense
A rival delight to the soul and the sense;
It is blissful to quaff the nectareous air;
To pluck from the branches ambrosial fare;
To list to the music of birds and of trees,
The chiming of waters, the song of the breeze;
To gaze on the Paradise blooming around,
And scent the rich breath of its flowery ground.
Lovely or rare, none can compare
With this heaven on earth so surpassingly fair!

The creatures now savage, not then beasts of prey,
'Mid the flocks and the herds fondly pasture and play:

The lion lies down with the kidling; the lamb
Disports with the tiger; the wolf with its dam;
The elephant, twining his trunk round the boughs
Of the palm, scatters dates for his friends to carouse;
The giraffe plucks the high-growing fruits; and each beast
Makes the banquet of Nature a fellowship feast.
Lovely or rare, none can compare
With this heaven on earth so surpassingly fair!

'Tis the garden of Eden, where joy, peace, and love,
Join the creatures below to their Maker above.
Behold! from you verdant alcove, hand in hand,
Wander Adam and Eve, till admiring they stand
Beneath the resplendent pre-eminent tree
Of knowledge, whose fruit is forbidden.   And see!
In the guise of a serpent, where Satan appears,
And whispers melodious guilt in their ears.
Lovely or rare, none can compare
With this heaven on earth so surpassingly fair!

O horror of horrors! the dark deed is done:
They have tasted the fruit.   Lo! the shuddering sun
Rushes out of the sky; all is terror and gloom.
The tears of the angels, bewailing man's doom,
Rain woe upon earth; the wild animals roar,
As their fangs, stainless once, are polluted with gore;
Flocks and herds fly before them, astounded, aghast;
Shrieks of anguish are borne on the terrible blast.
Fear and despair are on earth and in air,
For thunder has ravaged that garden so fair.

Degraded, ashamed, sinful Adam and Eve
From its precincts are driven to toil and to grieve;
Then earth gave a groan, a soul-harrowing sound,
And thrilled in her depths with a shudder profound,

That withered each Paradise tree to its root,
And shook down for ever and ever its fruit,
And scattered the rivers—till all was o'erthrown,
That the site of the garden might never be known.
And Record is all that is left, since the fall,
Its exquisite beauties and bliss to recall.

Then, then in the desert's profoundest abyss,
Where the winds o'er the waste fiercely whistle and hiss,
In the blackness of night, with convulsions and throes,
Did Earth her sepulchral recesses unclose,
And heave up a monster, the world to affright,
Terrific of purpose, tremendous in might,
Though his features to none might he ever reveal.
Gladness and mirth fled from the earth,
When that fearful invisible monster had birth.

The hopes and the courage of Adam to daunt,
It ceased not, the spectre, his footsteps to haunt;
His children it touched, and converted to dust
In a moment his tenderest objects of trust;
Birds and beasts fell around him; where'er Adam walked,
Before him, in fancy, the murderer stalked;
More dread to the heart when unseen by the eye,
'Twas vain from the phantom to hide or to fly;
Wrinkles and bloom met the same doom—
One touch of the Gorgon sent all to the tomb.

It lurked in the wave, in the air, in the bower—
An ubiquitous curse, an all withering power—
Still snatching from Adam his hope and his joy,
And scaring with dread when it failed to destroy;
Till weakened with age, worn with sorrow and fear,
He felt a cold hand on his heart, and his ear
Was chilled by the spectre's cadaverous breath,
As in accents sepulchral it groaned—I AM DEATH!

2

THE SANCTUARY.

In Israel was many a refuge city,
　　Whereto the blameless homicide might flee,
And claim protection, sustenance, and pity,
　　Safe from the blood-avenger's enmity,
Until the law's acquittal sent him thence,
　　　　Free from offence.

Round old cathedral, abbey-church, and palace,
　　Did we ourselves a sanctuary draw,
Where no stern creditor could glut his malice,
　　And even criminals might brave the law;
Nor judge nor justice in that chartered verge
　　　　Their rights could urge.

These times are gone; felons and knavish debtors
　　May mourn the change, but who bewails their case?
For why should God and King be made abettors
　　Of guilt and fraud, the champions of the base?
Never may such a desecration stain
　　　　Our land again!

But all are not divested of their charter;
　　One refuge still is left for human woes.
Victim of care! or persecution's martyr!
　　Who seek'st a sure asylum from thy foes,
Learn that the holiest, safest, purest, best,
　　　　Is man's own breast!

There is a solemn sanctuary founded
　　By God himself; not for transgressors meant;
But that the man oppressed, the spirit-wounded,
　　And all beneath the world's injustice bent,
Might turn from outward wrong, turmoil, and din,
　　　　To peace within.

Each bosom is a temple; when its altar,
  The living heart, is unprofaned and pure,
Its verge is hallowed; none need fear or falter
  Who thither fly; it is an ark secure,
Winning, above a world o'erwhelmed with wrath,
      Its peaceful path.

O Bower of Bliss! O Sanctuary holy!
  Terrestrial antepast of heavenly joy!
Never! oh, never may misdeed or folly
  My claim to thy beatitudes destroy!
Still may I keep this Paradise unlost,
      Where'er I'm tost.

Even in the flesh, the spirit disembodied,
  Unchecked by time and space, may soar elate,
In silent awe to commune with the Godhead—
  Or the millennium reign anticipate,
When earth shall be all sanctity and love,
      Like heaven above.

How sweet to turn from anguish, guilt, and madness,
  From scenes where strife and tumult never cease,
To that Elysian world of bosom'd gladness,
  Where all is silence, charity, and peace;
And sheltered from the storm the soul may rest
      On its own nest!

When, spleenful as the sensitive Mimosa,
  We shrink from Winter's touch and Nature's gloom,
There may we conjure up a Vallombrosa,
  Where groves and bowers in summer beauty bloom,
And the heart dances in the sunny glade
      Fancy has made.

But, would we dedicate to nobler uses,
  This bosom sanctuary, let us there
Hallow our hearts from all the world's abuses ;
  While high and charitable thoughts and prayer,
May teach us gratitude to God, combined
      With love of kind.

Reader ! this is no lay unfelt and hollow,
  But prompted by the happy, grateful heart
Of one who, having humbly tried to follow
  The path he counsels, would to thee impart
The love and holy quiet which have blest
      His own calm breast.

THE POPPY.

THE man who roams by wild-flowered ditch or hedge
        Skirting the mead,
Or treads the cornfield path—along its edge,
        May mark a weed,
Whose ragged scarlet gear might well denote
A road-side beggar in a soldier's coat.

Hence ! terms misplaced, and thoughts disparaging
        O Poppy Flower !
Thou art the Crœsus of the field—its king—
        A mystic power,
With emblems deep and secret blessings fraught,
And potent properties that baffle thought.

When thy hues catch, amid the growing corn,
        The traveller's eye,
"Weeds ! weeds !" he cries, and shakes his head in scorn :
        But when on high

The grain uplifts its harvest-bearing crest,
The Poppy's hidden, and the taunt suppressed.

So, when our early state is poor and mean,
     Our portion small,
Our scarlet-blushing moral weeds are seen,
     And blamed by all;
But as we rise in rank we win repute,
Our faults gold-hidden, our accusers mute.

Why does the Poppy with its chaliced store
     Of opiate rare,
Flush in the fields, and grace the hovel door,
     But to declare
That, from the City's palaces forlorn,
Sleep flies to bless the cottage in the corn?

And oh! how precious is the Anodyne
     Its cells exude,
Charming the mind's disquietude malign
     To peaceful mood,
Soothing the body's anguish with its balm,
Lulling the restless into slumbers calm.

What though the reckless suicide—oppressed
     By fell despair,
Turns to a poison-cup thy chalice, blessed
     With gifts so rare;
And basely flying, while the brave remain,
Deserts the post God gave him to maintain.

Such art perverted does but more enhance
     That higher power
Which, planting by the corn—(man's sustenance),
     The Poppy flower,

Both in one soil, one atmosphere their breath,
Rears, side by side, the means of life and death!

Who, who can mark thee, Poppy, when the air
　　　　　　　　　　　Fans thy lips bright,
Nor move his own in sympathetic prayer
　　　　　　　　　　　　To Him whose might
Combined the powers — O thought-bewildering deed!
Of death—sleep—health—oblivion—in a weed!

THE MURDERER'S CONFESSION.

I PAUSED not to question the Devil's suggestion,
　　But o'er the cliff, headlong, the living was thrown;
A scream and a plashing, a foam and a flashing,
And the smothering water accomplished his slaughter,
　　All was silent, and I was alone!

With heart-thrilling spasm I leant o'er the chasm;
　　There was blood on the wave that closed o'er his head,
And in bubbles his breath, as he struggled with death,
　　Rose up to the surface.　I shuddered and fled.

With footsteps that staggered and countenance haggard,
　　I stole to my dwelling, bewildered, dismayed,
Till whisperings stealthy said—" Psha! he was wealthy,
　　Thou'rt his heir—no one saw thee—then be not
　　　　afraid."

I summoned the neighbours, I joined in their labours.
　　We sought for the missing by day and by night;
We ransacked each single height, hollow, or dingle,
Till shoreward we wended, when starkly extended,
　　His corpse lay before us—O God! what a sight!

And yet was there nothing for terror or loathing.
The blood had been washed from his face and his clothing,
    But by no language, *no* pen, his life-like wide open
        Eyes can be painted;——
They stared at me, flared at me, angrily glared at me,
      I felt murder-attainted;
Yet my guilty commotion seemed truth and devotion,
      When I shuddered and fainted.

No hint finds emission that breathes of suspicion,
None dare utter a sound when an inquest has found
      His death accidental;
Whence then and wherefore, having nothing to care for,
      These agonies mental?
Why grieve and why sicken, frame-withered, soul-
      stricken?

Age-paralysed, sickly, he must have died quickly,
      Each day brought some new ill;
Why leave him to languish and struggle with anguish,
The deed that relieved him from all that aggrieved him,
      Was kindly, not cruel.

In procession extended a funeral splendid,
With bannered displays and escutcheons emblazoned,
      To church slowly passed,
When a dread apparition astounded my vision;
Like an aspen leaf shaking, dumfounded and quaking,
      I stood all aghast!

From its nailed coffin prison the corpse had arisen,
And in all its shroud vesture, with menacing gesture,
And eye-balls that stared at me, flared at me, glared
    at me,

It pointed—it flouted its slayer, and shouted
    In accents that thrilled me,
" That ruthless dissembler, that guilt-stricken trembler,
    Is the villain who killed me !"

'Twas fancy's creation—mere hallucination—
A lucky delusion, for again my confusion,
Guilt's evidence sinister, seemed to people and minister
The painful achievement of grief and bereavement.

Then why these probations, these self-condemnations
    Incessant and fearful ?
Some with impunity snatch opportunity,
Slay—and exult in concealment's immunity ;
Free from forebodings and heartfelt corrodings,
They fear no disclosure no public exposure,
And sleeping unhaunted and waking undaunted,
    Live happy and cheerful.

To escape the ideal let me dwell on the real ;
    I, a pauper so lately,
In abundance possessing life's every blessing,
Fine steeds in my stable, rare wines on my table,
Servants dressed gaily, choice banquets daily,
A wife fond and beautiful, children most dutiful,
I, a pauper so lately, live rich and greatly,
    In a mansion-house stately.

Life's blessings ?   O liar ! all are curses most dire ;
    In the midst of my revels,
His eyes ever stare at me, flare at me, glare at me,
Before me when treading my manors outspreading,
There yawns an abysmal cliff precipice dismal.
Isolation has vanished, all silence is banished,
Where'er I immew me his death-shrieks pursue me,
    I am hunted by devils.

My wine clear and ruddy seems turbid and bloody,
I cannot quaff water :——recalling his slaughter,
My terror it doubles——'tis beaded with bubbles,
   Each filled with his breath,
And every glass in each hisses——" Assassin !
My curse shall affright thee, haunt, harrow, and blight
  thee
   In life and in death !"

My daughters, their mother, contend with each other
Who shall show most affection, best soothe my dejec-
  tion :
Revolting endearments ! their garments seem cerements,
And I shudder with loathing at their grave-tainted
  clothing.
   Home and the mercies
That to others are dearest, to me are the drearest
   And deadliest curses.

When free from this error I thrill with the terror,
   (Thought horrid to dwell on!)
That the wretch whom they cherish may shamefully
  perish,
Be publicly gibbeted, branded, exhibited,
   As a murderous felon !

O punishment hellish ! the house I embellish
From centre to corner upbraids its adorner——
A door's lowest creaking swells into a shrieking,
Against me each column bears evidence solemn,
   Each statue 's a Nemesis.
They follow, infest me, they strive to arrest me,
Till in terrified sadness that verges on madness,
   I rush from the premises.

The country's amenity brings no serenity.
Each rural sound seeming a menace or screaming,
There is not a bird or beast but cries—" Murder !
    There goes the offender !
Dog him, waylay him, encompass him, stay him,
    And make him surrender !"

My flower-beds splendid seem eyes blood-distended,
His eyes, ever flaring, and staring, and glaring !
I turn from them quickly, but phantoms more sickly
    Drive me hither and thither.
I would forfeit most gladly wealth stolen so madly,
Quitting grandeur and revelry to fly from this devilry,
    But whither—O whither?

Hence idle delusions ! hence fears and confusions !
Not a single friend's severance lessens men's reverence,
No neighbour of rank quits my sumptuous banquets
    Without lauding their donor ;
Throughout the wide county I'm famed for my bounty,
    All hold me in honour.

Let the dotard and craven by fear be enslaven.
They have vanished ! How fast fly these images ghastly,
    When in firm self-reliance,
You determine on treating the brain's sickly cheating,
    With scorn and defiance !

Ha ha ! I am fearless henceforward and tearless,
No coinage of fancy, no dream's necromancy
Shall sadden and darken—God help me!—hist—hearken !
'Tis the shriek soul-appalling he uttered when falling !

By day thus affrighted, 'tis worse when benighted ;
With the clock's midnight boom, from the church on his
    tomb,

There comes a sharp screaming too fearful for dreaming;
Bone fingers unholy draw the foot curtains slowly,
O God! how they stare at me, flare at me, glare at me,
  Those eyes of a Gorgon!
Beneath the clothes sinking with shuddering shrinking,
A mental orgasm and bodily spasm
  Convulse every organ.

Nerves a thousand times stronger could bear it no longer,
Grief, sickness, compunction, dismay in conjunction,
Nights and days ghost-prolific, more grim and terrific
  Than judges and juries,
Make the heart writhe and falter more than gibbet and
  halter.
Arrest me, secure me, seize, handcuff, immure me!
I own my transgression—will make full confession,
Quick—quick! Let me plunge in some dark-vaulted
  dungeon,
Where, tho' tried and death-fated, I may not be baited
  By devils and furies!

THE CONTRAST.

WRITTEN UNDER WINDSOR TERRACE, THE DAY AFTER THE FUNERAL OF GEORGE
THE THIRD.

I saw him last on this Terrace proud,
 Walking in health and gladness,
Begirt with his Court; and in all the crowd
 Not a single look of sadness.

Bright was the sun, and the leaves were green,
 Blithely the birds were singing,
The cymbal replied to the tambourine,
 And the bells were merrily ringing.

THE CONTRAST.

I have stood with the crowd beside his bier,
    When not a word was spoken;
But every eye was dim with a tear,
    And the silence by sobs was broken.

I have heard the earth on his coffin pour
    To the muffled drum's deep rolling,
While the minute-gun with its solemn roar,
    Drowned the death-bell's tolling.

The time since he walked in his glory thus,
    To the grave till I saw him carried,
Was an age of the mightiest change to *us*,
    But to *him* a night unvaried.

We have fought the fight;—from his lofty throne
    The foe of our land we have tumbled;
And it gladdened each eye, save his alone,
    For whom that foe we humbled.

A daughter beloved—a Queen—a son—
    And a son's sole child have perished;
And sad was each heart, save the only one
    By which they were fondest cherished.

For his eyes were sealed, and his mind was dark,
    And he sat in his age's lateness,
Like a vision throned, as a solemn mark
    Of the frailty of human greatness.

His silver beard o'er a bosom spread,
    Unvexed by life's commotion,
Like a yearly-lengthening snow-drift shed
    On the calm of a frozen ocean.

THE BARD'S SONG TO HIS DAUGHTER.

O'er him oblivion's waters boomed,
   As the stream of time kept flowing;
And we only heard of our king when doomed
   To know that his strength was going.

At intervals thus the waves disgorge,
   By weakness rent asunder,
A part of the wreck of the Royal George,
   For the people's pity and wonder.

THE BARD'S SONG TO HIS DAUGHTER.

O DAUGHTER dear, my darling child,
   Prop of my mortal pilgrimage,
Thou who hast care and pain beguiled,
   And wreathed with Spring my wintry age—
Through thee a second prospect opes
   Of life, when but to live is glee,
And jocund joys, and youthful hopes,
   Come thronging to my heart through thee.

Backward thou lead'st me to the bowers
   Where love and youth their transports gave
While forward still thou strewest flowers,
   And bidst me live beyond the grave.
For still my blood in thee shall flow,
   Perhaps to warm a distant line,
Thy face my lineaments shall show,
   And even my thoughts survive in thine.

Yes, Daughter, when this tongue is mute—
   This heart is dust—these eyes are closed,
And thou art singing to thy lute
   Some stanza by thy sire composed,

To friends around thou may'st impart
 A thought of him who wrote the lays,
And from the grave my form shall start,
 Embodied forth to fancy's gaze.

Then to their memories will throng
 Scenes shared with him who lies in earth,
The cheerful page, the lively song,
 The woodland walk, or festive mirth;
Then may they heave the pensive sigh
 That friendship seeks not to control,
And from the fixed and thoughtful eye
 The half unconscious tears may roll:

Such now bedew my cheek—but mine
 Are drops of gratitude and love,
That mingle human with divine—
 The gift below, its source above.—
How exquisitely dear thou art
 Can only be by tears express'd,
And the fond thrilling of my heart
 While thus I clasp thee to my breast.

THE FLOWER THAT FEELS NOT SPRING.

FROM the prisons dark of the circling bark
 The leaves of tenderest green are glancing;
They gambol on high in the bright blue sky,
 Fondly with spring's young Zephyrs dancing,
While music and joy and jubilee gush
From the lark and linnet, the blackbird and thrush.

The butterfly springs on its new-born wings,
   The dormouse starts from his wintry sleeping;
The flowers of earth find a second birth,
   To light and life from the darkness leaping :
The roses and tulips will soon resume
Their youth's first perfume and primitive bloom.

What renders me sad when all nature glad
   The heart of each living creature cheers ?
I laid in the bosom of earth a blossom,
   And watered its bed with a father's tears;
But the grave has no spring, and I still deplore
That the floweret I planted comes up no more !

That eye whose soft blue, of the firmament's hue,
   Expressed all holy and heavenly things, —
Those ringlets bright, which scattered a light
   Such as angels shake from their sunny wings—
That cheek, in whose freshness my heart had trust—
All—all have perished—my daughter is dust !

Yet the blaze sublime of thy virtue's prime,
   Still gilds my tears and a balm supplies,
As the matin ray of the god of day
   Brightens the dew which at last it dries :
Yes, Fanny ! I cannot regret thy clay,
When I think where thy spirit has winged its way.

So wither we all—so flourish and fall,
   Like the flowers and weeds that in churchyards wave ;
Our leaves we spread over comrades dead,
   And blossom and bloom with our root in the grave ;—
Springing from earth into earth we are thrust,
Ashes to ashes and dust to dust !

If death's worst smart is to feel that we part
    From those we love and shall see no more,
It softens its sting to know that we wing
    Our flight to the friends who have gone before;
And the grave is a boon and a blessing to me,
If it waft me, O Fanny, my daughter, to thee!

MORAL RUINS.

ASIA's rock-hollowed Fanes, first-born of Time,
                In sculpture's prime,
Wrought by the ceaseless toil of many a race,
                Whom none may trace,
Have crumbled back to wastes of ragged stone,
And formless caverns, desolate and lone;——

Egypt's stern Temples, whose colossal mound,
                Sphinx-guarded, frowned
From brows of Granite challenges to Fate,
                And human hate,
Are giant ruins in a desert land,
Or sunk to sculptured quarries in the sand.

The marble miracles of Greece and Rome,
                Temple and Dome,
Art's masterpieces, awful in the excess
                Of loveliness,
Hallowed by statued Gods which might be thought
To be themselves by the Celestials wrought,——

Where are they now?—their majesty august
    Grovels in dust.
Time on their altars prone their ruins flings
    As offerings,
Forming a lair whence ominous bird and brute
Their wailful *Misereres* howl and hoot.

Down from its height the Druid's sacred stone
    In sport is thrown,
And many a Christian Fane have change and hate
    Made desolate,
Prostrating saint, apostle, statue, bust,
With Pagan deities to mingle dust.

On these dear sepulchres of buried days
    How sad to gaze!
Yet, since their substances were perishable,
    And hands unstable
Upreared their piles, no wonder that decay
Both man and monument should sweep away.

Ah me! how much more saddened is my mood,
    How heart-subdued,
The ruins and the wrecks when I behold
    By time unrolled,
Of all the Faiths that man has ever known,
World-worshipped once—now spurned and overthrown!

Religions—from the soul deriving breath,
    Should know no death;
Yet do they perish, mingling their remains
    With fallen fanes;
Creeds, canons, dogmas, councils, are the wrecked
And mouldering Masonry of intellect.——

Apis, Osiris, paramount of yore
                On Egypt's shore,
Woden and Thor, through the wide North adored,
                With blood outpoured;
Jove, and the multiform Divinities,
To whom the Pagan nations bowed their knees——

Lo! they are cast aside, dethroned, forlorn,
                Defaced, out-worn,
Like the world's childish dolls, which but insult
                Its age adult,
Or prostrate scarecrows, on whose rags we tread,
With scorn proportioned to our former dread.

Alas for human reason! all is change
                Ceaseless and strange;
All ages form new systems, leaving heirs
                To cancel theirs:
The future can but imitate the past,
And instability alone will last.——

Is there no compass left, by which to steer
                This erring sphere?
No tie that may indissolubly bind
                To God, mankind?
No code that may defy time's sharpest tooth?
No fixed, immutable, unerring truth?

There is! there is!——one primitive and sure
                Religion pure,
Unchanged in spirit, though its forms and codes
                Wear myriad modes,
Contains all creeds within its mighty span——
THE LOVE OF GOD, DISPLAYED IN LOVE OF MAN.——

This is the Christian's faith, when rightly read ;——
     Oh ! may it spread
Till Earth, redeemed from every hateful leaven,
     Makes peace with heaven :
Below——one blessed brotherhood of love ;
One Father——worshipped with one voice — above !

MORAL ALCHEMY.

THE toils of Alchemists, whose vain pursuit
     Sought to transmute
Dross into gold,——their secrets and their store
     Of mystic lore,
What to the jibing modern do they seem ?
An ignis fatuus chase, a phantasy, a dream !

Yet for enlightened *moral* Alchemists
     There still exists
A philosophic stone, whose magic spell
     No tongue may tell,
Which renovates the soul's decaying health,
And what it touches turns to purest mental wealth.

This secret is revealed in every trace
     Of Nature's face,
Whose seeming frown invariably tends
     To smiling ends,
Transmuting ills into their opposite,
And all that shocks the sense to subsequent delight.

Seems Earth unlovely in her robe of snow?
                Then look below,
Where Nature in her subterranean Ark,
                Silent and dark,
Already has each floral germ unfurled
That shall revive and clothe the dead and naked world.

Behold those perished flowers to earth consigned—
                They, like mankind,
Seek in their grave new birth.   By nature's power
                Each in its hour
Clothed in new beauty, from its tomb shall spring,
And from its tube or chalice heavenward incense fling.

Laboratories of a wider fold
                I now behold,
Where are prepared the harvests yet unborn
                Of wine, oil, corn.—
In those mute rayless banquet-halls I see
Myriads of coming feasts with all their revelry.

Yon teeming and minuter cells enclose
                The embryos
Of fruits and seeds, food for the feathered race,
                Whose chaunted grace,
Swelling in choral gratitude on high,
Shall with thanksgiving anthems melodize the sky.

And what materials, mystic Alchemist!
                Dost thou enlist
To fabricate this ever-varied feast,
                For man, bird, beast?
Whence the life, plenty, music, beauty, bloom?
From silence, languor, death, unsightliness and gloom!

From Nature's magic hand whose touch makes sadness
                 Eventual gladness,
The reverent moral Alchemist may learn
                 The art to turn
Fate's roughest, hardest, most forbidding dross,
Into the mental gold that knows not change or loss.

Lose we a valued friend ?—To soothe our woe
                 Let us bestow
On those who still survive an added love,
                 So shall we prove,
Howe'er the dear departed we deplore,
In friendship's sum and substance no diminished store.

Lose we our health ?—Now may we fully know
                 What thanks we owe
For our sane years, perchance of lengthened scope ;
                 Now does our hope
Point to the day when sickness, taking flight,
Shall make us better feel health's exquisite delight.

In losing fortune, many a lucky elf
                 Has found himself.—
As all our moral bitters are design'd
                 To brace the mind,
And renovate its healthy tone, the wise
Their sorest trials hail as blessings in disguise.

There is *no* gloom on earth ; for God above
                 Chastens in love,
Transmuting sorrows into golden joy
                 Free from alloy,
His dearest attribute is still to bless,
And man's most welcome hymn is grateful cheerfulness.

MORAL COSMETICS.

YE who would save your features florid,
Lithe limbs, bright eyes, unwrinkled forehead
From age's devastation horrid,
    Adopt this plan :—
'Twill make, in climates cold or torrid,
    A hale old man.

Avoid, in youth, luxurious diet,
Restrain the passions' lawless riot;
Devoted to domestic quiet,
    Be wisely gay :
So shall ye, spite of age's fiat,
    Resist decay.

Seek not in Mammon's worship pleasure,
But find your richest, dearest treasure,
In books, friends, music, polished leisure ;
    The mind, not sense,
Made the sole scale by which ye measure
    Your opulence.

This is the solace, this the science,
Life's purest, sweetest, best appliance,
That disappoints not man's reliance,
    Whate'er his state ;
But challenges, with calm defiance,
    Time, fortune, fate.

THE OLD MAN'S PÆAN.

VAINLY, ye libellers! your page
Assaults and villifies old age,
    'Tis still life's golden æra;
Its pleasures, wisely understood,
An unalloyed unfailing good,
    Its evils a chimæra.——

Time's victor, I am victor still——
Holding the privilege at will
    To seize him by the forelock;
On me would he return the grasp,
He finds there's nothing left to clasp——
    Not even a single hoar lock.——

We blame the idolatrous divine
Who gilds and decorates his shrine,
    The Deity neglected;
Yet our self-adoration blind
Is body-worship—to the mind
    No reverence directed.

Greybeards there are, who thinking art
Can conquer nature, play the part
    Of adolescent friskers;
Swindlers and counterfeits of truth,
They strive to cheat us by false youth,
    False teeth, hair, eyebrows, whiskers.

While to the frame due care I give,
No masquerader will I live,
    To no disguises pander;

THE OLD MAN'S PÆAN.

But rather seek to save from blight
My mind in all its pristine plight
    Of cheerfulness and candor.

A youthful cheer sustains us old,
As arrows best their course uphold
    Winged by a lightsome feather.——
Happy the young old man who thus
Bears, like a human arbutus,
    Life's flowers and fruit together.

To dark oblivion I bequeath
The ruddy cheek, brown hair, white teeth,
    And eyes that brightly twinkle ;——
Crows' feet may plough with furrows deep
My features, if I can but keep
    My mind without a wrinkle.

Young, I was never free——my soul
Still mastered by the stern control
    Of some tyrannic passion ;
While my poor body, servile tool !
The livery wore of fop and fool,
    An abject slave of fashion.

Thanks to thy welcome touch, old age !
Which strongest chains can disengage,
    The bondman 's manumitted :——
Released from labour, thraldom, strife,
I pasture in the park of life,
    Unsaddled and unbitted.

If drawn for the Militia——called
On Juries, where the heart is galled
    With crime, chicane, disaster,

" Begone," I cry—" avaunt! avast!
Thank heaven! I'm sixty, and at last
    Am of myself free master."

An actor once in every strife
That agitates the stage of life,
    A lover, fearer, hater,
Now in senility's snug box
I sit, aloof from all their shocks,
    A passive, pleased spectator.

Free-traders, Chartists, Puseyites!
Your warfare, with its wrongs and rights,
    In me no rage arouses;
I read the news, and cry, if hurt
At Whigs and Tories throwing dirt,
    " A plague on both your houses!"

Tailors! avaunt your bills and spells!
When fashion plays on folly's bells,
    No haddock can be deafer;—
Comfort and neatness all my care,
I stick to broadcloth, and forswear
    Both Macintosh and Zephyr.--

'Tis but our sensual pleasures' zest
That time can dull;—our purest, best
    Defy decay or capture.
A landscape—book—a work of art—
My friends, my home—still fill my heart
    With undiminished rapture.

Fled some few years, old Time may try
Again to wake my rhyme, when I,
    Obeying the vagary,

May thus subscribe the muse's frisk:
" My pensive public—yours !—A BRISK
   YOUNG SEPTUAGENARY !"

ANSWER TO "AN OLD MAN'S PÆAN."

WRITTEN (*invitâ Minervâ*) AT THE INSTIGATION OF J. H.

THOU greybeard gay ! whose muse—(perchance
In second childhood's ignorance,)
      Inspired " An Old Man's Pæan,"
Hear how a brother senior sings
Sexagenarian sufferings,
      In strains antipodean !

Young, I could take a morning's sport ;
Play matches in the Tennis Court,
      So strong was I and plastic ;
Dine out, and yet with spirit light
And body unfatigued, at night,
      Could sport the toe fantastic.

Behold me now !—my limbs are stiff :
An open door, an east-wind's whiff,
      Brings sharp rheumatic touches ;
A chamber-horse my only nag,
I mope at home, or slowly drag
      My gouty feet on crutches.

Once I devoured whatever came,
And never knew, except by name,
      The heartburn, bile, dyspepsy :
Now I must fast—eat what I hate,
Or all my ailments aggravate,
      From ache to epilepsy.

How starving Tantalus of old
Was punished by the gods, is told
    In many a classic stanza ;
And all must recollect the wand
That whisked the viands from the hand
    Of hungry Sancho Panza :—

Their fate without their fault is mine.
Champagne and claret, drinks divine
    As nectar or ambrosia,
I may not quaff, but—(horrid bore !)
My sherry from a cruet pour
    And think of past symposia.

At home my wife *will* supervise
Each meal I take.   I wish her eyes
    Were sometimes touched with blindness!
But no—they move not from my plate :
God bless her ! how I love, yet hate
    Her ever watchful kindness.

"My dear ! you know you 're bilious—pray
Avoid the turtle soup to-day,
    And do not touch the salmon ;
Just take a chicken wing, or leg,
But no rich sauce—and let me beg
    You will not taste the gammon."

Shell-fish—of yore my favourite food,
Are now my bane ; yet crabs eschew'd,
    Might make an angel crabbed—
No wonder if I quit the treat
Of dainties that I may not eat,
    Half starving and half rabid.

Debarred by fond affection's care
From all my palate yearns to share,
   A kindness still more cruel
Gives me *carte blanche* in all I loathe—
Bread-puddings, sago, mutton-broth,
   Rice-milk, and water-gruel!

INVOCATION.

[WRITTEN IN THE NEIGHBOURHOOD OF ABBOTSFORD DURING THE LAST ILLNESS
OF SIR WALTER SCOTT.

SPIRITS! Intelligences! Passions! Dreams!
   Ghosts! Genii! Sprites!
Muses, that haunt the Heliconian streams,
   Inspiring Lights!
Whose intellectual fires, in Scott combined,
Supplied the sun of his omniscient mind!

Ye who have o'er-informed and overwrought
   His teeming soul,
Bidding it scatter galaxies of thought
   From pole to pole;
Enlightening others till itself grew dark—
A midnight heaven, without one starry spark;—

Spirits of Earth and Air—of Light and Gloom!
   Awake! arise!
Restore the victim you have made—relume
   His darkling eyes.
Wizards! be all your magic skill unfurl'd,
To charm to health the Charmer of the World!

The scabbard, by its sword outworn, repair;
 Give to his lips
Their lore, than Chrysostom's more rich and rare :
 Dispel the eclipse
That intercepts his intellectual light,
And saddens all mankind with tears and night.

Not only for the Bard of highest worth,
 But best of men,
Do I invoke ye, Powers of Heaven and Earth !
 Oh ! where and when
Shall we again behold his counterpart—
Such kindred excellence of head and heart ?

So good and great—benevolent as wise—
 On his high throne
How meekly hath he borne his faculties !
 How finely shown
A model to the irritable race,
Of generous kindness, courtesy, and grace !

If he *must* die, how great to perish thus
 In glory's blaze ;
A world, in requiem unanimous,
 Weeping his praise !
While Angels wait to catch his parting breath—
Who would not give his life for such a death ?

THE MOTHER'S MISTAKE.

HEARD you that piercing shriek—the throe
Of fear and agonising woe?
It is a mother, who with wild
  Despairing looks and gasping breath,
Thinks she beholds her only child
  Extended on the floor in death!
That darling Babe whose natal cry
Had thrilled her heart with ecstacy,
As with baptizing tears of bliss
  Her nestling treasure she bedewed,
Then clasped him with a silent kiss,
  And heavenward looked her gratitude :——
That darling babe who, while he pressed
His rosebud lips around her breast,
Would steal an upward glance, and bless
With smiles his mother's tenderness ;
Confining laughter to his eyes,
Lest he should lose the teeming prize :——
That darling Babe who, sleeping, proved,
More than when waking, how she loved.
Then was her ever watchful ear
  Prepared to catch the smallest noise,
Which sometimes hope and sometimes fear
  Would liken to her infant's voice.
With beating heart and timid flush,
  On tiptoe to his cot she crept,
Lifting the curtain with a hush,
  To gaze upon him as he slept,
Then would she place his outstretched arm
Beside his body, close and warm ;

THE MOTHER'S MISTAKE.

Adjust his scattered clothes aright,
And shade his features from the light,
And look a thousand fond caressings
And move her lips in speechless blessings,
Then steal away with eyes that glisten,
Again to linger round and listen.
Oh! can she bear to think that he
Whom she has loved so tenderly,
Her only earthly hope and stay,
For ever should be wrenched away?
No, no!——to such o'erpowering grief
Oblivion brings a short relief:
She hears no sound; all objects swim
Before her sight confused and dim;
She feels each sickening sense decay,
Sinks shuddering down, and faints away!

Her child revives——its fit is o'er;
  When with affrighted zeal it tries
By voice and kisses to restore
  The mother's dormant faculties;
Till nature's tides with quickened force
Resume their interrupted course:
Her eyes she opens, sees her boy,
  Gazes with sense-bewildered start,
Utters a thrilling cry of joy,
  Clasps him in transport to her heart,
Stamps kisses on his mouth, his cheek,
Looks up to heaven, and tries to speak;
But voice is drowned in heaving throbs,
Outgushing tears, and gasping sobs.

THE SUN'S ECLIPSE.—July 8th, 1842.

'Tis cloudless morning, but a frown misplaced,
   Cold—lurid—strange,
The summer smile from Nature's brow hath chased.
   What fearful change,
What menacing catastrophe is thus
Ushered by such prognostics ominous?

Is it the light of day, this livid glare,
   Death's counterpart :—
What means the withering coldness in the air
   That chills my heart,
And what the gloom portentous that hath made
The glow of morning a funereal shade?

O'er the Sun's disc a dark orb wins its slow
   Gloom-deepening way,
Climbs—spreads—enshrouds—extinguishes—and lo !
   The god of day
Hangs in the sky, a corpse! the usurper's might
Hath stormed his throne, and quenched the life of light !

A pall is on the earth—the screaming birds
   To covert speed ;
Bewildered and aghast, the bellowing herds
   Rush o'er the mead ;
While men, pale shadows in the ghastly gloom,
Seem spectral forms just risen from the tomb.

Transient, though total, was that drear eclipse;
   With might restored
The Sun regladdened earth—but human lips
   Have never poured

In mortal ears the horrors of the sight
That thrilled my soul that memorable night.

To every distant zone and fulgent star
        Mine eyes could reach,
And the wide waste was one chaotic war;
        O'er all and each,
Above—beneath—around me—everywhere,
Was anarchy—convulsion—death—despair.

'Twas noon, and yet a deep unnatural night
        Enshrouded Heaven,
Save where some orb unsphered, or satellite
        Franticly driven,
Glared as it darted through the darkness dread,
Blind—rudderless—unchecked—unpiloted.

A thousand simultaneous thunders crashed,
        As here and there
Some rushing planet 'gainst another dashed,
        Shooting through air
Volleys of shattered wreck, when, both destroyed,
Foundered and sank in the engulfing void.

Others, self-kindled, as they whirled and turned
        Without a guide,
Burst into flames, and rushing as they burned
        With range more wide,
Like fire-ships that some stately fleet surprise,
Spread havoc through the constellated skies.

While stars kept falling from their spheres—as though
        The heavens wept fire,
Earth was a raging hell of war and woe
        Most deep and dire,

3*

Virtue was vice—vice virtue—all was strife,
Brute force was law—justice the assassin's knife.

From that fell scene my space-commanding eye
   Glad to withdraw,
I pierced the empyrean palace of the sky
   And shuddering saw
A vacant throne—a sun's extinguished sphere,
All else a void—dark, desolate, and drear.

"What mean," I cried, "these sights unparalleled,
   These scenes of fear?"
When lo! a voice replied, and Nature held
   Her breath to hear,
"Mortal, the scroll before thine eyes unfurled,
Displays a *soul eclipse*—an *atheist world.*"

I woke—my dream was o'er! What ecstacy
   It was to know
That God was guide and guardian of the sky,
   That man below
Deserved the love I felt—I could not speak
The thrilling joy, whose tears were on my cheek!

LACHRYMOSE WRITERS.

Ye human screech-owls, who delight
 To herald woe—whose day is night,
Whose mental food is misery and moans,
 If ye must needs uphold the pall,
 And walk at Pleasure's funeral,
Be Mutes—and publish not your cries and groans.

LACHRYMOSE WRITERS.

Near a menagerie to dwell,
Annoyed by ceaseless groan and yell,
Is sad, altho' we cannot blame the brutes ;
A far worse neighbour is the man
Whose study is a Caravan,
Whence the caged monster ever howls and hoots.

Ye say that Earth's a charnel—life
Incessant wretchedness and strife—
That all is doom below, and wrath above,
The sun and moon sepulchral lamps,
The sky a vault, whose baleful damps
Soon blight and moulder all that live and love.

Man, as your diatribes aver,
Only makes reason minister
To deeds irrational and schemes perverse ;
Human in name, he proves in all
His acts a hateful animal,
And woman (monstrous calumny) is worse.

This earth, whose walls are stony gloom,
Whose roof rains tears, whose floor 's a tomb
With its chain-rattling beach and lashing waves,
Is, ye maintain, a fitting jail
Where felon man the woes may wail,
From which no prudence guards, no mercy saves.

Even were it true, this lachrymose
List of imaginary woes,
Why from our sympathy extort more tears ?
Why blazon grief—why make the Press
Groan with repinings and distress,
Why knell despair for ever in our ears ?

Ungrateful and calumnious crew,
Whose plaints, as impious as untrue,
From morbid intellects derive their birth;
Away! begone to mope and moan,
And weep in some asylum lone,
Where ye may rail unheard at heaven and earth.

Earth! on whose stage in pomp arrayed
Life's joyous interlude is played,
Earth! with thy pageants ever new and bright,
Thy woods and waters, hills and dales,
How dead must be the soul that fails
To see and bless thy beauties infinite!

Man! whose high intellect supplies
A never-failing Paradise
Of holy and enrapturing pursuits,
Whose heart's a fount of fresh delight,
Pity the Cynics who would blight
Thy godlike gifts, and rank thee with the brutes.

Oh Woman! who from realms above
Hast brought to Earth the heaven of love,
Terrestrial angel, beautiful as pure!
No pains, no penalties dispense
On thy traducers—their offence
Is its own punishment most sharp and sure.

Father and God! whose love and might
To every sense are blazoned bright
On the vast three-leaved Bible—earth—sea—sky,
Pardon the impugners of thy laws,
Expand their hearts and give them cause
To bless the exhaustless grace they now deny.

WHY ARE THEY SHUT!

The following Stanzas were composed while the author was sitting *outside* a country church in Sussex, much regretting that, as it was week day, he could not gain admittance to the sacred edifice.

WHY are our Churches shut with jealous care,
　Bolted and barred against our bosom's yearning,
Save for the few short hours of Sabbath prayer,
　With the bell's tolling steadily returning?
　　　　　　　　　Why are they shut?

If with diurnal drudgeries o'erwrought,
　Or sick of dissipation's dull vagaries,
We wish to snatch one little space for thought,
　Or holy respite in our sanctuaries,
　　　　　　　　　Why are they shut?

What! shall the Church, the House of Prayer, no more,
　Give tacit notice from its fastened portals,
That for six days 'tis useless to adore,
　Since God will hold no communings with mortals?
　　　　　　　　　Why are they shut?

Are there no sinners in the churchless week,
　Who wish to sanctify a vowed repentance;
Are there no hearts bereft which fain would seek
　The only balm for Death's unpitying sentence?
　　　　　　　　　Why are they shut?

Are there no poor, no wronged, no heirs of grief,
　No sick, who when their strength or courage falters?
Long for a moment's respite or relief,
　By kneeling at the GOD OF MERCY'S altars?
　　　　　　　　　Why are they shut?

Are there no wicked, whom, if tempted in,
  Some qualm of conscience or devout suggestion
Might suddenly redeem from future sin?
  Oh! if there be, how solemn is the question,
                    Why are they shut?

In foreign climes mechanics leave their tasks
  To breathe a passing prayer in their Cathedrals:
There they have week-day shrines, and no one asks,
  When he would kneel to them, and count his bead-
    rolls,
                    Why are they shut?

Seeing them enter sad and disconcerted,
  To quit those cheering fanes with looks of gladness—
How often have my thoughts to ours reverted!
  How oft have I exclaimed in tones of sadness,
                    Why are they shut?

For who within a Parish Church can stroll,
  Wrapt in its week-day stillness and vacation,
Nor feel that in the very air his soul
  Receives a sweet and hallowing lustration?
                    Why are they shut?

The vacant pews, blank aisles, and empty choir,
  All in a deep sepulchral silence shrouded,
An awe more solemn and intense inspire,
  Than when with Sabbath congregations crowded.
                    Why are they shut?

The echoes of our footsteps, as we tread
  On hollow graves, are spiritual voices;
And holding mental converse with the dead,
  In holy reveries our soul rejoices.
                    Why are they shut?

If there be one—one only—who might share
This sanctifying week-day adoration,
Were but our churches open to his prayer,
Why—I demand with earnest iteration—
Why are they shut?

THE LIBELLED BENEFACTOR.

THEY warned me by all that affection could urge,
To repel his advances and fly from his sight,
They called him a fiend, a destroyer, a scourge,
And whispered his name with a shudder of fright.

They said that disease went as herald before,
While sorrow and severance followed his track,
They besought me if ever I came to his door,
Not a moment to pause, but turn instantly back.

"His breath," they exclaimed, "is a pestilence foul,
His aspect more hateful than language can tell,
His touch is pollution,—no Gorgon or Ghoul
In appearance and deeds is more loathsome and fell."

Such stern prohibitions, descriptions so dire,
By which the most dauntless might well be dismayed,
In me only wakened a deeper desire
To gaze on the monster so darkly portrayed.

I sought him—I saw him—he stood by a marsh,
Where henbane and hemlock with poppies entwined;
He was pale, he was grave, but no feature was harsh,
His eye was serene, his expression was kind.

"This stigmatized being," I cried in surprise,
    "Wears a face most benignant; but looks are not facts,
Physiognomy often abuses our eyes;
    I'll follow his footsteps and judge by his acts."

There came from a cottage a cry of alarm,
    An infant was writhing in agonies sore,
His hand rocked the cradle, its touch was a charm,
    The babe fell asleep, and its anguish was o'er.

He reached a proud mansion where, worn by the woe
    Of consumption, a Beauty lay withered, in bed;
Her pulse he compressed with his finger, and lo!
    The complaint of long years in a moment had fled!

He paused where he heard the disconsolate groan
    Of a widow with manifold miseries crushed;
Where a pauper was left in his sickness to groan:
    Both were healed at his sight, and their sorrows were
        hushed.

He sped where a king, sorely smitten with age,
    In vain sought relief from the pangs he endured;
"I come," said the stranger, "your woes to assuage;"
    He spoke, and the monarch was instantly cured.

Astounded by deeds which appeared to bespeak
    In the fiend a benevolent friend of mankind,
From himself I resolved a solution to seek
    Of the strange contradictions that puzzled my mind.

"Chase, mystical being," I cried, "this suspense;
    How comes it thou'rt blackened by every tongue,
When in truth thou'rt the champion, the hope, the
        defence
    Of the king and the beggar, the old and the young?"

"Thou hast witnessed"—he answered—(his voice and
 his face
 Were all that is musical, bland, and benign),
"Not a tithe of the blessings I shed on the race
 Who my form and my attributes daily malign.

"All distinctions of fortune, of birth, of degree,
 Disappear where my levelling banner I wave;
From his desolate dungeon the captive I free;
 His fetters I loose from the suffering slave.

"And when from their stormy probation on earth,
 The just and the righteous in peace I dismiss,
I give them a new and more glorious birth
 In regions of pure and perennial bliss."

"Let me bless thee," I cried, "for thy mission of love,
 Oh say to what name shall I fashion my breath?"
"THE ANGEL OF LIFE is my title above,
 But short-sighted mortals have christened me DEATH!"

DIRGE FOR A LIVING POET.*

WHAT! shall the mind of bard—historian—sage,
 Be prostrate laid upon oblivion's bier,
Shall darkness quench the beacon of our age,
 "Without the meed of one melodious tear?"
  Will none, with genius like his own,
  Mourn the fine intellect o'erthrown,
That died in giving life to deathless heirs?
  Are worthier voices mute? then I
  The Muse's humblest votary,
Will pour my wailful dirge and sympathising prayer.

  * Written during the last illness of Southey.

Well may I mourn that mental sun's eclipse,
  For in his study have I sate enshrined,
And reverently listened while his lips
  Mastered the master-spirits of mankind,
      As his expanding wisdom took
      New range from his consulted book.
Oh, to what noble thoughts didst thou give birth,
      Thou poet-sage, whose life and mind
      In mutual perfectness combined
The spirit's loftiest flight, with purest moral worth!

Behold the withering change! amid the rays
  That formed a halo round those volumed wits,
Amid his own imperishable lays
  In silent, blank fatuity he sits!
      Seeking a respite from his curse,
      His body, now his spirit's hearse,
Still haunts that book-charmed room, for there alone
      Thought-gleams illume his wandering eyes,
      As lightnings flicker o'er the skies
Where the departed sun in cloudless glory shone.

Oh withering, woeful change—oh living death!
  Lo! where he strays at Fancy's aimless beck,
On his dementate brow the titled wreath,
  A mournful mockery of reason's wreck.
      Roaming by Derwent's silent shore
      Or dark-hued Greta's rushing roar,
A human statue!   His unconscious stare
      Knows not the once familiar spot,
      Knows not the partner of his lot,
Who, as she guides him, sobs a broken-hearted prayer.

Oh flood and fell, lake, moorland, valley, hill!
  Mourn the dark bard who sang your praise of yore.

Oh Rydal-Falls, Lodore, and Dungeon Gill !
  Down the rock's cheek your tearful gushes pour.
    Ye crag-enveloped Tarns that sleep
    In your hushed craters, wake and weep.
Ye mountains ! hide your sorrowing heads in cloud :
    As sobbing winds around ye moan ;
    Helvellyn ! Skiddaw ! wail and groan,
And clothe your giant forms in vapour's mourning shroud.

Why make appeal to these ? Ye good and wise
  Who worshipped at his intellectual shrine,
Ye kindred natures, who can sympathise
  With genius 'reft of reason's light divine,
    Ye whom his learning, virtue, lays,
    Taught, guided, charmed in other days,
Let all your countless voices be combined,
    As on your knees, ye pour on high
    This choral supplicating cry—
Restore, restore, O God ! our poet's wandering mind !

CAMPBELL'S FUNERAL.*

'Tis well to see these accidental great,
  Noble by birth, or Fortune's favour blind,
Gracing themselves in adding grace and state
  To the more noble eminence of mind,
    And doing homage to a bard
    Whose breast by Nature's gems was starred,
Whose patent by the hand of God himself was signed.

* He was buried in Poets' Corner, Westminster Abbey, his pall
being supported by six noblemen.

While monarchs sleep, forgotten, unrevered,
 Time trims the lamp of intellectual fame:
The builders of the pyramids, who reared
  Mountains of stone, left none to tell their name.
   Though Homer's tomb was never known,
   A mausoleum of his own,
Long as the world endures his greatness shall proclaim.

What lauding sepulchre does Campbell want?
 'Tis his to give, and not derive renown.
What monumental bronze or adamant,
  Like his own deathless lays can hand him down?
   Poets outlast their tombs: the bust
   And statue soon revert to dust;
The dust they represent still wears the laurel crown.

The solid Abbey walls that seem time-proof,
 Formed to await the final day of doom;
The clustered shafts and arch-supported roof,
  That now enshrine and guard our Campbell's tomb,
   Become a ruined shattered fane,
   May fall and bury him again,
Yet still the bard shall live, his fame-wreath still shall
 bloom.

Methought the monumental effigies
 Of elder poets that were grouped around,
Leaned from their pedestals with eager eyes,
  To peer into the excavated ground
   Where lay the gifted, good, and brave,
   While earth from Kosciusko's grave
Fell on his coffin-plate with freedom-shrieking sound.

And over him the kindred dust was strew'd
 Of Poets' Corner. O misnomer strange!

The poet's confine is the amplitude
　　Of the whole earth's illimitable range,
　　　　O'er which his spirit wings its flight,
　　　　Shedding an intellectual light,
A sun that never sets, a moon that knows no change.

Around his grave in radiant brotherhood,
　　As if to form a halo o'er his head,
Not few of England's master-spirits stood,
　　Bards, artists, sages, reverently led
　　　　To waive each separating plea
　　　　Of sect, clime, party, and degree,
All honouring him on whom Nature all honours shed.

To me the humblest of the mourning band,
　　Who knew the bard through many a changeful year,
It was a proud sad privilege to stand
　　Beside his grave and shed a parting tear.
　　　　Seven lustres had he been my friend,
　　　　Be that my plea when I suspend
This all-unworthy wreath on such a poet's bier.

THE LIFE AND DEATH.

THE LIFE.

HATH Momus descended—the god of Mirth—
　　To glad the world with his triumphs thus ?
Or is it a mortal, who tastes on earth
　　An apotheosis rapturous !
While his worshippers hail him with choral cries,
And Laughter's reverberant ecstacies !

He moves like a mental sun, whose light
   Scatters around an electric ray,
Which every eye that beholds, is bright,
   And every bosom that feels, is gay—
A sun (it is own'd by a nation's lips),
That hath ne'er been dimmed—never known eclipse !

As this Spirit sits on his throne elate,
   They tender him homage from every sphere :
From the rich, the noble, the wise, the great—
   Nay, even the King is a courtier here ;
And vassal-like makes his crown submit
To the majesty of sceptred Wit.

They press him with flattering words and wiles
   To honour and grace their lordly halls,
And impart by his mirth, and songs, and smiles,
   A glory and zest to their festivals.
For they know that his presence can banish gloom,
And give light and life to the banquet-room.

On what aching hearts hath he gladness poured !
   In scenes unnumbered, what countless throngs,
From the public stage to the festive board,
   Have, enraptured, hung on his mirthful songs !
At his wit's incessantly flashing light,
What shouts have startled the ear of night !

Ask you the name of the gifted man,
   Whose genius thus could enchant the world ;
Whose fame through both the hemispheres ran—
   Whose flag of triumph was never furled ?—
You ask it not, for you know that none
But MATHEWS alone has such trophies won !

THE DEATH.

Hark to the toll of the passing bell,
    Which "swinging slow with solemn roar,"
Carries the dismal funeral knell
    O'er the thrilling waves of the Plymouth shore;
And is borne afar by the shuddering breeze,
From Wembury's cliffs to Mount-Edgecombe's trees.

Nature appears to have thrown a pall
    Over that landscape so rich and fair,
For a withering gloom and sadness fall
    Alike upon ocean, earth, and air,
And the darkling heights in the distance show
Like spectral mourners, grim with woe.

The bittern's wail and the sea-mew's cry,
    Seem to share the deep and wide distress,
As their wings they spread, and seaward fly
    Away from that scene of wretchedness:
And the booming moan of the distant surge
Falls on the ear like a doleful dirge.

Hark! 'tis a female cry—'tis the sound
    Of a widow's heart with anguish torn;
A groan succeeds, and the sob profound
    Of a sireless son, aghast, forlorn!
And oh! how loving and loved they were,
Their own 'reft hearts can alone declare.

Behold! from St. Andrew's Church appears
    A funeral train in its sad array,
Whose mourners, blind in their staunchless tears,
    With faltering footsteps feel their way
To the bones and mould thrown up in a heap
Beside a sepulchre dark and deep.

The coffin is sunk, the prayer is poured—
    " Ashes to ashes, and dust to dust."
They sprinkle earth on the rattling board,
    And they whose heads o'er the grave are thrust,
Draw back at the sound with a shuddering start,
For its awful echoes thrill their heart.

As if it were sent to reveal and bless,
    A ray through the lurid vapour beams—
Pierces the sepulchre's ghastliness,
    And lo! on the coffin's plate it gleams.
Th' inscription now may be plainly read—
" *Charles Mathews*"—*that's* the name of the dead.

God! can it be?—is that breath resigned
    Which rendered the brightest joy more bright?
Does that life of life, and mind of mind,
    The circle's soul, and the world's delight,
Lie stretched in the coffin's silence, dark,
Cold—lifeless—ghastly—stiff and stark?

What proofs of his friendship, wit, and worth,
    On memory crowd, and recall past years!
But I cannot give their record birth,
    For my heart and my eyes are both in tears:
Let me drop the pen—let me quit the lay,
And rush from my own sad thoughts away.

HOPE'S YEARNINGS.

How sweet it is, when wearied with the jars
    Of wrangling sects, each soured with bigot leaven,
To let the Spirit burst its prison bars
    And soar into the deep repose of Heaven!

How sweet it is, when sick with strife and noise
   Of the fell brood that owes to faction birth,
To turn to Nature's tranquillizing joys,
   And taste the soothing harmonies of Earth!

But though the lovely Earth, and Sea, and Air,
   Be rich in joys that form a sumless sum,
Filled with Nepenthes that can banish care,
   And wrap the senses in Elysium,

'Tis sweeter still from these delights to turn
   Back to our kind—to watch the course of Man,
And for that blessed consummation yearn,
   When Nature shall complete her noble plan;

When hate, oppression, vice, and crime, shall cease,
   When War's ensanguined banner shall be furled,
And to our moral system shall extend
   The perfectness of the material world.

Sweetest of all, when 'tis our happy fate
   To drop some tribute, trifling though it prove,
On the thrice-hallowed altar dedicate
   To Man's improvement, truth, and social love.

Faith in our race's destined elevation,
   And its incessant progress to the goal,
Tends, by exciting hope and emulation,
   To realise the aspirings of the soul.

4

TO A LOG OF WOOD UPON THE FIRE.

WHEN Horace, as the snows descended
On Mount Soracte, recommended
      That logs be doubled,
Until a blazing fire arose,
I wonder whether thoughts like those
Which in *my* noddle interpose,
      His fancy troubled.

Poor Log ! I cannot hear thee sigh,
And groan, and hiss, and see thee die,
      To warm a Poet,
Without evincing thy success,
And as thou wanest less and less,
Inditing a farewell address
      To let thee know it.

Peeping from earth—a bud unveiled,
Some " bosky bourne" or dingle hailed
      Thy natal hour ;
While infant winds around thee blew,
And thou wert fed with silver dew,
And tender sunbeams oozing through
      Thy leafy bower.

Earth—water—air— thy growth prepared ;
And if perchance some robin, scared
      From neighbouring manor,
Perched on thy crest, it rocked in air,
Making his ruddy feathers flare
In the sun's ray, as if they were
      A fairy banner.

TO A LOG OF WOOD UPON THE FIRE.

Or if some nightingale impressed
Against thy branching top her breast
   Heaving with passion,
And in the leafy nights of June,
Outpoured her sorrows to the moon,
Thy trembling stem thou didst attune
   To each vibration.

Thou grew'st a goodly tree, with shoots
Fanning the sky, and earth-bound roots
   So grappled under,
That thou whom perching birds could swing,
And zephyrs rock with lightest wing,
From thy firm trunk unmoved didst fling
   Tempest and thunder.

Thine offspring leaves—death's annual prey,
Which Herod Winter tore away
   From thy caressing,
In heaps, like graves, around thee blown,
Each morn thy dewy tears have strown,
O'er each thy branching hands been thrown,
   As if in blessing.

Bursting to life, another race
At touch of Spring in thy embrace,
   Sported and fluttered;
Aloft, where wanton breezes played,
In thy knit boughs have ringdoves made
Their nest, and lovers in thy shade
   Their vows have uttered.

How oft thy lofty summits won
Morn's virgin smile, and hailed the sun
   With rustling motion;

TO A LOG OF WOOD UPON THE FIRE.

How oft in silent depths of night,
When the moon sailed in cloudless light,
Thou hast stood awe-struck at the sight
     In hushed devotion—

'Twere vain to ask; for doomed to fall,
The day appointed for us all
     O'er thee impended;
The hatchet, with remorseless blow,
First laid thee in the forest low,
Then cut thee into logs—and so
     Thy course was ended.

But not thine use—for moral rules,
Worth all the wisdom of the schools,
     Thou may'st bequeath me;
Bidding me cherish those who live
Above me, and the more I thrive,
A wider shade and shelter give
     To those beneath me.

So when death lays his axe on me,
I may resign, as calm as thee,
     My hold terrestrial;
Like thine my latter end be found,
Diffusing light and warmth around,
And like thy smoke my spirit bound
     To realms celestial.

UNPOSSESSED POSSESSIONS.

WHOSE are Windsor and Hampton, the pride of the land,
With their treasures and trophies so varied and grand?
    The Queen's, you reply :
    Deuce a bit! you and I
Through their gates, twice a week, making privileged way,
    Tread their gilded saloons,
    View their portraits, cartoons,
And, like Crusoe, are monarchs of all we survey.

And whose are our nobles' magnificent homes,
With their galleries, gardens, their statues and domes?
    His Grace's, my Lord's ?
    Ay, in law and in words,
But in fact they are ours, for the master, poor wight!
    Gladly leaving their view
    To the visiting crew,
Keeps a dear exhibition for others' delight.

And whose are the stag-haunted parks, the domains,
The woods and the waters, the hills and the plains?
    Yours and mine, for our eyes
    Daily make them our prize :
What more have their owners?——The care and the cost!
    Alas! for the great,
    Whose treasures and state,
Unprized when possessed, are regretted when lost.

When I float on the Thames, or am whisked o'er the roads,
To the numerous royal and noble abodes
    Whose delights I may share,
    Without ownership's care,

TO THE FURZE BUSH.

With what pity the titled and rich I regard,
 And exultingly cry,
  Oh! how happy am I
To be only a poor unpatrician bard!

TO THE FURZE BUSH.

LET Burns and old Chaucer unite
 The praise of the Daisy to sing—
Let Wordsworth of Celandine write,
 And crown her the Queen of the Spring;
The Hyacinth's classical fame
 Let Milton embalm in his verse;
Be mine the glad task to proclaim
 The Charms of untrumpeted Furze!

Of all other bloom when bereft,
 And Sol wears his wintery screen,
Thy sunshining blossoms are left
 To light up the common and green.
O why should they envy the peer
 His perfume of spices and myrrhs,
When the poorest their senses may cheer
 With incense diffused from the Furze?

It is bristled with thorns, I confess;
 But so is the much-flattered Rose:
Is the Sweetbriar lauded the less
 Because amid prickles it grows?
'Twere to cut off an epigram's point,
 Or disfurnish a knight of his spurs,
If we foolishly wished to disjoint
 Its arms from the lance-bearing Furze.

Ye dabblers in mines, who would clutch
   The wealth which their bowels enfold;
See! Nature, with Midas-like touch,
   Here turns a whole common to gold;
No niggard is she to the poor,
   But distributes whatever is hers,
And the wayfaring beggar is sure.
   Of a tribute of gold from the Furze.

Ye worldlings! learn hence to divide
   Your wealth with the children of want,
Nor scorn, in your fortune and pride,
   To be taught by the commonest plant.
If the wisest new wisdom may draw
   From things humble, as reason avers,
We too may receive Heaven's law,
   And beneficence learn from the Furze!

THE FIRST OF MARCH.

THE bud is in the bough, and the leaf is in the bud,
And Earth's beginning now in her veins to feel the blood,
Which, warmed by summer suns in the alembic of the
     vine,
From her founts will overrun in a ruddy gush of wine.

The perfume and the bloom that shall decorate the
     flower,
Are quickening in the gloom of their subterranean bower;
And the juices meant to feed trees, vegetables, fruits,
Unerringly proceed to their pre-appointed roots.

How awful is the thought of the wonders underground,
Of the mystic changes wrought in the silent, dark profound;
How each thing upward tends by necessity decreed,
And a world's support depends on the shooting of a seed!

The summer's in her ark, and this sunny-pinion'd day
Is commissioned to remark whether Winter holds her
    sway;
Go back, thou dove of peace, with the myrtle on thy
    wing,
Say, that floods and tempests cease and the world is ripe
    for Spring.

Thou hast fanned the sleeping Earth till her dreams are
    all of flowers,
And the waters look in mirth for their overhanging
    bowers;
The forest seems to listen for the rustle of its leaves,
And the very skies to glisten in the hope of summer
    eves.

Thy vivifying spell has been felt beneath the wave,
By the dormouse in its cell, and the mole within its cave;
And the summer tribes that creep, or in air expand their
    wing,
Have started from their sleep at the summons of the
    Spring.

The cattle lift their voices from the valleys and the hills,
And the feathered race rejoices with a gush of tuneful
    bills,
And if this cloudless arch fills the poet's song with glee,
O thou sunny first of March! be it dedicate to thee.

INVOCATION TO THE CUCKOO.

O, PURSUIVANT and herald of the spring!
    Whether thou still dost dwell
    In some rose-laurelled dell
Of that charmed island, whose magician king
    Bade all its rocks and caves,
    Woods, winds, and waves,
Thrill to the dulcet chaunt of Ariel,
    Until he broke the spell,
And cast his wand into the shuddering sea—
    O hither, hither fleet,
    Upon the south wind sweet,
And soothe us with thy vernal melody!

Or whether to the redolent Azores,
    Amid whose tufted sheaves
    The floral goddess weaves
Her garland, breathing on the glades and shores
    Intoxicating air,
    Truant! thou dost despair;
Or lingerest still in that meridian nest,
    Where myriad piping throats
    Rival the warbler's notes,
The saffron namesakes of those islands blest—
    O hither, hither wing
Thy flight, and to our longing woodlands sing.

Or in those sea-girt gardens dost thou dwell,
    Of plantain, cocoa, palm,
    And that red tree, whose balm
Fumed in the holocausts of Israel;
    Beneath banana shades,
    Guava, and fig-tree glades,

Painting thy plumage in the sapphirine hue
   Thrown from the heron blue,
   Or rays of the prismatic parroquet—
   O, let the perfumed breeze
   From those Hesperides
Waft thee once more our eager ears to greet!

For lo! the young leaves flutter in the south,
   As if they tried their wings,
   While the bee's trumpet brings
News of each bud that pouts its honeyed mouth;
   Blue-bells, yellow-cups, jonquils,
   Lilies wild and daffodils
Gladden our meads in intertangled wreath;
   The sun enamoured lies,
   Watching the violets' eyes
On every bank, and drinks their luscious breath;
   With open lips the thorn
   Proclaims that May is born,
And darest thou, bird of spring, that summons scorn?

"Cuckoo! Cuckoo!" O welcome, welcome notes!
   Fields, woods, and waves rejoice
   In that recovered voice,
As on the wind its fluty music floats.
   At that elixir strain
   My youth resumes its reign,
And life's first spring comes blossoming again:
   Oh, wonderous bird! if thus
   Thy voice miraculous
Can renovate my spirits' vernal prime,
   Nor thou, my Muse, forbear
   That ecstacy to share—
I laugh at Fortune, and defy old Time.

MAN.

VERSIFIED FROM AN APOLOGUE BY DR. SHERIDAN.

AFFLICTION one day, as she harked to the roar
  Of the stormy and struggling billow,
Drew a beautiful form on the sands of the shore,
  With the branch of a weeping-willow.

Jupiter, struck with the noble plan,
  As he roamed on the verge of the ocean,
Breathed on the figure, and calling it Man,
  Endued it with life and motion.

A creature so glorious in mind and in frame,
  So stamped with each parent's impression,
Among them a point of contention became,
  Each claiming the right of possession.

He is mine, said Affliction; I gave him his birth,
  I alone am his cause of creation;
The materials were furnished by me, answered Earth;
  I gave him, said Jove, animation.

The gods, all assembled in solemn divan,
  After hearing each claimant's petition,
Pronounced a definitive verdict on Man,
  And thus settled his fate's disposition:

" Let Affliction possess her own child, till the woes
  Of life cease to harass and goad it;
After death give his body to Earth, whence it rose,
  And his spirit to Jove who bestowed it."

SPORTING WITHOUT A LICENSE.

THERE's a charm when Spring is young,
   And comes laughing on the breeze,
When each leaflet has a tongue,
   That is lisping in the trees,
When morn is fair and the sunny air
   With chime of beaks is ringing,
Through fields to rove with her we love,
   And listen to their singing.

The sportsman finds a zest,
   Which all others can outvie,
With his lightning to arrest
   Pheasants whirring through the sky;
With dog and gun from dawn of sun
   Till purple evening hovers,
O'er field and fen, and hill and glen,
   The happiest of rovers.

The hunter loves to dash
   Through the horn-resounding woods,
Or plunge with fearless splash
   Into intercepting floods;
O'er gap and gate he leaps elate,
   The vaulting stag to follow,
And at the death has scarcely breath
   To give the whoop and hallo!

By the river's margin dank,
   With the weeds and rushes mixed,

SPORTING WITHOUT A LICENSE.

Like a statue on a bank,
  See the patient angler fixed !
A summer's day he whiles away
  Without fatigue or sorrow,
And if the fish should baulk his wish,
  He comes again to-morrow.

In air let pheasants range,
  'Tis to me a glorious sight,
Which no fire of mine shall change
  Into grovelling blood and night ;
I am no hound, to pant and bound
  Behind a stag that's flying ;
Nor can I hook a trout from brook,
  On grass to watch its dying.

And yet no sportsman keen
  Can sweeter pastime ply,
Or enjoy the rural scene
  With more ecstacy than I :
There's not a view, a form, a hue,
  In earth, or air, or ocean,
That does not fill my heart, and thrill
  My bosom with emotion.

O clouds that paint the air !
  O fountains, fields, and groves !
Lights, sounds, and odours rare,
  Which my yearning spirit loves !
While thus I feel, and only steal
  From visions so enchanting,
In tuneful lays to sing your praise,
  What charm of life is wanting ?

THE QUARREL OF FAITH, HOPE, AND CHARITY.

ONCE Faith, Hope, and Charity traversed the land,
    In sisterhood's uninterrupted embraces,
Performing their office of love hand in hand,
    Of the Christian world the appropriate Graces.

But tiffs since those primitive days have occurred,
    That threaten to sever this friendly relation,
As may well be surmised when I state, word for word,
    The terms of their latest and worst altercation :

"Sister Charity, prythee allow me to state,"
    Cries Faith, in a tone of contemptuous sneering,
"That while you affect to be meek and sedate,
    Your conduct is cunning, your tone domineering.

" In the times that are gone, my world-harassing name,
    Received some accession of strength every hour ;
St. Bartholomew's Massacre hallowed my fame,
    And Sicily's Vespers asserted my power.

"When martyrs in multitudes rushed at my call,
    To peril their lives for Theology's sake,
Mine too was the voice that cried, ' Sacrifice all,
    With jail and with gibbet, with faggot and stake.'

" When the banner of orthodox slaughter was furled,
    And subjects no more from each other dissented,
I set them at war with the rest of the world,
    And for centuries national struggles fomented.

" What are all the great heroes on history's page,
  But puppets who figured as I pulled the strings?
Crusades I engendered in every age,
  And Faith was the leader of armies and kings.

" In those days of my glory Hope followed my track,
  In warfare a firm and impartial ally,
For she constantly patted both sides on the back,
  And promised them both a reward in the sky."

Here Charity, heaving disconsolate sighs,
  That said " I admit what I deeply deplore,"
Uplifted to heaven her tear-suffused eyes,
  Which seemed but to anger her sister the more.

" Nay, none of your cant, hypocritical minx !"
  She cried in a louder and bitterer tone,
" If you feel any fancy to whimper, methinks
  You might weep that the days of my glory are gone.

" What wreck of my palmy puissance is left ?
  What bravos and bullies my greatness declare ?
Of the holy and dear Inquisition bereft,
  All my fierce fulminations are impotent air.

" No racks and no pincers—no limbs piecemeal torn,
  No screams of the tortured my prowess display ;
And to crown all these slights, I am shamefully shorn
  Of my own proper triumph, an *auto da fé*.

" The Pope, who could once, in my terrible name,
  Spread warfare and havoc all Christendom round,
Is sunk to such pitiful dotage and shame,
  That the Vatican thunder 's a ridiculed sound.

" Nay, even in England, my latest strong-hold,
   And the firmest support of my paramount sway,
(In Gath or in Askelon be it not told,)
   All my orthodox bulwarks are crumbling away.

" Dissenters, untested, may now, nothing loth,
   As municipal officers feast and carouse;
And emancipate Catholics, taking the oath,
   O horror of horrors! may sit in the House.

" If Erin no longer my altar-flame fanned,
   By ceasing to murder for tithe now and then,
It might well be surmised that my paralysed hand
   Had lost all control o'er the actions of men.

" And what though each orthodox candidate swears
   To my thirty-nine Articles—'tis but a jest,
Since a bishop (*proh pudor !*), a bishop, declares
   That such oaths are a form—never meant as a test.

" And who is the cause that I'm laid on the shelf,
   Disowned and deserted by all but a few?
My downfall and ruin I trace to yourself,
   To you, I repeat, sister Charity—*you!*

" Your looks and your whining expressions of ruth,
   Your appeals—ever urged with insidious wiles,
To reason and justice—to love and to truth,
   Your tears of deceit, and your plausible smiles,

" Have inveigled the bulk of my subjects away,
   And have swelled your own ranks with deserters
      from mine:
Such conduct is base, and from this very day,
   Hope and I mean to leave you and take a new line."

With the look of an angel, the voice of a dove,
   Thus Charity answered——" Since Concord alone,
Can prosper our partnership mission of love,
   And exalt the attraction that calls her her own,

" I would not, dear sisters, even harbour a thought,
   That might peril a friendship so truly divine;
And if in our feelings a change has been wrought,
   I humbly submit that the fault is not mine.

" Christianity's attributes, holy and high,
   When first, sister Faith, you delighted to teach,
And Hope only wafted your words to the sky,
   I seconded gladly the labours of each :

" But when, in crusades! you began to affect
   A thousand disguises and masquerades new,
When you dressed yourself up in the badges of sect,
   Nay, even of Mussulman, Pagan, and Jew,

" And when in each garb, as yourself have just said,
   You scattered a firebrand wherever you went,
While Hope spent her breath as she followed or led,
   In fanning the flames of religious dissent,

" I raised up my voice in a solemn appeal
   Against your whole course of unchristian life,
Tho' its accents were drowned in the clashing of steel,
   In the clamour of councils, and schismatic strife ;

" But now when men, turning from dogmas to deeds,
   Bear the scriptural dictum of Jesus in mind,
That salvation depends not on canons and creeds,
   But on love of the Lord, and the love of our kind,

" My voice can be heard and my arguments weighed :
   Which explains why such numerous converts of late
Are under my love-breathing standard arrayed,
   Who once, beneath yours, were excited to hate.

" Superstition must throw off Religion's disguise ;
   For men, now enlightened, not darkling like owls,
While they reverence priests who are holy and wise,
   Will no longer be hoodwinked by cassocks or cowls.

" If, Sisters ! forgetting your primitive troth,
   You would still part the world into tyrants and slaves,
What wonder that sages should look on you both
   As the virtues of dupes, for the profit of knaves ?

" You would separate ?   Do so—I give you full scope ;
   But reflect, you are both of you naught when we part ;
While I, 'tis well known, can supply Faith and Hope,
   When I choose for my temple an innocent heart."

WINTER.

THE mill-wheel 's frozen in the stream,
   The church is decked with holly,
Misletoe hangs from the kitchen beam,
   To fright away melancholy ;
Icicles clink in the milkmaid's pail,
   Younkers skate on the pool below,
Blackbirds perch on the garden rail,
   And hark, how the cold winds blow !

There goes the squire to shoot at snipe,
   Here runs Dick to fetch a log;
You'd swear his breath was the smoke of a pipe
   In the frosty morning fog.
Hodge is breaking the ice for the kine,
   Old and young cough as they go,
The round red sun forgets to shine,
   And hark, how the cold winds blow!

THE CHOLERA MORBUS.

[ON HEARING IT SAID THAT THIS DISEASE ONLY ATTACKED THE POOR.]

IT comes! it comes! from England's trembling tongue
   One low and universal murmur stealeth:—
By dawn of day, each journal is o'erhung
   With startling eyes, to read what it revealeth,
And all aghast, ejaculate one word—
THE CHOLERA—no other sound is heard!

Had Death upon his ghastly horse revealed,
   From his throat-rattling trump a summons sounded,
Not more appallingly its blast had pealed
   Upon the nation's ear;—awe-struck, astounded,
Men strive in vain their secret fears to smother,
And gaze in blank dismay on one another.

Now are all cares absorbed in that of health;
   Hushed is the song, the dance, the voice of gladness,
While thousands in the selfishness of wealth,
   With looks of confidence, but hearts of sadness,
Dream they can purchase safety for their lives
By nostrums, drugs, and quack preventitives.

The wretch who might have died in squalid want,
   Unseen, unmourned by our hard-hearted blindness,
Wringing from fear what pity would not grant,
   Becomes the sudden object of our kindness,
Now that his betters he may implicate,
And spread infection to the rich and great.

Yet still will wealth presumptuously cry,
   " What though the hand of death be thus outstretched?
It will not reach the lordly and the high,
   But only strike the lowly and the wretched.
Tush! what have *we* to quail at?   Let us fold
Our arms, and trust to luxury and gold."

They do belie thee, honest Pestilence!
   Thou 'rt brave, magnanimous, not mean and dastard
Thou 'lt not assert thy dread omnipotence
   In mastering those already overmastered
By want and woe—trampling the trampled crowd,
To spare the unsparing, and preserve the proud.

Usurpers of the people's rights! prepare
   For death by quick atonement.—Stony-hearted
Oppressors of the poor!—in time beware!
   When the destroying angel's shaft is darted,
'Twill smite the star on titled bosoms set,
The mitre pierce, transfix the coronet.

Take moral physic, Pomp! not drugs and oil,
   And learn, to broad philanthropy a stranger,
That every son of poverty and toil,
   With whom thou sharest now an equal danger,
Should as a brother share, in happier hours,
The blessings which our common Father showers.

O thou reforming Cholera ! thou'rt sent
  Not as a scourge alone, but as a teacher—
That they who shall survive to mark the event
  Of thy dread summons thou death-dealing preacher !
By piety and love of kind may best
Requite the love that snatched them from the Pest.

THE RECANTATION.

YOUNG, saucy, shallow in my views,
The world before me—free to choose
    My calling or profession,
I canvassed, one by one, the list,
And thus, a tyro satirist,
    Condemned them in succession :

The Law ?—its sons cause half our ills,
By plucking clients in their bills,
    As sparrowhawks do sparrows ;
Shrinking the mind it whets, their trade
Acts as the grindstone on the blade,
    Which, while it sharpens, narrows.

What makes the Pleader twist and tear
Statutes to wrong the rightful heir,
    And bring the widow sorrow ?
A fee !—What makes him change his tack,
Eat his own words, and swear white's black ?—
    Another fee to-morrow.

A Curate ?—chained to some dull spot,
Even at church he mourns his lot,
    Repining with thanksgiving.

THE RECANTATION.

'Mid stupid clodpoles and their wives,
The Scholar's buried while he lives,
    And dies without a living.

And what are Bishops?——hypocrites
Who preach against the world's delights
    In purple and fine linen;
Who brand as crime, in humbler elves,
All vanities, while they themselves
    Have palaces to sin in.

A Soldier?——What! a bravo paid
To make man-butchery a trade——
    A Jack-a-dandy varlet,
Who sells his liberty——perchance
His very soul's inheritance——
    For feathers, lace, and scarlet!

A Sailor?——worse!——he's doomed to trace
With treadmill drudgery the space
    From foremast to the mizzen;
A slave to the tyrannic main,
Till some kind bullet comes to brain
    The brainless in his prison.

Physic?——a freak of times and modes,
Which yearly old mistakes explodes
    For new ones still absurder:
All slay their victims——disappear,
And only leave this doctrine clear,
    That "killing is no murder."

A Poet?——To describe aright
His lofty hopes and abject plight,
    The quickest tongue would lack words!

THE RECANTATION.

Still like a ropemaker, he twines
From morn to even lines on lines,
    And still keeps going backwards.

Older and wiser grown, my strain
Was changed, and thus did I arraign
    My crude and cynic sallies :
Railer !——like most satiric scribes,
Your world-condemning diatribes
    Smack less of truth than malice.

Abuse condemns not use——all good
Perverted or misunderstood,
    May generate all badness,
Reason itself——that gift divine,
To folly may be turned by wine,
    By long excess to madness.

From the professions thus portray'd,
As prone to stain, corrupt, degrade,
    Have sprung, for many ages,
All that the world with pride regards,
Our statesmen, patriots, heroes, bards,
    Philanthropists and sages.

Not from our callings do we take
Our characters :——men's actions make
    Or mar their reputations.
The good, the bad, the false, the true,
Would still be such, though all their crew
    Should interchange vocations.

Whate'er the compass-box's hue,
Substance, or form—the needle's true,
   Alike in calms or surges :
Even thus the virtuous heart, whate'er
Its owner's plight or calling—ne'er
   From honour's pole diverges.

DEATH.

FATE ! fortune ! chance ! whose blindness,
   Hostility or kindness,
Plays such strange freaks with human destinies,
   Contrasting poor and wealthy,
   The life-diseased and healthy,
The blessed, the cursed, the witless, and the wise,
   Ye have a master—one
   Who mars what ye have done,
Levelling all that move beneath the sun—
   Death !

   Take courage ye that languish
   Beneath the withering anguish
Of open wrong, or tyrannous deceit,
   There comes a swift redresser,
   To punish your oppressor,
And lay him prostrate—helpless at your feet.
   O champion strong !
   Righter of wrong,
Justice—equality to thee belong—
   Death !

   Where conquest crowns his quarrel,
   And the victor, wreathed with laurel,

While trembling nations bow beneath his rod,
   On his guarded throne reposes,
   In living apotheosis,
The Lord's anointed, and earth's demigod,
   What form of fear
   Croaks in his ear,
"The victor's car is but a funeral bier."——
     Death!

   Who——spite of guards and yeomen,
   Steel phalanx and cross-bowmen,
Leaps at a bound the shuddering castle's moat,
   The tyrant's crown down dashes,
   His brandished sceptre smashes,
With rattling fingers grasps him by the throat,
   His breath out-wrings,
   And his corpse down flings
To the dark pit where grave-worms feed on kings?——
     Death!

   When the murderer's undetected,
   When the robber's unsuspected,
And night has veiled his crime from every eye;
   When nothing living daunts him,
   And no fear of justice haunts him,
Who wakes his conscience-stricken agony?
   Who makes him start
   With his withering dart,
And wrings the secret from his bursting heart?
     Death!

   To those who pine in sorrow,
   Whose wretchedness can borrow
No moment's ease from any human act,
   To the widow comfort-spurning,
   To the slave for freedom yearning,

To the diseased with cureless anguish rack'd,
    Who brings release
    And whispers peace,
And points to realms where pain and sorrow cease ?—
    Death !

THE POET AMONG THE TREES.

Oak is the noblest tree that grows,
    Its leaves are freedom 's type and herald,
If we may put our faith in those
    Of Literary-Fund Fitzgerald.

Willow 's a sentimental wood;
    And many sonneteers, to quicken 'em,
A relic keep of that which stood
    Before Pope's Tusculum at Twickenham.

The Birch-tree, with its pendent curves,
    Exciting many a sad reflection,
Not only present praise deserves,
    But our posterior recollection.

The Banyan, though unknown to us,
    Is sacred to the Eastern Magi ;
Some like the taste of Tityrus,
    " Recubans sub tegmine fagi."

Some like the Juniper—in gin ;
    Some fancy that its berries droop, as
Knowing a poison lurks within,
    More rank than that distilled from th' Upas.

THE POET AMONG THE TREES.

But he who wants a useful word,
  To tag a line or point a moral,
Will find there 's none to be preferred
  To that inspiring tree—the Laurel.

The hero-butchers of the sword,
  In Rome and Greece, and many a far land,
Like Bravos, murdered for reward,
  The settled price—a laurel-garland.

On bust or coin we mark the wreath,
  Forgetful of its bloody story,
How many myriads writhed in death,
  That one might bear this type of glory.

Cæsar first wore the badge, 'tis said,
  'Cause his bald sconce had nothing on it,
Knocking some millions on the head,
  To get his own a leafy bonnet.

Luckily for the Laurel's name,
  Profaned to purposes so frightful,
'Twas worn by nobler heirs of fame,
  All innocent, and some delightful.

With its green leaves were victors crowned
  In the Olympic games for running,
Who wrestled best, or galloped round
  The Circus with most speed and cunning.

Apollo, crowned with Bays, gives laws
  To the Parnassian Empyrean ;
And every schoolboy knows the cause,
  Who ever dipped in Tooke's Pantheon.

Daphne, like many another fair,
   To whom connubial ties are horrid,
Fled from his arms, but left a rare
   . Memento sprouting on his forehead.

For Bays did ancient bards compete,
   Gathered on Pindus or Parnassus,
They by the leaf were paid, not sheet,
   And that's the reason they surpass us.

One wreath thus twines the heads about,
   Whose brains have brightened all our sconces,
And those who others' brains knocked out,
   'Cause they themselves were royal dunces.

Men fight in these degenerate days,
   For crowns of gold, not laurel fillets;
And bards who borrow fire from bays,
   Must have them in the grate for billets.

Laureats we have (for cash and sack)
   Of all calibres and diameters,
But 'stead of poetry, alack!
   They give us lachrymose Hexameters.

And that illustrious leaf for which
   Folks wrote and wrestled, sang and bluster'd,
Is now boiled down to give a rich
   And dainty flavour to our custard!

TO THE LADIES OF ENGLAND.

BEAUTIES!—(for, dressed with so much taste,
All may with such a term be graced,)—
  Attend the friendly stanza,
Which deprecates the threatened change
Of English modes for fashions strange,
  And French extravaganza.

What! when her sons renown have won
In arts and arms, and proudly shone
  A pattern to the nations,
Shall England's recreant *daughters* kneel
At Gallic shrines, and stop to steal
  Fantastic innovations?

Domestic—simple—chaste—sedate—
Your fashions now assimilate
  Your virtues and your duties:—
With all the dignity of Rome,
The Grecian Graces find a home
  In England's classic Beauties.

When we behold so fit a shrine,
We deem its inmate all divine,
  And thoughts licentious bridle;
But if the case be tasteless, rude,
Grotesque, and glaring—we conclude
  It holds some worthless idol.

Let Gallia's nymphs of ardent mind,
To every wild extreme inclined,
  In folly be consistent;

Their failings let their *modes* express,
From simpleness of soul and dress,
      For ever equi-distant.

True to your staid and even port,
Let mad extremes of every sort
      With steady scorn be treated;
Nor by art's modish follies mar
The sweetest, loveliest work by far
      That nature has completed :—

For oh ! if in the world's wide round
One peerless object may be found,
      A something more than human ;
The faultless paragon confessed
May in one line be all expressed—
      A WELL-DRESSED ENGLISH WOMAN.

NIGHT-SONG.

WRITTEN AT SEA.

'Tis night—my Bark is on the Ocean,
  No sound I hear, no sight I see,
Not even the darkened waves whose motion
  Still bears me, Fanny, far from thee !
But from the misty skies are gleaming
  Two smiling stars that look, my love !
As if thine eyes, though veiled, were beaming
  Benignly on me from above.

Good night and bless thee, Fanny dearest !
  Nor let the sound disturb thy sleep,
If, when the midnight wind thou hearest,
  Thy thoughts are on the distant deep :—

Thy Lover there is safe and fearless,
    For Heaven still guards and guides my track;
Nor can my dreaming heart be cheerless,
    For still to thee 'tis wafted back.

'Tis sweet on the benighted billow,
    To trust in Him whom all adore;
'Tis sweet to think that from her pillow
    Her prayers for me shall Fanny pour.
The winds, self-lullabied, are dozing,
    The winking stars withdraw their light.
Fanny! methinks thine eyes are closing—
    Bless thee, my love! good night, good night!

THE SONG-VISION.

Oh, warble not that fearful air!
    For sweet and sprightly though it be,
It wakes in me a deep despair
    By its unhallowed gaiety.

It was the last my Fanny sung,
    The last enchanting playful strain,
That breathed from that melodious tongue,
    Which none shall ever hear again.

From Memory's fount what pleasures past
    At that one vocal summons flow;
Bliss which I vainly thought would last—
    Bliss which but deepens present woe!

THE SONG-VISION.

Where art thou, Fanny! can the tomb
   Have chilled that heart so fond and warm—
Have turned to dust that cheek of bloom—
   Those eyes of light—that angel form?

Ah no! the grave resigns its prey:
   See, see! my Fanny's sitting there;
While on the harp her fingers play
   A prelude to my favourite air.

There is the smile which ever blessed
   The gaze of mine enamoured eye—
The lips that I so oft have pressed
   In tribute for that melody.

She moves them now to sing!—hark, hark!
   But ah! no voice delights mine ears:
And now she fades in shadows dark;—
   Or am I blinded by my tears?

Stay yet awhile, my Fanny, stay,
   Nor from these outstretched arms depart;—
'Tis gone! the vision's snatched away!
   I feel it by my breaking heart.

Lady, forgive this burst of pain,
   That seeks a sad and short relief,
In coining from a 'wildered brain
   A solace for impassioned grief.

But sing no more that fearful air,
   For sweet and sprightly though it be,
It wakes in me a deep despair,
   By its unhallowed gaiety.

THE POET'S WINTER SONG TO HIS WIFE.

THE birds that sang so sweet in the summer skies are
 fled,
And we trample 'neath our feet leaves that fluttered o'er
 our head ;
The verdant fields of June wear a winding-sheet of white,
The stream has lost its tune, and the glancing waves
 their light.

We too, my faithful wife, feel our winter coming on,
And our dreams of early life like the summer birds are
 gone ;
My head is silvered o'er, while thine eyes their fire have
 lost,
And thy voice, so sweet of yore, is enchained by age's
 frost.

But the founts that live and shoot through the bosom of
 the earth,
Still prepare each seed and root to give future flowers
 their birth ;
And we, my dearest Jane, spite of age's wintry blight,
In our bosoms will retain Spring's florescence and de-
 light.

The seeds of love and lore that we planted in our youth,
Shall develop more and more their attractiveness and
 truth ;
The springs beneath shall run, though the snows be on
 our head,
For Love's declining sun shall with Friendship's rays be
 fed.

5*

Thus as happy as when young shall we both grow old,
     my wife,
On one bough united hung of the fruitful Tree of Life;
May we never disengage through each change of wind
     and weather,
Till in ripeness of old age we both drop to earth together !

SONG TO FANNY.

NATURE ! thy fair and smiling face
     Has now a double power to bless,
For 'tis the glass in which I trace
     My absent Fanny's loveliness.

Her heavenly eyes above me shine,
     The rose reflects her modest blush,
She breathes in every eglantine,
     She sings in every warbling thrush.

That *her* dear form alone I see
     Need not excite surprise in any,
For Fanny's all the world to me,
     And all the world to me is Fanny.

SONG TO FANNY.

THY bloom is soft, thine eyes are bright,
     And rose-buds are thy lips, my Fanny,
Thy glossy hair is rich with light,
     Thy form unparagoned by any;

But thine is not the brief array
   Of charms which time is sure to borrow,
Which accident may blight to-day,
   Or sickness undermine to-morrow.

No—thine is that immortal grace
   Which ne'er shall pass from thy possession,
That moral beauty of the face
   Which constitutes its sweet expression;
This shall preserve thee what thou art,
   When age thy blooming tints has shaded,
For while thy looks reflect thy heart,
   How can their charms be ever faded?

Nor, Fanny, can a love like mine
   With time decay, in sickness falter;
'Tis like thy beauty—half divine,
   Born of the soul, and cannot alter:
For when the body's mortal doom
   Our earthly pilgrimage shall sever,
Our spirits shall their loves resume,
   United in the skies for ever.

THE BIRTHDAY OF SPRING.

CRY Holiday! Holiday! let us be gay,
   And share in the rapture of heaven and earth;
For see! what a sunshiny joy they display,
   To welcome the Spring on the day of her birth;
While the elements, gladly outpouring their voice,
Nature's Pæan proclaim, and in chorus rejoice!

Loud carols each rill as it leaps in its bed;
The wind brings us music and balm from the south,
And Earth in delight calls on Echo to spread
The tidings of joy with her many-tongued mouth;
O'er sea, and o'er shore, over mountain and plain,
Far, far does she trumpet the jubilee strain.

Hark! hark to the cuckoo! its magical call
Awakens the flowerets that slept in the dells;
The snow-drop, the primrose, the hyacinth, all
Attune at this summons their silvery bells.
Hush! ting-a-ring-ting! don't you hear how they sing!
They are pealing a fairy-like welcome to Spring.

The love-thrilling hedge-birds are wild with delight;
Like arrows loud whistling the swallows flit by;
The rapturous lark, as he soars out of sight,
Sends us sun-lighted melody down from the sky.
In the air that they quaff, all the feathery throng
Taste the spirit of Spring that out-bursts in a song.

To me do the same vernal whisperings breathe
In all that I scent, that I hear, that I meet,
Without and within me, above and beneath,
Every sense is imbued with a prophecy sweet,
Of the pomp and the pleasantness Earth shall assume
When adorned, like a bride, in her flowery bloom.

In this transport of nature each feeling takes part;
I am thrilling with gratitude, reverence, joy;
A new spring of youth seems to gush from my heart,
And the man's metamorphosed again to a boy,
Oh! let me run wild, as in earlier years;
If my joy be suppressed, I shall burst into tears.

AN OLD MAN'S ASPIRATION.

O GLORIOUS Sun! whose car sublime
Unerring since the birth of time,
In glad magnificence hath run its race;
O day's delight—God-painted sky,
O moon and stars, whose galaxy
Illuminates the night thro' all the realms of space.

O poetry of forms and hues,
Resplendent Earth! whose varied views
In such harmonious beauty are combined;—
And thou, O palpitating Sea,
Who holdest this fair mystery
In the wide circle of thy thrilling arms enshrined—

Hear me, O hear while I impart
The deep conviction of my heart,
That such a theatre august and grand,
Whose author, actors, awful play,
Are God, mankind, a judgment day,
Was for some higher aim, some holier purpose plann'd.

I will not, nay I cannot, deem
This fair creation's moral scheme,
That seems so crude, mysterious, misapplied,
Meant to conclude as it began,
Unworthy the material plan
With whose perfections rare its failures are allied.

As in our individual fate,
Our manhood and maturer date,
Correct the faults and follies of our youth,

So will the world, I fondly hope,
With added years give fuller scope
To the display and love of wisdom, justice, truth.

'Tis this that makes my feelings glow,
My bosom thrill, my tears o'erflow,
At any deed magnanimous—sublime;
'Tis this that re-assures my soul,
When nations shun the forward goal,
And retrograde awhile in ignorance and crime.

Mine is no hopeless dream of some
Impeccable Millennium,
When saints and angels shall inhabit earth;
But a conviction deep, intense,
That man was meant by Providence
Progressively to reach a higher moral worth.

On this dear faith's sustaining truth
Hath my soul brooded from its youth,
As heaven's best gift, and earth's most cheering dower.
O! may I still in life's decline,
Hold unimpaired this creed benign,
And mine old age attest its meliorating power!

GIPSIES.

WHETHER from India's burning plains,
Or wild Bohemia's domains,
    Your steps were first directed;
Or whether ye be Egypt's sons,
Whose stream, like Nile's, for ever runs
    With sources undetected:

Arabs of Europe! Gipsy race!
Your Eastern manners, garb, and face,
    Appear a strange chimæra;
None, none but you can now be styled
Romantic, picturesque, and wild,
    In this prosaic æra.

Ye sole freebooters of the wood,
Since Adam Bell and Robin Hood:
    Kept everywhere asunder
From other tribes—King, Church, and State
Spurning; and only dedicate
    To freedom, sloth, and plunder;

Your forest-camp—the forms one sees
Banditti-like amid the trees,
    The ragged donkeys grazing,
The Sybil's eye prophetic, bright
With flashes of the fitful light
    Beneath the caldron blazing,—

O'er my young mind strange terrors threw:
Thy History gave me, Moore Carew!
    A more exalted notion
Of Gipsy life; nor can I yet
Gaze on your tents, and quite forget
    My former deep emotion.

For " auld lang syne" I'll not maltreat
Yon pseudo-tinker, though the cheat,
    As sly as thievish Reynard,
Instead of mending kettles, prowls,
To make foul havoc of my fowls,
    And decimate my hen-yard.

Come thou, too, black-eyed lass, and try
That potent skill in palmistry,
    Which sixpences can wheedle;
Mine is a friendly cottage—here
No snarling mastiff need you fear,
    No Constable or Beadle.

'Tis yours, I know, to draw at will
Upon futurity a bill,
    And Plutus to importune;—
Discount the bill—take half yourself,
Give me the balance of the pelf,
    And both may laugh at fortune.

LIFE.

THERE are who think this scene of life
A frightful gladiatorial strife,
    A struggle for existence,
Where class contends with class, and each
Must plunder all within his reach,
    To earn his own subsistence.

Shocked at the internecine air
Of this Arena, they forswear
    Its passions and its quarrels;
They will not sacrifice, to live,
All that to life its charms can give,
    Nor sell for bread their morals

Enthusiasts! check your reveries,
Ye cannot always pluck at ease
    From Pleasure's cornucopia;

Ye cannot alter Nature's plan,
Change to a perfect being Man,
   Nor England to Utopia.

Plunge in the busy current—stem
The tide of errors ye condemn,
   And fill life's active uses;
Begin reform yourselves, and live
To prove that Honesty may thrive
   Unaided by abuses.

TO A LADY.

[ON GIVING THE WRITER A LITTLE BRONZE CUPID FROM POMPEII.]

Thanks for thy little God of Love,
   Dug from Pompeii—whose fate 'tis
Henceforth to be installed above
   My household Lares and Penates.

Oh! could its lips of bronze unclose,
   How sad a tale might they recall!
How thrill us with the appalling woes
   Of the doomed City's burial!

Perchance, on that benighted day
   This tiny imp the table graced
Of one whose mansion might display
   The choicest stores of classic taste.

Of some one whose convivial board
   With all embellishments was deck'd,
While her rich cabinets outpoured
   A constant feast of Intellect.

TO A LADY.

Of one who, tho' she ne'er declined
   In social chat to bear a part',
Loved more to fill her house and mind
   With lettered lore, and varied art.

Of one who thus could give delight
   To guests of every mental hue,
Whether unlearned or erudite—
   Of one, in short, resembling *You!*

To the dark tomb, thou Pagan Sprite!
   For many centuries consigned,
Thrice welcome to this world of light,
   Where worshippers thou still wilt find.

Methinks thy new abode is one
   Thou wilt not, Cupid! disapprove,
For all my married life has run
   A lengthened course of constant love.

Prompt me, thou type of higher hope!
   To spread that love from me and mine,
Until, in its ascending scope,
   It soar to social and divine.

So, little Elf! shalt thou be eyed
   With doubled favour by thine owner,
Both as a tutelary guide,
   And a memorial of thy donor.

THE CHARMS OF LIFE.

WHAT hath life to charm us? Flowers
 Whose sweet lips have ever sung
Carols from the fields and bowers,
 In perfume's universal tongue.
Choral fairies bright and merry!
 Hark! I hear your silver bells,
 Chiming from the tufted dells
A May-day welcome—hey down derry!

Hark again! those jocund calls
 Are Echo's voice, who loves to mock
The laughter of the waterfalls
 That leap for joy from rock to rock.
And now the winds their organ ply,
 Tuned to the music of the birds,
 And rustling leaves and lowing herds,
O! what a thrilling harmony!

Joys there are of wider scope,—
 Our social and domestic ties,
Faith, love, charity, and hope,
 With all their mingled ecstacies.
And mental bliss that never cloys,
 But charms the head and thrills the heart;
 Life! how grand a boon thou art!
Life! how sumless are thy joys!

A HINT TO CYNICS.

YOUTH, beauty, love, delight,
 All blessings bright and dear,
Like shooting stars by night,
 Flash, fall, and disappear.

Let Cynics doubt their worth,
 Because they 're born to die,
The wiser sons of earth
 Will snatch them ere they fly.

Tho' mingled with alloy,
 We throw not gold away;
Then why reject the joy
 That 's blended with decay?

MUSIC.

PEACE to the tenants of the tomb
 Whom oft we met in hall and bower,
Peace to the buried friends with whom
 We shared the charm of Music's hour;
Tho' dead, they are not mute, for still
 Does memory wake some favoured strain
That makes our yearning bosoms thrill
 As if they lived and sang again.

Health to the friends we still possess;
 O! long and often may we meet,
Our yet remaining years to bless
 With Music's pleasures pure and sweet;

And praises to the power divine
    That gave to man the precious boon,
Which make's life's-social evening shine
    As brightly as its morn and noon.

THE BARD'S INSCRIPTION IN HIS DAUGHTER'S ALBUM.

THE thoughtful reader here may see
A little world's epitome
    In turning each successive folio;—
Names, drawings, music, poems, prose,
From kindred and from friends compose
    This Album's multifarious olio.

Its owner, from her circle wide
Of friends, may here survey with pride
    A cherished tributary Cento;
And when they 're absent—altered—dead—
Each contribution will be read
    With double zest as a memento.

Here with a smile will she recall
The walk, the concert, or the ball,
    Shared with the young and merry-hearted;—
And here, perchance, while brooding o'er
The song of one who sings no more,
    A tear may drop for the departed.

Yet—daughter dear! my heart foretells
That thou wilt quit all other spells,
    Of friends, however loved—and rather
Hang o'er the page that thus records,
With feelings ill-expressed by words,
    The fervent blessing of a Father!

STANZAS

WRITTEN FOR THE BAZAAR OF THE NATIONAL ANTI-CORN LAW LEAGUE, COVENT GARDEN THEATRE, 1845.

WHY with its ring has the connecting sea
    Married the Hemispheres and joined their hands,
Why has the Magnet's guiding ministry
    Made paths athwart the deep to distant lands?

Why are the winds to our control resigned?
    Why does resistless steam our will obey,
Why are all arts, all elements, combined
    To speed us o'er the ocean-world's highway?

That from wide earth, and from the watery waste,
    Creation's sacred flag may be unfurled,
Whereon the finger of the Lord hath traced
    Creation's law—" FREE TRADE WITH ALL THE
        WORLD !"

Thus nature—her maternal hands untied,
    Shall scatter fresh supplies of wealth and food,
And from each varied soil and clime provide
    Some separate blessing for the common good.

So shall the severed races of mankind,
    Bidding all barriers and restrictions cease,
By constant intercourse become combined
    In one vast family of love and peace.

Let no man part whom God would thus unite!
    They who would speed this high and holy aim,
Leagued in the cause of universal right,
    All factious ends, all party views disclaim.

Their weapons, Faith, and Charity, and Hope,
    Justice and Truth the champions of their cause,
Firmly but peaceably they seek to cope
    With selfish interests and mistaken laws.

Ye who love man's advancement—peace—free trade,
    Ye who would blessings win from every land,
Oh! give the liberating League your aid,
    And speed its course with zealous heart and hand !

A HINT TO THE FARMERS.

FARMERS, whose income, day by day,
Slides on the Sliding Scale away,
    Whatever its direction ;
When favoured most still most forlorn,
Starved by monopoly of Corn,
    And ruined by protection ;—

Farmers ! who dying, seldom see
One penny left for Charon's fee,
    When o'er the Styx ye're ferried,
But in your landlord's pocket trace
(Like Mecca to the Turks) the place
    Wherein your *profit*'s buried—

Farmers ! who find in Cobden's breath,
And Bright's harangues, a menaced death
    For all of yeoman station,
And most appropriately brand
The Corn-law Leaguers as a band
    Prone to *ass*—*ass*—ination :—

A HINT TO THE FARMERS.

When landlords cry, " *We* must be fed,
  Go—grind your bones to make our bread,
     From Earth more harvests ravish ;
Study Liebig, ye clodpole elves !
Buy Guano—Soda—stint yourselves,
     That we may still be lavish :"—

Farmers ! ye ought to patronise
Whate'er improvements may arise
     To lessen your expenses,
So hear my tale—there's little in 't,
'Tis merely meant to give a hint
     For making cheap field fences.

Queen Bess—I mean Elizabeth,
Favoured, as the historian saith,
     The handsome Earl of Leicester,
To whom she made large grants of land,
For which he doubtless kissed her hand,
     And duly thanked and blessed her.

These lands were commons, on whose turf,
Many a cottager and serf
     Had fed his goose or donkey ;
And being dispossessed, the crowd
Began to murmur in a loud,
     I need n't add a *wrong* key.

What cared his lordship ! down he came,
With carpenters to fence the same,
     And shut out clowns and cattle ;
Riding each morn the men to watch,
So that no moment they might snatch
     For drink or tittle-tattle.

One day, a peasant by his side
Bowed his gray head and humbly cried,
  "I ax your lorship's pardon,
I've got a notion in my nob,
Whereby this here expensive job
  Need hardly cost a farden."

"Not cost a farthing, doting clown!"
Exclaimed his lordship with a frown,
  Half angry and half comic;—
"Braggart most vain and over free,
Think'st thou that I can learn from thee
  A plan more economic?"

"Yes," quoth the rustic—"yes, my lord,
You need n't buy another board,
  Or oaken plank or paling,
Think not my words are brags and boasts,
For if your lordship finds the posts,
  The public will find *railing!*"

DISAPPOINTMENT.

Joy! joy! my lover's bark returns,
  I know her by her bearing brave:
How gallantly the foam she spurns,
  And bounds in triumph o'er the wave!

Why dost thou veil the glorious sight,
  In lurid rain, thou summer cloud?
See! see! the lightning flashes bright!
  Hark! to the thunder long and loud!

The storm is past—the skies are fair,
  But where's the bark?—there was but *one:*—
Ha! she is yonder, shattered—bare—
  She reels—she—sinks—O Heaven! she's gone!

6

THE DYING POET'S FAREWELL.

Animula vagula, blandula,
Hospes comesque corporis
Quæ nunc abibis in loca?

ADRIAN.

O THOU wondrous arch of azure,
 Sun, and starry plains immense!
Glories that astound the gazer,
 By their dread magnificence!
O thou ocean, whose commotion
Awes the proudest to devotion!
Must I—must I from ye fly,
Bid ye all adieu—and die?

O ye keen and gusty mountains,
 On whose top I braved the sky!
O ye music-pouring fountains,
 On whose marge I loved to lie!
O ye posies—lilies, roses,
All the charms that earth discloses!
Must I—must I from ye fly,
Bid ye all adieu—and die?

O ye birds whose matin chorus
 Taught me to rejoice and bless!
And ye herds, whose voice sonorous
 Swelled the hymn of thankfulness!
Learned leisure, and the pleasure
Of the Muse, my dearest treasure;
Must I—must I from ye fly,
Bid ye all adieu—and die?

O domestic ties endearing,
 Which still chain my soul to earth!

THE DYING POET'S FAREWELL.

O ye friends whose converse cheering,
   Winged the hours with social mirth!
Songs of gladness, chasing sadness,
Wine's delight, without its madness;
Must I, must I from ye fly,
Bid ye all adieu—and die?

Yes—I now fulfil the fiction
   Of the swan that sings in death;—
Earth, receive my benediction,
   Air, inhale my parting breath;
Hills and valleys, forest alleys,
Prompters of my muse's sallies,
Fields of green and skies of blue,
Take, O! take my last adieu.

Yet perhaps when all is ended,
   And the grave dissolves my frame,
The elements from which 'twas blended
   May their several parts reclaim;
Waters flowing, breezes blowing,
Earth, and all upon it growing,
Still may have my altered essence,
Ever floating in their presence;

While my disembodied spirit
   May to fields Elysian soar,
And some lowest seat inherit
   Near the mighty bards of yore;
Never, never to dissever,
But to dwell in bliss for ever,
Tuning an enthusiast lyre
To that high and laurelled quire.

SONNETS.

Eternal and Omnipotent Unseen !
  Who badest the world, with all its lives complete,
Start from the void and thrill beneath thy feet,
Thee I adore with reverence serene ;
  Here, in the fields, thine own cathedral meet,
Built by thyself, star-roofed, and hung with green,
  Wherein all breathing things in concord sweet,
  Organed by winds, perpetual hymns repeat :
Here hast thou spread that book to every eye,
  Whose tongue and truth all, all may read and prove,
On whose three blessèd leaves—Earth, Ocean, Sky,
  Thine own right hand hath stamped might, justice,
      love ;
Grand Trinity, which binds in due degree,
God, man, and brute, in social unity.

MORNING.

Beautiful Earth ! O how can I refrain
  From falling down to worship thee ? Behold,
Over the misty mountains springs amain
  The glorious Sun ; his flaming locks unfold
Their gorgeous clusters, pouring o'er the plain
  Torrents of light. Hark ! Chanticleer has tolled
His matin bell, and the lark's choral train
  Warble on high hosannas uncontrolled.

All nature worships thee, thou new-born day!
Blade, flower, and leaf, their dewy offerings pay
   Upon the shrine of incense-breathing earth;
Birds, flocks, and insects, chaunt their morning lay;
   Let me, too, join in the thanksgiving mirth,
And praise, through thee, the God that gave thee birth.

TO THE SETTING SUN.

Thou central Eye of God, whose lidless ball
   Is vision all around, dispensing heat,
And light and life, and regulating all
   With its pervading glance—how calm and sweet
   Is thine unclouded setting! Thou dost greet,
With parting smiles, the earth; night's shadows fall,
   But long where thou hast sunk shall splendours meet,
And, lingering there, thy glories past recall.
Oh! may my heart, like thee, unspotted, clear,
Be as a sun to all within its sphere;
   And when beneath the earth I seek my doom,
May I with smiling calmness disappear,
   And friendship's twilight, hovering o'er my tomb,
   Still bid my memory survive and bloom.

ON THE STATUE OF A PIPING FAUN.

Hark! hearest thou not the pipe of Faunus, sweeping,
   In dulcet glee, through Thessaly's domain?
Dost thou not see embowered wood-nymphs peeping
   To watch the graces that around him reign;

While distant vintagers, and peasants reaping,
   Stand in mute transport, listening to the strain;
And Pan himself, beneath a pine-tree sleeping,
   Looks round, and smiles, and drops to sleep again?
O happy Greece! while thy blest sons were rovers
Through all the loveliness this earth discovers,
   They in their minds a brighter region founded,
Haunted by gods and sylvans, nymphs and lovers,
   Where forms of grace through sunny landscapes
        bounded,
   By music and enchantment all surrounded.

ON A STUPENDOUS LEG OF GRANITE.

DISCOVERED STANDING BY ITSELF IN THE DESERTS OF EGYPT, WITH THE
INSCRIPTION INSERTED BELOW.

In Egypt's sandy silence, all alone,
   Stands a gigantic Leg, which far off throws
   The only shadow that the Desert knows.
"I am great Ozymandias," saith the stone,
   "The King of kings; this mighty city shows
The wonders of my hand." The city 's gone!
   Naught but the leg remaining to disclose
The site of that forgotten Babylon.
We wonder, and some hunter may express
Wonder like ours, when through the wilderness
   Where London *stood*, holding the wolf in chase,
He meets some fragment huge, and stops to guess
   What wonderful, but unrecorded, race
   Once dwelt in that annihilated place.

ON A GREEN HOUSE.

HERE, from earth's dædal heights and dingles lowly,
  The representatives of Nature meet ;
Not like a Congress, or Alliance Holy
  Of Kings, to rivet chains, but with their sweet
  Blossomy mouths to preach the love complete,
That with pearled misletoe, and beaded holly,
  Clothed them in green unchangeable, to greet
Winter with smiles, and banish melancholy.
I envy not the Emathian madman's fame,
Who won the world, and built immortal shame
  On tears and blood ; but if some flower, new found,
In its embalming cup might shroud my name,
  Mine were a tomb more worthily renowned
  Than Cheops' pile, or Artemisia's mound.

WRITTEN IN THE PORCH OF BINSTEAD CHURCH, ISLE OF WIGHT.

FAREWELL, sweet Binstead ! take a fond farewell
  From one unused to sight of woods and seas,
Amid the strife of cities doomed to dwell,
  Yet roused to ecstacy by scenes like these,
Who could for ever sit beneath thy trees,
  Inhaling fragrance from the flowery dell ;
Or listening to the murmur of the breeze,
  Gaze with delight on Ocean's awful swell.
Again farewell ! nor deem that I profane
Thy sacred porch ; for while the Sabbath strain
  May fail to turn the sinner from his ways,
These are impressions none can feel in vain—
  These are the wonders that perforce must raise
  The soul to God, in reverential praise.

THE WORLD.

OH, what a palace rare hast thou created,
　　Almighty Architect, for man's delight!
With sun, and moon, and stars illuminated;
　　Whose azure dome with pictured clouds is bright,
　　Each painted by thy hand—a glorious sight!
Whose halls are countless landscapes, variegated,
　　All carpeted with flowers; while all invite
Each sense of man to be with pleasure sated.
Fruits hang around us; music fills each beak;
The fields are perfumed; and to eyes that seek
　　For Nature's charms, what tears of joy will start.
So let me thank thee, God, not with the reek
　　Of sacrifice, but breathings poured apart,
　　And the blood-offering of a grateful heart.

TO A ROSE.

THOU new-born Rose, emerging from the dew,
　　Like Aphrodite, when the lovely bather
Blushed from the sea, how fair thou art to view,
　　And fragrant to the smell!　The Almighty Father
Implanted thee, that men of every hue,
　　Even a momentary joy might gather;
And shall he save one people, and pursue
　　Others to endless agony?　O rather
Let me believe in thee thou holy Rose,
Who dost alike thy lips of love unclose,
　　Be thy abode by saint or savage trod.
Thou art the priest whose sermons soothe our woes,
　　Preaching, with nature's tongue from every sod,
　　Love to mankind, and confidence in God.

ON AN ANCIENT LANCE, HANGING IN AN ARMOURY.

ONCE in the breezy coppice didst thou dance,
  And nightingales amid thy foliage sang;
Formed by man's cruel art into a lance,
  Oft hast thou pierced, (the while the welkin rang
  With trump and drum, shoutings and battle clang,)
Some foeman's heart. Pride, pomp, and circumstance,
  Have left thee, now, and thou dost silent hang,
From age to age, in deep and dusty trance.
  What is thy change to ours? These gazing eyes,
To earth reverting, may again arise
  In dust to settle on the self-same space;
Dust, which some offspring, yet unborn, who tries
To poise thy weight, may with his hand efface,
  And with his mouldered eyes again replace.

THE NIGHTINGALE.

LONE warbler! thy love-melting heart supplies
  The liquid music-fall, that from thy bill
Gushes in such ecstatic rhapsodies,
  Drowning night's ear. Yet thine is but the skill
Of loftier love, that hung up in the skies
  Those everlasting lamps, man's guide, until
Morning return, and bade fresh flowers arise,
  Blooming by night, new fragrance to distil.
Why are these blessings lavished from above
  On man, when his unconscious sense and sight
Are closed in sleep; but that the few who rove,
  From want or woe, or travels urge by night,
  May still have perfumes, music, flowers, and light;
So kind and watchful is celestial love!

6*

SUNSET.

'Tis sweet to sit beneath these walnut-trees,
   And pore upon the sun in splendour sinking,
And think upon the wond'rous mysteries
   Of this so lovely world, until, with thinking,
   Thought is bewildered, and the spirit, shrinking
Into itself no outward object sees,
   Still, from its inward fount, new visions drinking,
Till the sense swims in dreamy reveries.
Awaking from this trance, with gentle start,
'Tis sweeter still to feel the o'erflowing heart
   Shoot its glad gushes to the thrilling cheek;
To feel as if the yearning soul would dart
Upwards to God, and by its flutters speak
   Homage for which all language is too weak.

CHARADE.

Sordid and narrow and mean is my First,
   Where in tenements rank with tobacco and gin,
Dwells the toiling mechanic with poverty cursed,
   'Mid the breakers of law and the victims of sin.
'Tis gone!—a hall uprises—view
Yon clamorous prize-fighting crew,
Wrangling, jangling, sense entangling,
Law new-fangling, justice mangling—
'Tis not Bedlam, but as bad,
For money-mania makes them mad.
Hey presto pass! a graced saloon behold
   Where to a brighter star bright stars repair,
And beauty decked in jewelry and gold,
   Curtsey to grace and beauty still more rare.

CHARADE.

From each and all of these, at times,
 Prisoned within my second's bound,
The sick—the sad—the doomed for crimes,
 The idle and the gay are found,
Swiftly their wingless flight is flown,
 Their guide a lady's plaything, beckoned
By hand unseen from spot unknown :—
 What urges thee so fast my second?
What hurts the eye, yet mocks the sight,
 Feels not, yet sighs and makes lament ;—
As any floating feather light,
 And yet at times omnipotent.
Guarded, my Second, thus, thy might
 Would seem to challenge fate and death,
Yet doom and danger track thy flight,
 Threatening around—above—beneath.
See, see, the lightning's angry flash ;
 Hark ! what an elemental roar ?
A shuddering cry—a thunder crash—
 My Second's gone—'tis seen no more !
Let none but pleasant sights appear,
 Naught but the turtle-dove be heard,
Where Passion-flowers, to lovers dear,
 Enwreathe an arbour for my Third.—
There the heart vents in tender sighs
 The feeling that no words can reach,
Or makes the love-revealing eyes
 More fond and eloquent than speech.
Fulfilled be all the hopes ye raise,
 Enamoured inmates of the bower,
And oh ! may all your future days
 Be blissful as the present hour !

       [COURTSHIP.

CHARADE.

GIN-PALACE Circe! quit the niche
    Or den that constitutes my *First*,
Nor from below, thou fair foul witch!
    Call spirits baleful and accursed.
She's gone!—Beware! your pouch to pick,
    Yon crew throws dust into your eyes:
Distrust their flowers of rhetoric,
    They garland whom they victimize.
Now to our dearest hopes opposed,
    My changeful *First!* thou'rt all we dread;
And now, in solid gold disclosed,
    How eagerly thou'rt coveted!
But ah! most fatal art thou when
    Thou'rt formed beneath the 'whelming wave,
Of women fair and gallant men,
    The Sacrificer and the grave!

The friend, the lover, are on thee,
    My *Second!* source of many a tear,
When their vexed souls they cannot free
    From dark suspense, and jealous fear.
On thee, within this prison lone,
    The doomed assassin or the thief,
Vents, in his agony, the groan,
    Or prays for death as a relief.
I see thee speeding overhead,
    As if thou hadst an eagle's wing,
I see thee in the cattle shed,
    A lifeless and unmoving thing.

My *Third* is fashioned to enfold
Strange implements of war.——Behold
    Those frames with human features,
By time and artificial means
They 're manufactured to machines
    For killing human creatures.
Obedient moves——east, west, north, south,
Up to the breach, or cannon's mouth:
    Each automatic figure——
'Gainst friend or foe, whate'er the cause,
With equal nonchalance he draws
    His death-dispensing trigger.
Enslaved alike in frame and mind,
Life's object for its means resigned,
    What gains the unlucky varlet?
Dying, he sleeps on honour's couch,
And living, flaunts with empty pouch,
    In outward gold and scarlet.
Never were muscles, bones, and will,
By such self-sacrificing skill,
    Made neuter, passive, active.
Machine! thou 'rt mechanism's pride,
But never was its art applied
    To purpose less attractive!

                [BARRACK.]

CHARADE.

Oh! what a glorious city!——behold
  Its obelisks, pyramids, sphinx-guarded fanes,
You gaze on Bubastis in Egypt of old,
  And hark! to those sacred melodious strains!

The dulcimer, harp, shawm, and tabret combine
    With the choral rejoicings and anthems that burst
From yon temple's august and magnificent shrine,
    Where prostrated crowds are adoring my *First*.
How strange the conflicting caprices and whims
    Of blind superstition ! some ages are fled,
And the object which living was worshipped with hymns,
    And graced with an apotheosis when dead,
In Europe is marked for proscription and ban,
    As leagued with the foul and unsanctified crew
Who ply the black art that's forbidden to man,
    And with spirits of darkness dark courses pursue.

And where is my changeable *Second* displayed ?
    In the belle and the bird, in the damsel and crone,
In the foul and the fair, in the matron and maid,
    In the dabbler in mud, in the queen on her throne.
Who can reckon its changes of form and abode ?
    Arched and square, low and dirty, distorted and strait,
It is seen in the ditch, on the dunghill, the road,
    In the huts of the poor, in the halls of the great.
It is pure flesh and blood, when from Nature's own hand:
    Made by man, its diversified substance is found
In the fish of the deep, in the beasts of the land,
    In the trees of the field, in the ore under ground.
If sometimes 'tis worn unembellished and plain,
    By the wives or the daughters of niggardly churls,
At others 'tis decked with a glittering train
    Of diamonds and amethysts, rubies and pearls.

In my populous *Third* what a withering change
    From the bushy Bubastis my first gave to sight :
No sunbeam, no moon gilds its desolate range ;
    All is silence profound and perpetual night.

It has numberless houses and each one contains
  A single inhabitant ever asleep,
No footfall is heard in its streets and its lanes,
  In the midst of a crowd there is solitude deep.
Here lovers whose union has long been denied,
  Often meet, but no love-breathing whisper is heard;
Here bitterest foemen are placed side by side,
  But the warfare is over : there's peace in my *Third!*

[CATACOMB.]

ADDRESS TO THE ALABASTER SARCOPHAGUS,

LATELY DEPOSITED IN THE BRITISH MUSEUM.

Thou alabaster relic ! while I hold
  My hand upon thy sculptured margin thrown,
Let me recall the scenes thou couldst unfold,
  Mightst thou relate the changes thou hast known,
For thou wert primitive in thy formation,
Launched from th' Almighty's hand at the Creation.

Yes—Thou wert present when the stars and skies
  And worlds unnumbered rolled into their places;
When God from Chaos bade the spheres arise,
  And fixed the blazing sun upon its basis,
And with his finger on the bounds of space
Marked out each planet's everlasting race.

How many thousand ages from thy birth
  Thou sleptst in darkness, it were vain to ask,
Till Egypt's sons upheaved thee from the earth,
  And year by year pursued their patient task;
Till thou wert carved and decorated thus,
Worthy to be a King's Sarcophagus.

What time Elijah to the skies ascended,
   Or David reigned in holy Palestine,
Some ancient Theban monarch was extended
   Beneath the lid of this emblazoned shrine,
And to that subterranean palace borne
Which toiling ages in the rock had worn.

Thebes from her hundred portals filled the plain
   To see the car on which thou wert upheld :—
What funeral pomps extended in thy train,
   What banners waved, what mighty music swelled,
As armies, priests, and crowds, bewailed in chorus
Their King—their God—their Serapis—their Orus !

Thus to thy second quarry did they trust
   Thee and the Lord of all the nations round.
Grim King of Silence ! Monarch of the dust !
   Embalmed—anointed—jeweled—sceptered – crowned,
Here did he lie in state, cold, stiff, and stark,
A leathern Pharaoh grinning in the dark.

Thus ages rolled—but their dissolving breath
   Could only blacken that imprisoned thing
Which wore a ghastly royalty in death,
   As if it struggled still to be a King ;
And each revolving century, like the last,
Just dropped its dust upon thy lid—and passed.

The Persian conqueror o'er Egypt poured
   His devastating host—a motley crew ;
The steel-clad horsemen—the barbarian horde—
   Music and men of every sound and hue—
Priests, archers, eunuchs, concubines and brutes—
Gongs, trumpets, cymbals, dulcimers, and lutes.

Then did the fierce Cambyses tear away
  The ponderous rock that sealed the sacred tomi
Then did the slowly penetrating ray
  Redeem thee from long centuries of gloom,
And lowered torches flashed against thy side
As Asia's king thy blazoned trophies eyed.

Plucked from his grave, with sacrilegious taunt,
  The features of the royal corpse they scanned :—
Dashing the diadem from his temple gaunt,
  They tore the sceptre from his graspless hand
And on those fields, where once his will was la
Left him for winds to waste and beasts to gnaw.

Some pious Thebans, when the storm was past,
  Unclosed the sepulchre with cunning skill,
And nature, aiding their devotion, cast
  Over its entrance a concealing rill.
Then thy third darkness came, and thou didst sleep
Twenty-three centuries in silence deep.

But he from whom nor pyramid nor sphinx
  Can hide its secrecies, Belzoni, came ;
From the tomb's mouth unloosed the granite links,
  Gave thee again to light, and life, and fame,
And brought thee from the sands and desert forth
To charm the pallid children of the North.

Thou art in London, which, when thou wert new,
  Was, what Thebes is, a wilderness and waste,
Where savage beasts more savage men pursue—
  A scene by nature cursed—by man disgraced.
Now—'tis the world's metropolis — the high
Queen of arms, learning, arts, and luxury.

Here, where I hold my hand, 'tis strange to think
    What other hands perchance preceded mine ;
Others have also stood beside thy brink,
    And vainly conned the moralizing line.
Kings, sages, chiefs, that touched this stone, like me,
Where are ye now ?—where all must shortly be !

All is mutation ;—he within this stone
    Was once the greatest monarch of the hour :—
His bones are dust—his very name unknown.
    Go—learn from him the vanity of power :
Seek not the frame's corruption to control,
But build a lasting mansion for thy soul.

COMIC POEMS.

THE CULPRIT AND THE JUDGE.

THE realm of France possessed, in days of old,
   A thriving set of literati,
Or men of letters, turning all to gold :——
   The standard works they made less weighty
By new abridgments——took abundant
   Pains their roughnesses to polish,
   And plied their scissors to abolish
The superficial and redundant.

And yet, instead of fame and praise,
Hogsheads of sack, and wreaths of bays,
The law, in those benighted ages,
   By barbarous edicts did enjoin
That they should cease their occupation,
Terming these literary sages
   Clippers and filers of the coin;
(Oh! what a monstrous profanation!)
Nay, what was deeper to be dreaded,
These worthies were, when caught, beheaded!

But to the point.   A story should
   Be like a coin——a head and tail,
In a few words enveloped.   Good!
   I must not let the likeness fail.——

A gascon who had long pursued
  This trade of clipping,
And filing the similitude
  Of good King Pepin,
Was caught by the police, who found him
   With file and scissors in his hand
   And ounces of Pactolian sand
Lying around him.
The case admitting no denial,
They hurried him forthwith to trial;
When the judge made a long oration,
About the crime of profanation,
And gave no respite for repentance,
But instantly pronounced his sentence,
     " Decapitation!"

" As to offending powers divine,"
  The culprit cried—" be nothing said :
Yours is a deeper guilt than mine.
  I took a portion from the head
Of the king's image; you, oh fearful odds!
Strike the whole head at once from God's !"

SONNET TO MY OWN NOSE.

O NOSE! thou rudder in my face's centre,
  Since I must follow thee until I die—
Since we are bound together by indenture,
  The master thou, and the apprentice I,
O be to your Telemachus a Mentor,
  Though oft invisible, for ever nigh ;
Guard him from all disgrace and misadventure,

From hostile tweak, or love's blind mastery.
So shalt thou quit the city's stench and smoke,
For hawthorn lanes and copses of young oak,
Scenting the gales of heaven that have not yet
Lost their fresh fragrance, since the morning broke,
And breath of flowers "with rosy May-dews wet,"
The primrose, cowslip, blue-bell, violet.

THE MILKMAID AND THE BANKER.

A MILKMAID, with a very pretty face,
    Who lived at Acton,
Had a black Cow the ugliest in the place,
    A crooked-backed one,
A beast as dangerous, too, as she was frightful,
    Vicious, and spiteful;
And so confirmed a truant, that she bounded
Over the hedges daily, and got pounded:
'Twas all in vain to tie her with a tether,
For then both Cow and cord eloped together.
Armed with an oaken bough—(what folly!
It should have been of thorn, or prickly holly.)
Patty one day was driving home the beast,
    Which had, as usual, slipped its anchor,
    When on the road she met a certain Banker,
Who stopped to give his eyes a feast,
By gazing on her features crimsoned high
By a long Cow-chase in July.

"Are you from Acton, pretty lass?" he cried;
"Yes"—with a curtesy she replied.

"Why, then you know the laundress, Sally Wrench?"
"Yes, she's my cousin, sir, and next-door neighbour."
"That's lucky—I've a message for the wench,
    Which needs dispatch, and you may save my labour.
Give her this kiss, my dear, and say I sent it:
But mind, you owe me one—I've only lent it."
"She shall know," cried the girl, as she brandish'd her
      bough,
    "Of the loving intentions you bore me;
But since you're in haste for the kiss, you'll allow,
That you'd better run forward and give it my Cow,
For she, at the rate she is scampering now,
    Will reach Acton some minutes before me."

THE FARMER'S WIFE AND THE GASCON.

At Neufchâtel, in France, where they prepare
    Cheeses that set us longing to be Mites,
There dwelt a farmer's wife, famed for her rare
    Skill in these small quadrangular delights.—
Where they were made, they sold for the immense
    Price of three sous a-piece;
But as salt water made their charms increase,
    In England the fixed rate was eighteen-pence.

This damsel had to help her in the farm,
    To milk her cows, and feed her hogs,
A Gascon peasant, with a sturdy arm
    For digging, or for carrying logs;
But in his noddle weak as any baby,
    In fact a gaby,

And such a glutton when you came to feed him,
  That Wantley's dragon, who " ate barns and churches,
As if they were geese and turkeys,"
  (Vide the Ballad,) scarcely could exceed him.

One morn she had prepared a monstrous bowl
  Of cream, like nectar,
And would n't go to Church (good careful soul!)
  Till she had left it safe with a protector;
So she gave strict injunctions to the Gascon
  To watch it while his mistress was to mass gone.

Watch it he did—he never took his eyes off,
  But licked his upper, then his under lip,
And doubled up his fist to drive the flies off,
  Begrudging them the smallest sip,
      Which if they got,
Like my Lord Salisbury, he heaved a sigh,
  And cried,—" O happy, happy fly,
      How I do envy you your lot !"

Each moment did his appetite grow stronger;
  His bowels yearned;
At length he could not bear it any longer,
  But on all sides his looks he turned,
And finding that the coast was clear, he quaffed
  The whole up at a draught.——
Scudding from church, the farmer's wife
  Flew to the dairy;
But stood aghast, and could not, for her life,
  One sentence utter,
Until she summoned breath enough to mutter,
  " Holy St. Mary !"

And shortly, with a face of scarlet,
The vixen (for she *was* a vixen) flew
  Upon the varlet,
Asking the when, and where, and how, and who
  Had gulped her cream, nor left an atom ;
To which he gave not separate replies,
  But with a look of excellent digestion,
  One answer made to every question,
    " The Flies !"

" The flies, you rogue ! the flies, you guzzling dog !
  Behold your whiskers still are covered thickly ;
Thief—liar—villain—gormandizer—hog !
  I'll make you tell another story quickly."
So out she bounced, and brought, with loud alarms,
  Two stout *Gens-d'armes,*
Who bore him to the judge—a little prig,
  With angry bottle nose
  Like a red cabbage rose,
While lots of white ones flourished on his wig.—
Looking at once both stern and wise,
  He turned to the delinquent,
And 'gan to question him and catechise
  As to which way the drink went :
Still the same dogged answers rise,
" The flies, my Lord—the flies, the flies !"

" Psha !" quoth the judge, half peevish and half pomp-
    ous,
  " Why, you're *non compos.*
You should have watched the bowl as she desired,
  And killed the flies, you stupid clown."
" What, is it lawful then," the dolt enquired,
  " To kill the flies in this here town ?"—

"The man's an ass! a pretty question this!
Lawful, you booby? to be sure it is.——
You've my authority, whene'er you meet 'em
To kill the rogues, and if you like it, eat 'em."
    "Zooks!" cried the rustic, "I'm right glad to hear it.
    Constable, catch that thief! may I go hang
If yonder blue-bottle, (I know his face,)
    Is n't the very leader of the gang
That stole the cream, let me come near it!"
    This said, he started from his place,
And aiming one of his sledge-hammer blows
At a large fly upon the Judge's nose,
The luckless blue-bottle he smashed,
    And gratified a double grudge,
For the same catapult completely mashed
    The bottle-nose belonging to the Judge!

THE AUCTIONEER AND THE LAWYER.

A city Auctioneer, one Samuel Stubbs,
    Did greater execution with his hammer,
    Assisted by his puffing clamour,
Than Gog and Magog with their clubs,
Or that great Fee-fa-fum of War,
The Scandinavian Thor,
Did with his mallet, which (see Bryant's
Mythology,) felled stoutest giants;——
For Samuel knocked down houses, churches,
And woods of oak, and elms, and birches,
With greater ease than mad Orlando
Tore the first tree he set his hand to.——

7

THE AUCTIONEER AND THE LAWYER.

He ought in reason to have raised his own
Lot by knocking others' down.
And had he been content with shaking
His hammer and his hand, and taking
Advantage of what brought him grist, he
Might have been as rich as Christie;
But somehow when thy midnight bell, Bow,
    Sounded along Cheapside its knell,
    Our spark was busy in Pall-Mall
Shaking his elbow;——
Marking, with paw upon his mazzard,
The turns of hazard;
Or rattling in a box the dice,
    Which seemed as if a grudge they bore
To Stubbs; for often in a trice,
Down on the nail he was compelled to pay
All that his hammer brought him in the day,
    And sometimes more.
Thus like a male Penelope, our wight
What he had done by day undid by night:
No wonder, therefore, if like her
    He was beset by clamorous brutes,
Who crowded round him to prefer
    Their several suits.

One Mr. Snipps, the tailor, had the longest
    Bill for many suits—of raiment,
And naturally thought he had the strongest
    Claim for payment.
But debts of honour must be paid,
Whate'er becomes of debts of trade;
And so our stylish auctioneer,
From month to month throughout the year,

Excuses, falsehoods, pleas, alleges;
Or flatteries, compliments, and pledges,
When in the latter mood one day,
He squeezed his hand, and swore to pay.

"But when?" "Next month, you may depend on't,
My dearest Snipps, before the end on't;
Your face proclaims, in every feature,
You would n't harm a fellow creature—
You 're a kind soul, I know you are, Snipps."—
"Ay, so you said six months ago;
But such fine words, I'd have you know,
Butter no parsnips."
This said, he bade his lawyer draw
    A special writ,
    Serve it on Stubbs, and follow it
Up with the utmost rigour of the law.

This lawyer was a friend of Stubbs;
    That is to say
    In a civic way,
Where business interposes not its rubs;
For where the main chance is in question,
    Damon leaves Pythias to the stake,
    Pylades and Orestes break,
And Alexander cuts Hephæstion;
But when our man of law *must* sue his friends,
Tenfold politeness made amends.

So when he meets our Auctioneer,
    Into his outstretched hand he thrust his
Writ, and said with friendly leer,
    "My dear, dear Stubbs, pray do me justice;

In this affair I hope you see
No censure can attach to me—
 Don't entertain a wrong impression;
I'm doing now what must be done
 In my profession."—
  " And so am I," Stubbs answered with a frown;
So crying, " Going—going—going—gone !"
 He knocked him down.

THE GOUTY MERCHANT AND THE STRANGER.

In Broad Street Buildings, on a winter night,
Snug by his parlour fire a gouty wight
Sat all alone, with one hand rubbing
 His leg wrapped up in fleecy hose,
 While t'other held beneath his nose
The Public Ledger, in whose columns, grubbing,
 He noted all the sales of hops,
 Ships, shops, and slops,
Gums, galls, and groceries, ginger, gin,
Tar, tallow, turmeric, turpentine, and tin;

When lo! a decent personage in black
 Entered, and most politely said—
" Your footman, sir, has gone his nightly track,
 To the King's Head,
And left your door ajar, which I
Observed in passing by,
And thought it neighbourly to give you notice."

  " Ten thousand thanks ! how very few get,
  In time of danger,
  Such kind attentions from a stranger !

Assuredly that fellow's throat is
     Doomed to a final drop at Newgate,
He knows too, the unconscionable elf!
That there 's no soul at home except myself."

"Indeed!" replied the stranger, looking grave;
"Then he 's a double knave.
He knows that rogues and thieves by scores
Nightly beset unguarded doors;
And see how easily might one
     Of these domestic foes,
     Even beneath your very nose,
Perform his knavish tricks,
Enter your room as I have done,
Blow out your candles—*thus*, and *thus*
Pocket your silver candlesticks—
     And walk off *thus!*"

So said, so done—he made no more remark;
     Nor waited for replies,
     But marched off with his prize,
Leaving the gouty merchant in the dark.

THE FAT ACTOR AND THE RUSTIC.

CARDINAL WOLSEY was a man
     Of an unbounded stomach, Shakespeare says:
Meaning, (in metaphor,) for ever puffing
To swell beyond his size and span;
     But had he seen a player of our days
Enacting Falstaff without stuffing,

He would have owned that Wolsey's bulk ideal
   Equalled not that within the bounds
   This actor's belt surrounds,
Which is, moreover, all alive and real.

This player, when the Peace enabled shoals
   Of our odd fishes
To visit every clime between the poles,
Swam with the stream, a histrionic Kraken:
   Although his wishes
Must not in this proceeding be mistaken,
For he went out professionally bent
To see how money might be made, not spent.

In this most laudable employ
   He found himself at Lille one afternoon;
And that he might the breeze enjoy,
   And catch a peep at the ascending moon,
Out of the town he took a stroll,
Refreshing in the fields his soul
With sight of streams, and trees, and snowy fleeces,
And thoughts of crowded houses and new pieces.

   When we are pleasantly employed, time flies;——
   He counted up his profits in the skies,
   Until the moon began to shine,
On which he gazed awhile, and then,
   Pulled out his watch, and cried—" Past nine !
Why, zounds, they shut the gates at ten !"
Backwards he turned his steps *instanter*,
   Stumping along with might and main,
   And though 'tis plain
He could n't gallop, trot, or canter,
(Those who had seen it would confess it,) he
Marched well for one of such obesity.

Eyeing his watch, and now his forehead mopping,
He puffed and blew along the road,
Afraid of melting, more afraid of stopping;
When in his path he met a clown,
Returning from the town.——
"Tell me," he panted in a thawing state,
"Dost think I can get in friend, at the gate?"
    "Get in?" replied the hesitating loon,
Measuring with his eye our bulky wight:
"Why yes, sir, I should think you might——
    A load of hay got in this afternoon!"

THE BANK CLERK AND THE STABLE KEEPERS:

SHOWING how Peter was undone
By taking care of Number One.——

OF PETER PRIM (so Johnson would have written.)
    Let me indulge in the remembrance;——Peter!
Thy formal phiz has oft my fancy smitten,
    For sure the Bank had never a completer
Quiz among its thousand clerks,
Than he who elicits our remarks.——

Prim was a formalist, a prig,
    A solemn fop, an office Martinet,
One of those small precisians who look big
    If half an hour before their time they get
To an appointment, and abuse those elves
Who are not over-punctual like themselves.

If you should mark his powdered head betimes,
    And polished shoes in Lothbury,
You knew the hour—for the three quarters' chimes
    Invariably struck as he went by;
From morning fines he always saved his gammon,
Not from his hate of sloth, but love of Mammon.

For Peter had a special eye
To Number One—his charity
    At home beginning, ne'er extends,
But where it started had its end too;
    And as to lending cash to friends,
Luckily he had none to lend to.

No purchases so cheap as his,
    While no one's bargains went so far,
And though in dress a deadly quiz,
    No Quaker more particular.

This live automaton, who seemed
    To move by clockwork, ever keen
    To live upon the saving plan,
Had soon the honour to be deemed
    That selfish, heartless, cold machine,
    Called in the City—a warm man.

A Bank Director once, who dwelt at Chigwell,
    PRIM to a turtle-feast invited,
And as the reader knows the prig well,
    I need not say he went, delighted;
For great men, when they let you slice their meat,
May give a slice of loan—a richer treat.

No stage leaves Chigwell after eight,
    Which was too early to come back,
So, after much debate,
    Peter resolved to hire a hack;
The more inclined to this, because he knew
In London Wall, at Number Two,
An economic stable-keeper,
From whom he hoped to get one cheaper.

Behold him mounted on his jade,
    A perfect Johnny Gilpin figure;
But the good bargain he had made
    Compensating for sneer and snigger,
He trotted on—arrived—sat down,
    Devoured enough for six or seven,
His horse remounted, and reached town
    As he had fixed, exactly at eleven.
But whether habit led him, or the Fates
    To give a preference to Number One,
    (As he had always done,)
Or that the darkness jumbled the two gates,
Certain it is he gave *that* bell a drag,
    Instead of Number Two,
Rode in—dismounted—left his nag,
    And homeward hurried without more ado.

Some days elapsed, and no one came
To bring the bill, or payment claim;
He 'gan to hope 'twas overlooked,
Forgotten quite, or never booked,
An error which the honesty of PRIM
Would ne'er have rectified, if left to him.
After six weeks, however, comes a pair
    Of groom-like looking men,

Each with a bill, which Peter they submit to ;
One for the six weeks' *hire* of a bay mare,
And one for six weeks' *keep* of ditto :
    Together—twenty-two pounds ten !

The tale got wind.   What ! Peter make a blunder ?
There was no end of joke, and quiz, and wonder,
Which, with the loss of cash, so mortified
    PRIM, that he suffered an attack
    Of bile, and bargained with a quack,
Who daily swore to cure him—till he died ;
    When, as no will was found,
        His scraped, and saved, and hoarded store,
        Went to a man to whom, some months before,
He had refused to lend a pound !

PIRON, AND THE JUDGE OF THE POLICE.

PIRON, a Poet of the Gallic nation,
    Who beat all waggish rivals hollow,
Was apt to draw his inspiration
    Rather from Bacchus than Apollo.
His hostess was his deity,
His Hippocrene was *eau-de-vie ;*
And though 'tis said
    That poets live not till they die,
When living he was often dead—
That is to say, dead drunk.   "While I,"
Quoth Piron, "am by all upbraided
    With drunkenness, the vilest, worst,
Most base, detestable, degraded,
Of sins that ever man repented,
        None of you blames this cursed thirst

With which I'm constantly tormented.——
Worse than a cholic or a phthisic,
    Even now it gripes me so severely,
  That I must fly to calm it, merely
Swallowing brandy as a physic."

To cure this unrelenting fever
  He poured such doses through his lips, he
Was shortly what the French call *irre,*
    Anglic?—tipsy ;
And while the midnight bell was pealing
    Its solemn tolling,
Our Bacchanal was homeward reeling,
    Tumbling and rolling,
Until at last he made a stop,
    Suffering his noddle, which he could not keep
Upright, upon the ground to drop,
    And in two minutes was asleep,
      Fast as a top.

Round came the guard, and seeing him extended
    Across the gutter
    Incompetent to move or utter,
They thought at first his days were ended ;
But finding that he was not dead,
Having lost nothing but his head,
They popped him on a horse's back,
    Just like a sack,
And shot him on the guard-house floor,
To let him terminate his snore.

Next morning when our tippling bard
    Had got his senses,
They brought a coach into the yard,
    And drove him off to answer his offences,

Before the Judge of the Police,
    Who made a mighty fuss and clamour;
But, like some Justices of peace,
    Who know as much of law as grammar,
Was an egregious ninny-hammer.
" Well, fellow," cried the magistrate,
    " What have you got to say for boozing,
Then lying in the street and snoozing
All night in that indecent state ?"
" Sir," quoth the culprit to the man of law,
    " It was a frost last night in town,
And tired of tripping, sliding, and slipping,
    Methought I might as well lie down,
And wait until there came a thaw."
    " Pooh ! nonsense ! psha !
Imprisonment must be the lot
Of such a vagabond and sot.
But, tell me, fellow, what's your name ?"
    " PIRON."—" The dramatist ?"—" The same."
    " Ah, well, well, well, Monsieur PIRON,
Pray take your hat and quit the court,
For wags like you must have their sport;
But recollect, when you are gone,
You'll owe me one and thus I shew it:
I have a brother who's a poet,
    And lives as you do, by his wits."
Quoth PIRON, " that can never pass,
For I've a brother who's an ass,
    So we are quits."

THE FARMER AND THE COUNSELLOR.

A COUNSEL in the Common Pleas,
　　Who was esteemed a mighty wit,
　　Upon the strength of a chance hit
Amid a thousand flippancies,
And his occasional bad jokes
　　In bullying, bantering, browbeating,
　　Ridiculing, and maltreating
Women, or other timid folks,
　　In a late cause resolved to hoax
A clownish Yorkshire farmer—one
　　Who, by his uncouth look and gait,
　　Appeared expressly meant by Fate
For being quizzed and played upon :
So having tipped the wink to those
　　In the back rows,
Who kept their laughter bottled down,
　　Until our wag should draw the cork,
He smiled jocosely on the clown,
　　And went to work.

" Well, Farmer Numscull, how go calves at York ?"
　　" Why—not, sir, as they do wi' you,
　　But on four legs, instead of two."
" Officer !" cried the legal elf,
Piqued at the laugh against himself,
　　" Do pray keep silence down below there.
Now look at me, clown, and attend ;
Have I not seen you somewhere, friend ?"
　　" Yees—very like—I often go there."
" Our rustic 's waggish—quite laconic,"
The counsel cried, with grin sardonic ;

"I wish I'd known this prodigy,
This genius of the clods, when I
On circuit was at York residing.
Now, Farmer, do for once speak true—
Mind, you're on oath, so tell me, you,
Who doubtless think yourself so clever,
Are there as many fools as ever
In the West Riding?"
"Why—no, sir, no; we've got our share,
But not so many as when *you* were there!"

THE COLLEGIAN AND THE PORTER.

AT Trin. Coll. Cam.—which means, in proper spelling,
Trinity College, Cambridge, there resided
One Harry Dashington—a youth excelling
In all the learning commonly provided
For those who choose that classic station
For finishing their education:
That is, he understood computing
The odds at any race or match;
Was a dead hand at pigeon-shooting;
Could kick up rows, knock down the watch—
Play truant and the rake at random—
Drink—tie cravats—and drive a tandem.

Remonstrance, fine, and rustication,
So far from working reformation,
Seemed but to make his lapses greater,
Till he was warned that next offence
Would have this certain consequence—
Expulsion from his Alma Mater.

One need not be a necromancer
    To guess that, with so wild a wight,
    The next offence occurred next night,
    When our incurable came rolling
    Home as the midnight chimes were tolling,
And rung the College bell.——No answer.

The second peal was vain—the third
    Made the street echo its alarum;
When to his great delight he heard
The sordid Janitor, old Ben,
Rousing and growling in his den.
    "Who's there?—I s'pose young Harum Scarum."
"'Tis I, my worthy Ben, 'tis Harry."
"Aye, so I thought—and there you'll tarry.
    'Tis past the hour—the gates are closed,
You know my orders; I shall lose
    My place if I undo the door."
"And I (young Hopeful interposed)
"Shall be expelled if you refuse;
    So prythee"—Ben began to snore.

"I'm wet," cried Harry, "to the skin;
    Hip! hallo! Ben!—don't be a ninny;
    Beneath the gate I've thrust a guinea,
So tumble out and let me in."——

"Humph!" growled the greedy old curmudgeon,
Half overjoyed and half in dudgeon,
    "Now, you may pass, but make no fuss,
On tiptoe walk, and hold your prate."
    "Look on the stones, old Cerberus,"
Cried Harry as he passed the gate,
"I've dropped a shilling—take the light,
You'll find it just outside:——good night."

Behold the porter in his shirt,
 Cursing the rain which never stopped,
Groping and raking in the dirt,
And all without success ; but that
Is hardly to be wondered at,
 Because no shilling had been dropped ;
So he gave o'er the search at last,
Regained the door and found it fast !

With sundry oaths, and growls, and groans,
 He rang, once, twice, and thrice ; and then,
Mingled with giggling, heard the tones
 Of Harry, mimicking old Ben.

" Who 's there ?—'Tis really a disgrace
 To ring so loud.—I've locked the gate—
 I know my duty—'tis too late,
You would n't have me lose my place ?"
 " Psha ! Mr. Dashington : remember,
 This is the middle of November,
  I'm stripped, 'tis raining cats and dogs."
" Hush, hush !" quoth Hal, " I'm fast asleep ;"
And then he snored as loud and deep
 As a whole company of hogs :
 " But, harkye, Ben, I'll grant admittance
 At the same rate I paid myself."
 " Nay, master, leave me half the pittance,"
 Replied the avaricious elf.
 " No : all or none—a full acquittance :
 The terms, I know, are somewhat high ;
 But you have fixed the price, not I—
I won't take less, I can't afford it."
So, finding all his haggling vain,
Ben, with an oath and groan of pain,
 Drew out the guinea, and restored it.

" Surely you 'll give me," growled the outwitted
Porter, when again admitted,
    " Something, now you 've done your joking,
  For all this trouble, time, and soaking."
     " Oh surely, surely," Harry said ;
    " Since, as you urge, I broke your rest,
  And you 're half drowned, and quite undress'd,
    I'll give you—leave to go to bed !"

THE MAYOR OF MIROBLAIS.

WHILE he was laying plans for getting
  The honours of the *Chapeau rouge*,
The Cardinal Dubois was ever fretting ;
All his days and nights allotting
To bribes and schemes, intriguing, plotting,
  Until his face grew yellow as gamboge,
His eyes sepulchral, dull, and gummy,
And his whole frame a walking mummy.

Meanwhile his steward, De la Vigne,
  Seemed to be fattening on his master,
For, as the one grew lank and lean,
  The other only thrived the faster.

Enjoying, as he swelled in figure,
Such constant spirits, laugh, and snigger,
That it e'en struck his Excellency,
Who called him up and asked him whence he
Contrived to get so plump and jolly,
  While he himself, a man of rank,
     Visibly shrank,
And daily grew more melancholy.

THE MAYOR OF MIROBLAIS.

" Really, my lord," the steward said,
    " There 's nothing marvellous in that;
You have a hat for ever in your head,
    My head is always in my hat."

Dubois, too wealthy to be marred in all
His plots, was presently a Cardinal,
    And wore what he had pined to win;
When *pasquinades* soon flew about,
Hinting his sconce was *deeper red* without,
    Than 'twas within.

Perhaps it was, but that's no matter,
The Pope, like any other hatter,
Makes coverings, not heads; and this
    With its new guest agreed so well,
That he soon wore an altered phiz:
    Ate heartily, began to swell,
Recovered from his ails and ills,
And grew quite rosy in the gills.

'Tis strange, but true, our worthy wore
    Fine robes, and waxed both plump and fresh,
From the first moment he forswore
    All pomps and appetites of flesh.——
His Eminence, on this inflation
Both of his stomach and his station,
    His old Château resolved to visit,
Accompanied by one Dupin,
A sandy-headed little man,
    Who daily managed to elicit
Jokes from some French Joe Miller's page,
Old, and but little of their age;

Though they drew forth as never-failing
  A roar of laughter every time,
  As if they were as new and prime
As those which we are now retailing.

To the Château in Languedoc,
  Whole deputations
From the surrounding districts flock,
  With odes, addresses, gratulations,
  And long orations;
And amongst others, the *Préfet*
  Of Miroblais,
  Famed for its annual Fair of Asses,
Began a speech which, by its dull
Exordium, threatened to be full
  As long and dry as fifty masses.

Dupin, who saw his yawning master
Somewhat annoyed by this disaster,
And thought it might be acceptable
To quiz the bore, and stop his gabble,
  Abruptly cried—" Pray Mr. Mayor,
  How much did asses fetch, last Fair ?"

" Why, sir," the worthy mayor replied,
As the impertinent he eyed—
" Small sandy ones, like you, might each
  Sell for three crowns, and plenty too ;".
Then quietly resumed his speech,
  And mouthed it regularly through.

RABELAIS AND THE LAMPREYS.

WHEN the eccentric Rabelais was physician
   To Cardinal Lorraine, he sat at dinner
   Beside that gormandizing sinner;
Not like the medical magician
Who whisked from Sancho Panza's fauces
The evanescent meats and sauces,
   But to protect his sacred master
      Against such diet as obstructs
   The action of the epigastre,
      O'erloads the biliary ducts,
The peristaltic motion crosses,
And puzzles the digestive process.

The Cardinal, one hungry day,
   First having with his eyes consumed
   Some lampreys that before him fumed,
Had plunged his fork into the prey,
When Rabelais gravely shook his head,
Tapped on his plate three times and said—
   "Pah!—hard digestion! hard digestion!"
And his bile-dreading Eminence,
Though sorely tempted, had the sense
   To send it off without a question.—

"Hip! Hallo! bring the lampreys here!"
   Cried Rabelais, as the dish he snatched;
And gobbling up the dainty cheer,
   The whole was instantly dispatched.

Redden'd with vain attempts at stifling
   At once his wrath and appetite,

His patron cried, "Your conduct's rude,
This is no subject, sir, for trifling;
　How dare you designate this food
　As indigestible and crude,
　　Then swallow it before my sight?"

Quoth Rabelais, "It may soon be shown
　That I don't merit this rebuff:
I tapped *the plate*, and that you'll own,
　Is indigestible enough;
　But as to this unlucky fish,
With you so strangely out of favour,
　Not only 'tis a wholesome dish,
But one of most delicious flavour!"

THE BITER BIT.

Jack Dobson, honest son of tillage,
The Toby Philpot of his village,
Laugh'd and grew fat, Time's gorgon visage braving;
　To hear him cackle at a hoax,
　Or new edition of old jokes,
You'd think a Roman Capitol was saving.
　Not Boniface, when at a mug
　Of ale he gave a hearty tug,
Was fuller of his subject-matter;
　And Dobson had a better plea
　For boasting of its pedigree;
　For his was brewed at home, and he
Was infinitely fatter.

THE BITER BIT.

One cask he had better and stronger
 Than all the rest brewed at a christening;
 To pass it set his eyes a glistening;
In short he could n't tarry longer,
But seizing spiggot and a faucet,
He tapp'd it—quaffed a luscious posset—
Then, like a hospitable fellow,
Sent for his friends to make them mellow.——

Among them he invited one
 Called Tibbs, a simple-minded wight,
 Whom waggish Dobson took delight
To make the subject of his fun:
For Nature such few brains had put
In neighbour Tibbs's *occiput*,
 That all the rustic wags and wits
Found him a most convenient butt
 For their good hits;
Though sometimes, as both great and small aver,
He gave them Roland for their Oliver.

The guests all met, and dinner spread,
Dobson first tipped the wink, then said,
" Well, now, my lads, we'll all draw lots,
 To settle which of us shall go
 Into the cellerage below,
 To fill the pots."
So saying, he adroitly wriggled
 The shortest into Tibbs's paw,
Whereat the others hugely giggled,
 And Tibbs, obedient to the law,
 Went down, the beverage to draw.

Now, Farmer Dobson, wicked wag!
   Over the cellar door had slung
   A water-bowl, so slily hung,
That whoso gave the door a drag,
   Was sure to shower down at once
   A quart of liquid on his sconce.

Our host and all his brother wits,
   Soon as they heard their victim's tramp,
Who looked half-drowned, burst into fits,
Which in fresh peals of laughter flamed,
When Tibbs in drawling tone, exclaimed:
   " Is n't your cellar rather damp ?"

Grace being said, quick havoc followed;
Many good things were said and swallowed;—
Joking, laughing, stuffing, and quaffing,
For a full hour they pushed about
   The cans, and when there came a pause,
   From mere exhaustion of their jaws,
Tibbs with his nasal twang drawled out —
" Suppose we now draw lots again,
   Which of us shall go down to put
   The spiggot back into the butt."
" Why, zounds!" the farmer roared amain—
" The spiggot back! come, come, you 're funning,
You have n't left the liquor running ?"

" I did as I was ordered, Jack,"
   Quoth Tibbs ;—" and if it was intentioned
That I should put the spiggot back,
   'Tis a great pity 'twas n't mentioned :—
You 've lost a cask of precious stuff,
But I, for one, have drunk enough."

THE PARSON AT FAULT.

" Ass ! numskull ! fool !" the farmer cried—
  " What can one get, confound your souls !
    By asking such half-witted lubbers ?"—
" This lesson, neighbour," Tibbs replied—
  " That those who choose to play at bowls
    Must expect rubbers !"

THE PARSON AT FAULT.

A COUNTRY parson took a notion
  Into his head, one Whitsuntide,
That it was more like true devotion
  To preach extempore ;—he tried :
Succeeded once—twice—thrice—but, lo !
  His fourth discourse was not forthcoming ;
  Spite of his hawing and his humming,
Not a word further could he go ;
So that the worthy man perforce
  Was fain to leave them in the lurch,
  And say, that, since he came to church,
He'd lost the thread of his discourse.

Whereat a man below exclaimed,
  " Lock the doors, beadle ! search us round,
  All, every one, until it 's found ;
The thief should really be ashamed.—
  Here are *my* pockets—ransack both !
  I have it not, I 'll take my oath."

BLIND MAN'S BUFF.

THREE wags, (whom some fastidious carpers
Might rather designate three sharpers)
   Entered, at York, the Cat and Fiddle,
And finding that the host was out
   On business for two hours or more,
   While Sam, the rustic waiter, wore
The visage of a simple lout,
   Whom they might safely try to diddle,
They ordered dinner in a canter—
   Cold or hot, it mattered not,
Provided it were served *instanter* ;
And as the heat had made them very
   Dry and dusty in their throttles,
   They bade the waiter bring three bottles
Of prime old port and one of sherry.——

Sam ran with ardour to the larder,
   Then to the kitchen ;
And, as he briskly went to work, he
Drew from the spit a roasting turkey,
   With sausages embellished, which in
A trice upon the board was spread,
Together with a nice cold brisket,
Nor did he even obliviscate
   Half a pig's head.
To these succeeded puddings, pies,
   Custards and jellies,
All doomed to fall a sacrifice
   To their insatiable bellies ;
As if, like camels, they intended

8

To stuff into their monstrous craws
   Enough to satisfy their maws,
Until their pilgrimage was ended.
Talking, laughing, eating, quaffing,
   The bottles stood no moment still;
They rallied Sam with joke and banter,
And, as they drained the last decanter,
   Called for the bill.——

'Twas brought——when one of them who eyed
And added up the items, cried,
   " Extremely moderate indeed !
I'll make a point to recommend
This inn to every travelling friend ;
   And you, Sam, shall be doubly fee'd."
This said, a weighty purse he drew,
   When his companion interposed——
" Nay, Harry, that will never do,
   Pray let your purse again be closed ;
You paid all charges yesterday,
'Tis clearly now *my* turn to pay."

Harry, however, would n't listen
   To any such insulting offer,
His generous eyes appear to glisten
   Indignant at the very proffer ;
And though his friend talked loud, the clangour
Served but to aggravate Hal's anger,
   " My worthy fellow," cried the third,
   " Now really this is too absurd ;
What ! do both of ye forget
I have n't paid a farthing yet ?
Am I eternally to cram

At your expense? 'tis childish quite;
  I claim this payment as my right—
Here—how much is the money, Sam?"

To this most rational proposal
  The others gave such fierce negation,
One might have fancied they were foes all,
  So hot became the altercation,
Each in his purse his money rattling,
Insisting, arguing, and battling.

One of them cried at last—"A truce!—
  This point we will no longer moot;
Wrangling for trifles is no use,
  And thus we 'll finish the dispute.—
That we may settle what we three owe,
  We 'll blindfold Sam, and whichsoe'er
He catches of us first shall bear
The whole expenses of the trio,
With half-a-crown (if that 's enough,)
To Sam for playing Blindman's Buff."

Sam liked it hugely—thought the ransom,
For a good game of fun was handsome;
Gave his own handkerchief beside,
To have his eyes securely tied,
And soon began to grope and search;
  When the three knaves, I need n't say,
Adroitly left him in the lurch,
  Slipped down the stairs and stole away.

Poor Sam continued hard at work;—
  Now o'er a chair he gets a fall;
Now floundering forwards with a jerk,
  He bobs his nose against the wall;

THE POET AND THE ALCHEMIST.

And now encouraged by a subtle
  Fancy, that they 're near the door,
  He jumps behind it to explore,
And breaks his shins against the scuttle.—
Crying, at each disaster—" Drat it !
Dang it ! 'od rabbit it ! and rat it !''—
Just in this crisis of his doom,
The host, returning, sought the room ;
And Sam no sooner heard his tread,
  Than, pouncing on him like a bruin,
  He almost shook him into ruin,
And with a shout of laughter said—
  " By gom, I've cotched thee now, so down
  With cash for all, and my half crown !''—
Off went the bandage, and his eyes
  Seemed to be goggling o'er his forehead,
  While his mouth widened with a horrid
Look of agonised surprise.

" Gull !'' roared his master, " Gudgeon ! dunce !
Fool as you are you 're right for once,
'Tis clear that I must pay the sum ; —
  But this one thought my wrath assuages—
That every halfpenny shall come
  Out of your wages !''

———————

THE POET AND THE ALCHEMIST.

AUTHORS of modern date are wealthy fellows ;—
  'Tis but to snip his locks and follow
  Now the golden-haired Apollo
Invoking Plutus to blow up the bellows

Of inspiration, they distil
The rhymes and novels which cajole us,
    Not from the Heliconian rill,
But from the waters of Pactolus.

Before this golden age of writers,
    A Grub-street Garreteer existed,
One of the regular inditers
    Of odes and poems to be twisted
    Into encomiastic verses,
    For patrons who have heavy purses.
Besides the Bellman's rhymes, he had
Others to let both gay and sad,
    All ticketed from A to Izzard;
And living by his wits, I need not add,
    The rogue was lean as any lizard.

Like a rope-maker's were his ways,
    For still one line upon another
    He spun, and, like his hempen brother,
Kept going backwards all his days.

Hard by his attic lived a Chemist,
    Or Alchemist, who had a mighty
    Faith in the Elixir Vitæ;
And though unflattered by the dimmest
    Glimpses of success, kept groping
And grubbing in his dark vocation,
    Stupidly hoping
To find the art of changing metals,
And guineas coin from pots and kettles,
By mystery of transmutation.

THE POET AND THE ALCHEMIST.

Our starving poet took occasion
    To seek this conjuror's abode ;
    Not with encomiastic ode,
Or laudatory dedication,
But with an offer to impart,
For twenty pounds, the secret art,
Which should procure, without the pain
    Of metals, chemistry, and fire,
What he so long had sought in vain,
    And gratify his heart's desire.

The money paid, our bard was hurried
    To the philosopher's sanctorum,
Who, somewhat sublimized and flurried
    Out of his chemical decorum,
Crowed, capered, giggled, seemed to spurn his
Crucibles, retort, and furnace,
And cried as he secured the door,
    And carefully put to the shutter,
" Now, now, the secret I implore ;
    For God's sake speak, discover, utter !"

With grave and solemn air the Poet
Cried—" List—oh, list ! for thus I show it :—
Let this plain truth those ingrates strike,
    Who still, though blessed, new blessings crave,
That we may all have what we like,
    Simply by liking what we have !"

THE ASTRONOMICAL ALDERMAN.

THE pedant or scholastikos became
   The butt of all the Grecian jokes;——
With us, poor Paddy bears the blame
   Of blunders made by other folks;
Though we have certain civic sages
    Termed Aldermen, who perpetrate
    Bulls as legitimate and great,
As any that the classic pages
   Of old Hierocles can show,
Or Mr. Miller's, commonly called Joe.——

One of these turtle-eating men,
Not much excelling in his spelling,
   When ridicule he meant to brave,
Said he was more PH. than N.
    Meaning thereby, more *phool* than *nave*.
Though they who knew our cunning Thraso,
Pronounced it flattery to say so.
His Civic brethren to express
    His "double, double, toil and trouble,"
And bustling noisy emptiness,
    Had christened him Sir Hubble Bubble.

This wight ventripotent was dining
Once at the Grocers' Hall, and lining
   With calipee and calipash
That tomb omnivorous—his paunch,
Then on the haunch
   Inflicting many a horrid gash,
When having swallowed six or seven

Pounds, he fell into a mood
  Of such supreme beatitude,
That it reminded him of Heaven,
And he began with mighty *bonhomie*
To talk Astronomy.——

"Sir," he exclaimed, between his bumpers,
  "Copernicus and Tycho-Brahe,
  And all those chaps, have had their day;
They 've written monstrous lies, sir, thumpers!——
Move round the sun?——it 's talking treason;
The earth stands still——it stands to reason.——
Round as a globe? stuff——humbug——fable!
It 's a flat sphere, like this here table,
And the sun overhangs this sphere,
Ay——just like that there chandelier."

"But," quoth his neighbour, "when the sun
From East to West his course has run,
How comes it that he shows his face
Next morning in his former place?"
"Ho! there's a pretty question, truly!"
Replied our wight, with an unruly
  Burst of laughter and delight,
So much his triumph seemed to please him;
  "Why, blockhead! he goes back at night,
And that 's the reason no one sees him!"

SOUTH-DOWN MUTTON.

IF men, when in a rage, inspected
  Before a glass, their angry features,
Most likely they would stand corrected
  At sight of such distorted creatures;

So we may hold a moral mirror
  Before these myrmidons of passion,
And make ill temper see its error,
  By gravely mimicking its fashion.

A sober Cit of Sweeting's Alley,
  Deemed a warm man on 'Change, was what
In temper might be reckoned hot,
Indulging many an angry sally
Against his wife and servants :——(this
  Is no unprecedented state
  For man and wife, when, *tête-à-tête,*
They revel in domestic bliss,)——
But to show off his freaks before his
Guests, was *contra bonos mores.*

Our Cit was somewhat of a glutton,
Or epicure, at least in mutton ;
Esteeming it a more delicious
Feast, than those of old Apicius,
Crassus' savoury symposia,
Or even Jupiter's ambrosia.

One day a leg arrived from Brighton,
  A true South Down legitimate,
When he enlarged with much delight on
  The fat and grain, and shape and weight ;
Pronounced on each a learned stricture,
Declared the joint a perfect picture,
And as his eye its outline followed,
  Called it a prize—a lucky hit—
  A gem—a pearl more exquisite
Than ever Cleopatra swallowed ;
Promulging finally, this fiat——
" I'll dine at five, and ask Jack Wyatt."
                    s*

The cover raised, the meat he eyed
   With new enjoyment——next the cloth he
Tucked in his button-hole, and cried,
   " Done to a tittle——brown and frothy !''
Then seized the carving-knife, elate,
But lo ! it would not penetrate
The skin——(the anatomic term is
The what-d'-ye-call?——ay--epidermis.)

He felt the edge——'twas like a dump ;
   Whereat with passion-crimson'd frown,
He reached the stair-head at a jump,
   And threw the blade in fury down,
Venting unnumbered curses on
His thoughtless lazy servant——John.

His guest, observing this disclosure
Of temper, threw with great composure
The dish, with mutton, spoons and all,
Down helter-skelter to the hall,
Where it arrived with fearful clatter.
" Zounds !'' cried the Cit, " why, what's the matter?''
" Nothing whatever,'' with a quiet
Look and accent, answered Wyatt :
   " I hope I have n't unawares
Made a mistake ; but when you threw
The knife below, in such a stew,
   I thought you meant to dine down stairs !''

EVENING : AN ELEGY.

BY A POETICAL CARMAN.

APOLLO now, Sol's carman, drives his stud
 Home to the mews that 's seated in the West,
And Customs' clerks, like him, through Thames-street
   mud,
 Now westering wend, in Holland trowsers dress'd.

So from the stands the empty carts are dragged,
 The horses homeward to their stables go,
And mine, with hauling heavy hogsheads fagged,
 Prepare to taste the luxury of—"Wo!"

Now from the slaughter-houses cattle roar,
 Knowing that with the morn their lives they yields,
And Mr. Sweetman's gig is at the door,
 To take him to his house in Hackney Fields.

Closed are the gates of the West India Docks,
 Rums, Sugars, Coffee, find at length repose,
And I, with other careless carmen, flocks
 To the King's Head, the Chequers, or the Rose.

They smoke a pipe—the shepherd's pipe I wakes,
 Them skittles pleases—me the Muse invites,
They in their ignorance to drinking takes,
 I, blessed with learning, takes a pen and writes.

PATENT BROWN STOUT.

A BREWER, in a country town,
   Had got a monstrous reputation;
No other beer but his went down;——
   The hosts of the surrounding station
Engraved his name upon their mugs,
   And painted it on every shutter;
   And though some envious folks would utter
Hints, that its flavour came from drugs,
Others maintained 'twas no such matter,
   But owing to his monstrous vat,
   At least as corpulent as that
At Heidelberg——and some said fatter.

His foreman was a lusty Black,
   An honest fellow;
But one who had an ugly knack
Of tasting samples as he brewed,
   Till he was stupefied and mellow.
One day, in this top-heavy mood,
Having to cross the vat aforesaid,
   (Just then with boiling beer supplied,)
O'ercome with giddiness and qualms, he
Reeled——fell in—and nothing more said,
But in his favourite liquor died,
   Like Clarence in his butt of Malmsey.

In all directions round about
   The negro absentee was sought;
   But as no human noddle thought
That our Fat Black was now Brown Stout,
They settled that the rogue had left
The place for debt, or crime or theft.

PATENT BROWN STOUT.

Meanwhile the beer was, day by day,
Drawn into casks and sent away,
    Until the lees flowed thick and thicker;
When lo! outstretched upon the ground,
Once more their missing friend they found,
    As they had often done – in liquor.

"See!" cried his moralizing master,
    "I always knew the fellow drank hard,
And prophesied some sad disaster;
His fate should other tipplers strike:
Poor Mungo! there he welters, like
    A toast at bottom of a tankard!"
Next morn a publican, whose tap
    Had helped to drain the vat so dry,
Not having heard of the mishap,
    Came to demand a fresh supply,
Protesting loudly that the last
All previous specimens surpassed,
Possessing a much richer *gusto*
Than formerly it ever used to,
And begging, as a special favour,
Some more of the exact same flavour.——
"Zounds!" cried the Brewer, "that's a task
More difficult to grant than ask :——
Most gladly would I give the smack
    Of the last beer to the ensuing,
But where am I to find a Black,
    And boil him down at every brewing?"

YORK KIDNEY POTATOES.

ONE Farmer Giles, an honest clown
   From Peterborough, had occasion
To travel up to London town,
   About the death of a relation,
And wrote, his purpose to explain,
To cousin Jos. in Martin's lane ;
Who quickly sent him such an answer, as
   Might best determine him to dwell
   At the Blue Boar—the Cross—the Bell,
Or some one of the caravanseras
To which the various coaches went—
All which, he said, were excellent.

Quoth Giles, " I think it rather odd he
   Should write me thus, when I have read
   That London hosts will steal at dead
   Of night, to stab you in your bed,
Pocket your purse, and sell your body ;
To 'scape from which unpleasant process,
I'll drive at once to cousin Jos.'s."

Now cousin Jos. (whose name was Spriggs)
Was one of those punctilious prigs
   Who reverence the *comme il faut ;*
Who deem it criminal to vary
From modes prescribed, and thus " Monstrari
   Pretereuntium digito."

Conceive him writhing down the Strand
With a live rustic in his hand,
   At once the gaper and gapee ;

And pity his unhappy plight,
Condemned when, tête-à-tête, at night
To talk of hogs, nor deem it right
    To show his horrible *ennui*.

Jos. was of learned notoriety,
    One of the male Blue-stocking clan,
Was registered of each Society,
    Royal and Antiquarian;
Took in the Scientific Journal,
And wrote for Mr. Urban's Mag.
(For fear its liveliness should flag,)
A thermometrical diurnal,
With statements of old tombs and churches,
And such unreadable researches.

Wearied to death, one Thursday night,
With hearing our agrarian wight
    Prose about crops, and farms and dairies,
Spriggs cried——"A truce to corn and hay——
Somerset House is no great way,
    We'll go and see the Antiquaries."——

"And what are they?" inquired his guest:——
"Why, sir," said Jos., somewhat distress'd
    To answer his interrogator——
"They are a sort——a sort——a kind
    Of commentators upon Nature."——
"What, common 'tatoes!" Giles rejoin'd,
    His fist upon the table dashing:
"Take my advice——don't purchase one,
Not even at a groat a ton,——
    None but York kidneys does for mashing."

THE JESTER CONDEMNED TO DEATH.

ONE of the Kings of Scanderoon,
    A royal jester,
Had in his train a gross buffoon,
    Who used to pester
The court with tricks inopportune,
Venting on the highest folks his
Scurvy pleasantries and hoaxes.

It needs some sense to play the fool;
    Which wholesome rule
Occurred not to our jackanapes,
    Who consequently found his freaks
Lead to innumerable scrapes,
    And quite as many kicks and tweaks,
Which only seemed to make him faster
Try the patience of his master.

Some sin at last beyond all measure,
Incurred the desperate displeasure
    Of his serene and raging highness :
Whether the wag had twitched his beard,
Which he was bound to have revered,
    Or had intruded on the shyness
Of the seraglio, or let fly
An epigram at royalty,
None knows—his sin was an occult one ;
But records tell us that the sultan,
Meaning to terrify the knave,
    Exclaimed—" 'Tis time to stop that breath ;
Thy doom is sealed ;—presumptuous slave !
    Thou stand'st condemned to certain death.

Silence, base rebel !——no replying !——
  But such is my indulgence still,
    That, of my own free grace and will,
I leave to thee the mode of dying."

"Thy royal will be done——'tis just,"
Replied the wretch, and kissed the dust ;
  "Since my last moments to assuage,
Your majesty's humane decree
Has deigned to leave the choice to me,
  I'll die, so please you, of old age."

LAUS ATRAMENTI,
Or the Praise of Blacking.

A NEW SONG.

Our Sires were such pedagogue blockheads of yore,
  That they sent us to college instruction to seek,
Where we bothered our brains with pedantical lore,
  Law, Logic, and Algebra, Latin and Greek ;
But now, wiser grown, leaving learning alone,
And resolving to shine by a light of our own,
Our cares we transfer from the head to the foot,
Leave the brain to be muddied, and polish the boot.

On the banks of the Isis, ye classical fools,
  Who with Lycophron's crabbedness puzzle your ear,
And ye who learn logarithmetical rules
  At Cambridge, from tables of Baron Napier,
Renounce Aristotle, and take to the bottle
That wears " Patent Blacking" inscribed on its throttle ;
For Napier and Greek are by few understood,
While all can decide when your blacking is good.

When a gentleman dubbed by the wight of the brush,
　　Which has set up your foot in Corinthian style,
For the rest of your wardrobe you care not a rush,
　　Secure of the public's distinguishing smile.
Though your dress may be dusty, and musty, and fusty,
You're whitewashed by blacking, and cannot be rusty;——
Such errors as these are but venial and small,
People look at your boot, which atones for them all.

And ye who are struggling your fortune to make
　　By the brief or the bolus, law, commerce, or trade,
Your pitiful schemes of ambition forsake,
　　And be makers of blacking, by taunts undismayed;
For what is auguster than giving a lustre
To those who without you would hardly pass muster,
And by selling your "brilliant and beautiful jet,"
A name and a fortune together to get?

Day and Martin now laugh as they ride in their coach,
　　Till they're black in the face as their customers' boots;
Warren swears that his blacking 's beyond all approach,
　　Which Turner's advertisement plumply refutes;
They hector and huff, print, publish, and puff,
And write in the papers ridiculous stuff,
While Hunt, who was blackened by all, and run down,
Takes a thriving revenge as he blackens the town.

Their labels belibel each other—each wall
　　With the feuds of these rivals in blacking is white;
But the high polished town seems to patronise all,
　　And the parties get rich in each other's despite;
For my own part, I think I shall mix up my ink,
In a bottle with lamp-black and beer to the brink,
And set up at once for a shiner of shoes,
Since I never shall shine by the aid of the muse.

THE TWO BRACELETS.

A FARMER GENERAL, one Monsieur B——,
  Who dwelt in France when Louis held the throne,
Lived like a prince from every trouble free,
  Except a wife—(the exception's large, I own)
For she was fat as any marchioness,
And given to extravagance in dress.——

One day she bought a pair of bracelets—such
  As few but royal damsels would bespeak;
They cost—I cannot recollect how much,
  But they were quite magnificent—*unique*—
And having clasped them on, away she flies
Off to the Opera to show her prize.

It happened that the queen was there that night,
  Just opposite the box that Madame took,
And on the bracelets with intense delight
  Frequently looked—or else appeared to look;
For she took special care to have them seen,
As if on purpose to outvie the queen.

Soon to the box door came a Page, attired
  In the Queen's proper livery, all in style,
And in the name of Majesty required
  One of the bracelets for a little while,
That by her eye she might the pattern take,
And order some of the exact same make.

Off went the sparkling bauble in a trice,
  While her rouged cheeks with exultation burn,
As, bowing to the Royal party thrice,
  She patiently awaited its return;

But when the Queen retired, and none was sent,
Our dame began to wonder what it meant.—

A Lord in waiting soon confirmed her fears :
   "Oh, that pretended Page I've often seen—
A noted sharper—has been such for years.
   Madame, you're robbed—he came not from the Queen;
I knew the rogue, and should have had him taken,
But that he slipped away and saved his bacon."

Boiling with anger, Madame called her coach,
   And drove to the *Bureau de la Justice,*
Where, with loud tongue, and many a keen reproach,
   About the shameful state of the police,
She called upon the Provost for relief,
And bade him send his men to catch the thief.

Early next morn she heard the knocker's din ;
   Her heart beat high, with expectation big,
When lo ! the Provost's Clerk was ushered in—
   A formal consequential little prig,
Who, with a mighty magisterial air,
Hemmed, and began his errand to declare :—

"Madame, a man is brought to our bureau,
   On whom was found a bracelet of great cost,
And we are all anxiety to know
   Whether or not it is the one you lost ;
Wherefore I'll take the other, if you please,
Just to compare, and see if it agrees."

"Dear sir, I'm overjoyed—'tis mine, I'm sure ;
   Such a police as ours how few can boast !
Here, take the bracelet—keep the rogue secure,
   I'll follow you in half an hour at most ;
Ten thousand thanks—I hope you'll trounce the spark,
Open the door, there, for the Provost's Clerk !"

Oh! how she chuckled as she drove along,
   Settling what pangs the pilferer should feel :
No punishment appeared to her too strong,
   Even should the wretch be broken on the wheel ;
For what infliction could be reckoned cruel,
To one who would purloin so rich a jewel ?

Arrived at the bureau, her joy finds vent :
   " Well, Mr. Provost, where 's the guilty knave ?
The other bracelet by your clerk I sent,
   Doubtless it matches with the one you have ;
Why, then, outstretch your mouth with such surprise,
And goggle on me thus with all your eyes ?"

" La ! bless me, Ma'am, you' re finely hoaxed——good
     lack !
I sent no clerk, no thief have we found out,
And the important little prig in black
   Was the accomplice of the page no doubt ;
Methinks the rascals might have left you one,
But *both* your bracelets now are fairly gone !"

MARSHAL SAXE AND HIS PHYSICIAN.

FEVER 's a most audacious varlet ;——
     Now in a general's face he shakes
     His all-defying fist, and makes
His visage like his jacket——scarlet ;
Now o'er surrounding guards he throws
     A summerset, and never squeaks
     " An' please your Majesty," but tweaks
The Lord's anointed by the nose.

With his inflammatory finger,
   (Much like the heater of an urn)
   He makes the pulses boil and burn,
  Puts fur upon the tongue, (not ermine,)
And leaves his prey to die or linger,
   Just as the doctors may determine.

Though this disorder sometimes seems
   Mild and benignant,
It interferes so with our schemes,
Imparting to our heads a dizziness,
Just when we want them clear for business,
    That it may well be termed malignant.

Of these inopportune attacks,
One fiercely fell on Marshal Saxe,
Just as his troops had opened trenches
    Before a fortress; (what a pity!)
Not only did it make his heart ache
To be condemned to pill, cathartic,
Bolus, and blister, drugs and drenches,
But shocked his military notions,
To make him take unwished-for potions,
    Instead of taking, as he wished——the city.

SENAC, however, his physician,
Soon gave our invalid permission
    To be coached out an easy distance,
First stipulating one condition—
That whatsoe'er the when and where,
The Doctor should be then and there,
Lest any syncope, relapse,
Or other unforeseen mishaps,
    Should call for medical assistance.

SAXE gives consent with all his heart,
   Orders the carriage in a minute,
   Whispers the coachman—mounts within it,
SENAC the same, and off they start,
   Joking, smiling, time beguiling,
   In a facetious *tête-à-tête.*——
The subject of their mutual chatter is
   Nothing to us ;——enough to state
That Marshal Saxe at length got out
To reconnoitre a redoubt,
Projecting from a range of batteries.

Left in the carriage, our physician,
By no means relished his position,
When he discovered they had got
Nearly within half cannon shot;
Wherefore he bawled, with fear half melted,
   " For God's sake move me from this spot !——
Doubtless they've noticed our approach,
And, when they recognize your coach,
Shan't I be fired at, peppered, pelted,
(When I can neither fly nor hide)
   From some of yonder bristling masses ?"
" It's not unlikely," SAXE replied;
" And war I know is not your trade,
So if you feel the least afraid,
   Pull up the glasses !''

STANZAS TO PUNCHINELLO.

THOU lignum-vitæ Roscius, who
  Dost the old vagrant stage renew,
Peerless, inimitable, Punchinello!
  The Queen of smiles is quite out-done
  By thee, all-glorious king of fun,
Thou grinning, giggling, laugh-extorting fellow!

At other times mine ear is wrung
  Whene'er I hear the trumpet's tongue,
Waking associations melancholic;
  But that which heralds thee recalls
  All childhood's joys and festivals,
And makes the heart rebound with freak and frolic.

Ere of thy face I get a snatch,
  Oh! with what boyish glee I catch
Thy twittering, cackling, bubbling, squeaking gibber—
  Sweeter than syren voices—fraught
  With richer merriment than aught
That drops from witling mouths, though uttered glibber.

What way was ever known before
  To keep the circle in a roar,
Nor wound the feelings of a single hearer!
  Engrossing all the jibes and jokes,
  Unenvied by the duller folks,
A harmless wit—an unmalignant jeerer.

The upturned eyes I love to trace
  Of wondering mortals, when their face
Is all alive with an expectant gladness;

To mark the flickering giggle first,
The growing grin—the sudden burst,
And universal shout of merry madness.

I love those sounds to analyse,
From childhood's shrill ecstatic cries,
To age's chuckle with its coughing after;
To see the grave and the genteel
Rein awhile the mirth they feel,
Then loose their muscles, and let out the laughter.

Sometimes I note a henpecked wight
Enjoying thy marital might,
To him a beatific *beau idéal;*
He counts each crack on Judy's pate,
Then homeward creeps to cogitate
The difference 'twixt dramatic wives and real.

But, Punch, thou'rt ungallant and rude,
In plying thy persuasive wood;
Remember that thy cudgel's girth is fuller
Than that compassionate, thumb-thick,
Established wife-compelling stick,
Made legal by the dictum of Judge Buller.

When the officious doctor hies
To cure thy spouse, there's no surprise;
Thou should'st receive him with nose-tweaking
    grappling;
Nor can we wonder that the mob
Encores each crack upon his nob,
When thou art feeing him with oaken sapling.

As for our common enemy,
Old Nick, we all rejoice to see
The *coup de grace* that silences his wrangle;

But, lo! Jack Ketch!—ah, welladay!
Dramatic justice claims its prey,
And thou in hempen handkerchief must dangle.

Now helpless hang those arms which once
Rattled such music on the sconce;
Hushed is that tongue which late out-jested Yorick;
That hunch behind is shrugged no more,
No longer heaves the paunch before,
Which wagged with such a pleasantry plethorick.

But Thespian deaths are transient woes,
And still less durable are those
Suffered by lignum-vitæ malefactors;
Thou wilt return alert, alive,
And long, oh long mayest thou survive,
First of head-breaking and side-splitting actors!

THE PLEASANT TETE-A-TETE.

THE Isle of Saint Eustatia, which the Dutch
First colonized, was governed long ago—
(I mean *mis*-governed)—by the Herr Van Gutch,
As great a rogue as one would wish to know,
Who should, instead of ruling at Eustatia,
Have shared a convict's fate in Australasia.

No excellency could the knave pretend to,
Save in his title, which the folks about him
Lavished upon him as an innuendo,
Ironically meant to mock and flout him;
For he had proved himself in every case
Sordid, corrupt, extortionate, and base.

Lord Bacon urged that when in bribes he *did* err,
  Justice, but not injustice, he had sold;
Van Gutch sold either to the highest bidder;
  So that each criminal possessed of gold
Became, of course, more daring and more hardened,
Knowing beforehand that he should be pardoned.

Our governor was in fact an island Pope,
  (But not, I ween, Pope Innocent or Pius,)
Selling indulgences that gave full scope
  To him who fostered any lawless bias,
To sear his conscience, so that nought should shock it,
By purchased absolutions in his pocket.

As he sat waiting for this odious traffic,
  Ready for hire to pardon or condemn,
Smoking his pipe in vacancy seraphic,
  'Twixt stupid sottishness and native phlegm,
An Englishman, named Tate, made application
To buy a pardon by anticipation.

"May 't please your Excellency," whispered Tate,
  "I want to horsewhip, kick, and clapper-claw
A fellow that I hold in special hate;
  But as the knave will doubtless take the law,
I wish beforehand to inquire the pittance
That I must pay to purchase an acquittance."

"That," said Van Gutch, "on circumstance must rest;
  Does the man merit such a deep disgrace?"—
"Richly; he stands recorded and confessed
  The most notorious scoundrel in the place."—
"Nay, then, I'll not be hard in my condition:
I promise, for ten ducats, full remission."—

"Take them," said Tate, and threw them on the table;
  Then drew a whip prepared for the occasion,
And laid it on as if he would disable
  His victim from all further malversation,
So thick a storm he raised of kicks and lashes,
With curses, sandwich-like, between the slashes.

Cried Tate, " Your Excellency 's the convicted
  And flagrant knave to whom I made allusion,
And this unmeasured scourging I 've inflicted,
  Because your back claims lengthened retribution.
There !—there 's no harm done—all is honest barter :
I 've trimmed a scoundrel :—you have caught a Tartar."

This said, he bowed politely and departed ;
  Hied to the shore, embarked and hoisted sail ;
And in some half hour's space had fairly started
  From St. Eustatia with a favouring gale,
Leaving the writhing Dutchman in a fluster
Of anguish, rage, oaths, bullying, and bluster.

AN EASY REMEDY.

An honest tailor, whose baptismal
  And patronymic appellations
Were William Button, had a dismal
  Tendency to deep potations ;
And though, as he was over-mated,
Like Jerry Sneak, our snip was fated
In spite of all his hungry heavings,
To drink the tea and coffee leavings,
And eat cold mutton-flaps at dinner ;
Yet sometimes the rebellious sinner,

Asserting his marital rights,
Would on the wages-paying nights,
Betake him to the public-house,
To smoke, and tipple, and carouse;
   And as with each new dram and sip he
     Still more and more pot-valiant grew,
At last he fairly braved his spouse,
    Called her a vixen and a shrew,
A Jezebel and a Xantippe!

Returning home one night, our varlet
   Bold with his wife-compelling liquor,
   Rattled the knocker quick and quicker,
When with fierce eye and face of scarlet
His tender spouse appeared, and shrilly
Vented reproaches on her Willy.
" So, Jackanapes, you've come at last !
No doubt the evening has been passed
In tippling purl, you drunken sot,
Mulled ale and amber, hot and hot;
While your poor wife is left to slave,
   And drink cold water from the can,
Cold water, ye remorseless knave !"
   " Cold !" cried the husband, who began
In turn to wrangle and to storm it——
" Cold ! ye poor lazy slattern ;——cold !
Then why, ye good-for nothing scold,
Why don't you warm it ?"

MADAME TALLEYRAND AND THE TRAVELLER.

THE famous Talleyrand, who knew
   The secret of avoiding execution,
And kept his head upon his shoulders, through
   All the convulsions of the Revolution,
When heads were cropped by the prevailing powers,
      Like cauliflowers,
Till they themselves endured the keen
Infliction of the Guillotine,
And made way for another faction,
To undergo the same reaction :—
This Talleyrand possessed a wife,
Selected in his humbler life—
   A rich bourgeois of homely breeding,
Neither *bas bleu*, nor *femme savante*,
But rather, as I freely grant,
   Deficient in her general reading.

One day—'twas when he stood elate,
Napoleon's minister of state—
Having invited to his house
   Some literati to confer
   With a great foreign traveller,
The husband thus addressed his spouse :
   " My dear, at dinner you will meet
A foreigner, a man of note.
These authors like that you should quote
   From their own works ; therefore, to greet
Our guest, suppose you learn by rote
A sentence here and there. that when
He prates, like other travelled men,

Of his exploits on land and ocean,
You may not be completely gravelled,
  But have at least some little notion
Of how, and when, and where he travelled.
Take down his book, you'll find it yonder;
Its dull contents you need not ponder;
  Read but the headings of the chapters,
Refer to them with praise and wonder,
  And our vain guest will be in raptures."

Madame, resolved to play her part
So as to win the stranger's heart,
Studied the book; but far from dull,
She found it quite delightful;—full
Of marvellous adventures, fraught
With perilous escapes, which wrought
So deep an interest in her mind,
She really was surprised to find,
As to the dinner-room she tripped,
How rapidly the time had slipped.

The more to flatter and delight her,
  When at the board she took her place,
The famous traveller and writer
  Was seated by her side;—the grace
Was hardly said, or soup sent round,
  'Ere with a shrug and a grimace,
Eager to show her lore profound,
A la Française, she raised her eyes,
And hands, and voice, in ecstacies—
" *Eh, Mons'eur Robinson, mon Dieu,*
Voil? un conte merveilleux !
Ah, par exemple! it appals
  The mind to think of your attacks

On those terrific cannibals—
   Those horrid savages and blacks,
Who, if they once had gained the upper
Hand, had eaten you for supper,
And so prevented your proceeding
With that sweet book I've just been reading.
   Mais, quel bonheur! to liberate
Poor FRIDAY from the murderous crew,
   And gain in your deserted state,
   So lonely and disconsolate
A servant and companion too!"

The visitants were all astounded;
The stranger stared aghast, dumfounded:
Poor Talleyrand blushed red as flame,
Till having catechised the dame,
The mystery was quickly cleared;
The simple woman it appeared,
Instead of the intended book
In which she had been urged to look,
From the same shelf contrived to take
Robinson Crusoe by mistake!

PROJECTS AND COMPANIES.

"Some were condensing air into a dry tangible substance by extracting the nitre, and letting the aqueous or fluid particles percolate; others softening marble for pillows and pincushions; others petrifying the hoofs of a living horse to preserve them from foundering."—*Gulliver's Travels.*

A NATION'S wealth that overflows,
Will sometimes in its course disclose
   Fantastical contortions:
'Tis like the rising of the Nile,
Which fats the soil, but breeds the while
   Strange monsters and abortions.

Better our superflux to waste
On peaceful schemes, howe'er misplaced,
 Than war and its abuses;
But better still if he could guide
And limit the Pactolian tide,
 To salutary uses.

Our sires, poor unambitious folks!
Had but an individual hoax,
 A single South-sea bubble:
Each province *our* delusion shares,
From Poyais down to Buenos-Ayres—
 To count them is a trouble.

The gold that's sent out ready made
To the new world, must be repaid
 By help of Watt and Boulton,
Who from their mines, by aid of pumps,
Will raise up ore, and lumps, and dumps,
 Whence sovereigns may be molten!

Others, not roaming quite so far,
In stocks and bonds Peninsular,
 Find all their treasure vanish;
Leaving a warning to the rash,
That the best way to keep their cash,
 Is *not* to touch the Spanish.

Gilded by Eldorado dreams,
No wonder if our foreign schemes
 Assume a tint romantic;
But even at home, beneath our eyes,
What *ignes fatui* arise,
 Extravagant and antic!

9*

PROJECTS AND COMPANIES.

Bridges of iron, stone, and wood,
Not only, Thames, bestride thy flood,
   As if thou wert a runnel;
But terraces must clog thy shore,
While underneath thy bed we bore
   A subterranean tunnel.

Now bursts a fiercer mania—all
From every shire, the great, the small,
   For Railroad shares are scrambling :
Peers, paupers, countesses, their maids,
With equal ardour ply the trades
   Of jobbing, scheming, gambling.

Decoyed by projects wild and rash,
Some find their rail-devoted cash
   Is lost beyond retrieval ;
Others, who profitably sold,
Will tell you that the age of gold
   And iron are coeval.

With each new moon new bubbles rise,
Each, as it flits before our eyes,
   Its predecessor smashing ;
All at their rivals freely throw
Their dirt, to which we doubtless owe
   The Company for washing.

These are but weeds, the rich manure
Of overflowing wealth is sure
   To generate the thistle :——
They who would learn its nobler use,
May Pope's majestic lines peruse
   That close his Fourth Epistle.

ELEGY.

TO THE MEMORY OF MISS EMILY KAY, COUSIN TO MISS ELLEN GEE, OF KEW, WHO DIED LATELY AT EWELL, AND WAS BURIED IN ESSEX.

"They fool me to the top of my bent."—SHAKSPEARE.

SAD nymphs of U L, U have much to cry for,
   Sweet M L E K U never more shall C!
O S X maids! come hither and D, o,
   With tearful I, this M T L E G.

Without X S she did X L alway,
   Ah me! it truly vexes 1 2 C
How soon so D R a creature may D K,
   And only leave behind X U V E!

Whate'er 1 0 to do she did discharge,
   So that an N M E it might N D R:
Then why an S A write?—then why N
   Or with my briny tears B D U her B R?

When her Piano-40 she did press,
   Such heavenly sounds did M N 8, that she
Knowing her Q, soon 1 U 2 confess
   Her X L N C in an X T C.

Her hair was soft as silk, not Y R E,
   It gave no Q, nor yet 2 P to view:
She was not handsome; shall I tell U Y?
   U R 2 know her I was all S Q.

L 8 she was, and prattling like a J;
   How little, M L E! did you 4 C,
The grave should soon M U U, cold as clay,
   And you should cease to be an N T T!

PITT'S BON-MOT.

While taking **T** at **Q** with **L N G**,
    The **M T** grate she rose to put a :
Her clothes caught fire—no **1** again shall see
    Poor **M L E**; who now is dead as Solon.

O L N G! in vain you set at **O**
    G R and reproach for suffering her **2 B**
Thus sacrificed; to **J L U** should be brought,
    Or burnt **U O 2 B** in **F E G**.

Sweet **M L E K** into **S X** they bore,
    Taking good care the monument **2 Y 10**,
And as her tomb was much **2** low **B 4**,
    They lately brought fresh bricks the walls to **10**
        (heighten.)

PITT'S BON-MOT.

Though William Pitt (nick-named the Tory
In Morris's facetious story,)
    Retains the honours of his name
    As a Debates-man,
Who in the House of Commons, "*ore
Rotundo*," cried up England's glory,
    Yet as a statesman,
Or as a financier, his fame
May be compared to his own sinking fund,
Which, if not quite extinct, is *moribund*.

Seeing this heaven-born minister's renown
    In his political capacity,
Thus tumbling down,
    An instance of his smart dicacity,

Ought in justice to be stated,
 In order that the reader may bestow
Due praise on the defunct for a *bon-mot*,
 The only one he ever perpetrated.

When the French threatened in flat-bottomed boats
 To come and cut our throats,
Pitt—then Lord Warden of the Cinque Ports—held
 A meeting in the town of Dover,
 To settle, should the French come over,
How they might best and soonest be repell'd;
 Which said assemblage, being fierce and loyal,
Declared that England might discard her fears,
 For they themselves would promise to destroy all
The French, if they might form a corps, the Mayor
To be commander, and the whole to bear
The name of Royal Dover Volunteers.

The Premier, when the cheering ceased,
 Smiled, for he knew the dictum true,
That greatest boasters do the least,
And whispered to himself —"The Dover traders
 Are most insufferable gasconaders;
 If any folks deserve an *innuendo*,
By way of a rebuke, I'm sure these men do."
 However no remark was made,
Until the secretary reading o'er
The rules and regulations of the corps,
 Broke off, and to the chairman said,
 "Sir, I respectfully submit
 That it were well on this occasion,
Among our standing rules and laws,
To insert the customary clause,
Not to serve out of England."—"Yes," said Pitt,
 "*Except in case of an invasion!*"

HOBBS AND DOBBS.

Adrian.—" Your jest is somewhat of the oldest, Master Giles."
Giles.—" Hush ! do you think I would offer a new joke, any more than new wine, to your Worship ?"—*The Unknown.*

Love in a village, where the parties revel
  In all the neighbourly civility
  Of cheerful, social amiability,
    Is vastly pleasant ;
But hatred in a village is the devil !
    Because each peasant
Is ever meeting in that narrow circle,
The very man on whom he longs to work ill.
How sad the pity that our *beau idéal*
    Is never real ;—
That envy, hatred, jealousy, and malice,
  Should hold their chalice
Up to the lips of rustics, who were meant
By Nature to be innocent,
And harmless as the household dove,
    That type of love !

After this pretty bit of flummery,
  Or moral sentimental proem,
  (An apt exordium to my poem,)
I must be quick, concise, and summary,
And without any more preparative,
  Commence my narrative.

At Oakley, in the Western Riding
Of Yorkshire, were two men residing,
Named Hobbs and Dobbs, whose constant quarrels,
  Springing from rivalry in trade,
  A sort of village warfare made,
Which sadly spoilt the people's morals,

Splitting them into furious factions;
  Some warmly advocating Hobbs,
While others, both by words and actions,
  Supported Dobbs.
And yet these foolish fellows ought
  In their two leaders to have found
Men of strong understanding, taught
    With friendly stitches,
To patch up, not occasion breaches,
  And mend the *soles* of all the rustics round,
For they were both shoemakers, and their labours
  Should have been circumscribed to putting
Their friends and customers, and neighbours,
  On a good footing.

They lived, unfortunately, *vis-à-vis*,
  And soon began the work of emulation,
By flaming shopboards, where in gilt
And lackered lustre, you might see
  The symbols of their occupation,
Much paint in blue and crimson being spilt,
That each might be more splendid than the other,
And win all custom from his baffled brother.

Hobbs, who had somehow given handle
For undeserved reproach and scandal,
  When he new-dizened out his board,
Wrote at its foot this Latin scrap—
  "*Mens conscia recti*," which he took
  From some heraldic motto-book,
Meaning thereby to have a slap
  At his maligners and afford
Proof that his path he still pursued,
Strong in a conscious rectitude.

This was a source of envious dolour
    To Dobbs, who, in his first confusion,
Knowing his rival was no scholar,
    Deduced the natural conclusion
That " *conscia recti* " doubtless meant
    Some article of trade, perchance,
    Some fashion just arrived from France,
    And being resolutely bent
His hated rival to eclipse,
He sent forthwith for Mr. Cripps
        Painter and glazier,
    When thus ejaculated Dobbs—
" Paint me a still more flaming board,
    Of green, and gold, and azure;
What! do you think I can't afford
    To pay for it as well as Hobbs?
Be these French kickshaws what they will,
I am resolved to beat him still,
        To which effect I
Desire you 'll print in gold at bottom,
(That folks may fancy I have got 'em,)
    Men's AND WOMEN'S *conscia recti!*"

MONSIEUR LE BRUN.

Monsieur le Brun (who must not be confused
    With the great painter) jointly cultivated
Apollo's laurel and the grape of Bacchus,
    And into *mediocre* verse translated,
Or rather, as the French would say, *traduced*
    The odes of Flaccus.

The work, I must confess, was badly done,
    For poor Le Brun,
Still scribbling, and unable still to win
  A living for himself and wife,
Was like a rope-maker, condemned to spin
  Long lines, yet still go backward all his life.

Le Brun asserted that an author loses
By quaffing with the water-drinking Muses,
  Wherefore he held in small account
    Castalia's fount,
  And not a solitary sip he
  Ever quaffed from Aganippe,
Maintaining that champagne and other wine,
  With, now and then, a draught of liquor,
  Produced an inspiration quicker,
As well as more delightful and divine.——
If to his cups his couplets he had suited,
  They *must* have sparkled—and 'tis strange to me,
That want of life should ever be imputed
  To poetry inspired by *eau-de-vie.*

But so it was—his poems, every one,
    Were like a flintless gun,
  Which won't go off for want of fire;
And poor Le Brun who took to deeper drinking
    Instead of thinking,
  Sunk daily deeper in oblivion's mire.
While swallowing compound spirits, still the faster
  He lost his own, till he became a prey
To hypochondria; and one disaster
  Another following, his health gave way.
His stomach, it was said, had lost its coat,

Or thrown it off, perhaps, from being hot,
For his old trick he never had forgot,
Of pouring ardent spirits down his throat :
Which daily system of potation
Most deleterious,
Brought fever first, then inflammation,
When his poor wife so much his aspect shocked her,
Called in the doctor,
And now the case grew serious.

Bolus, a man of fees, not feeling,
Finding his purse was low, though high his fever,
Bolted, but sent a priest, who, kneeling,
Thus comforted the bibulous believer :—
" My son, 'tis clear you have not long to live,
So you must use this unction,
Confess your sins with due compunction,
And freely all your enemies forgive—
Bestowing on them, if they 're nigh,
The kiss of peace before you die !"

" Kiss what I hated most—my deadliest foes !
Surely, good father, you impose
A penance too revolting to be just,
'Tis ten times worse than fasts, hair shirts, and whips ;
However, if I must, I must ;
So put a glass of water to my lips !"

ST. GEORGE'S PENITENTIARY.

THE learned and facetious Dr. Airy
    Preached, 'tother day, a sermon so pathetic,
For the St. George's Penitentiary,
    That it seemed just like giving an emetic
To every purse of Christian bowels:
    Folks sobbed and blubbered
So fast that hankerchiefs were turned to towels;
    And the last tear seemed squeezed from out its cup-
        board.
The Doctor smiled (within his sleeve)
    At these salt tributes to his oratory,
Sure that the Institution would receive
    A sum redounding to his proper glory,
    From the soul-melted auditory.

The sermon o'er, he bent his keen
    Ear to the tinklings of the plate;—
    Alas they came with pause deliberate
        'Twixt each donation,
"Like angel visits, few and far between,"
        (I like a new quotation,)
    But, as he caught the sounds, he thought
Each had a golden echo, which in fairness
Made full atonement for its rareness.
    "Ay, ay," soliloquized the preacher,
"I told them charity atoned
For multitudes of sins;—they've owned
    For once the wisdom of their teacher.
And, for their many crimes untold,
Are doing penance with their gold."

With this auriferous impression,
    Proud and elate,
    He move towards the plate;
But ah! how changed was his expression,
When, 'stead of the expected prize,
Nothing but shillings met his eyes,
And those, alas! too few in number
    Each other to encumber.
" Ah!" cried the parson——" addle-pated
Dolts and dunces! when I stated,
' Love of our species is the just
Measure of charity, they must
Have understood the phrase to be,
    Love of our specie.'
Nothing but shillings, shillings still!
    A strange vagary!
Now on my credit, if I had my will,
Their Institution's title I would vary,
Into the *Twelve-*PENNY*-tentiary.*"
Doctor! 'tis my opinion humble,
You had not any right to grumble,
For he who in this penny age can touch
A shilling, gets twelve times as much
As other folks;——I state no hoax,
But simple fact, devoid of jokes,
Or amphibological equivoques;
Yes, since the penny banner was unfurled,
In this two-halfpenny four-farthing world,
Have we not thousands who are willing
    To place unlimited reliance,
    For learning, news, and science,
Upon the twelfth part of a shilling?
Have we not Penny Cyclopedias,
    Penny Magazines and books,

Penny Tracts, less good than tedious,
 For *penitents* of rueful looks,
And penny classics that give scope
 To boys at penny schools, and misses,
 To sympathize with poor Ulysses
And his beloved *Penny-lope?*

 With such economy,
Where every cottage is a college,
What wonder, in the march of knowledge,
 That ploughboys understand astronomy?
Cries Hodge—"How comes it that the sun,
 Who nightly seeks the western shore,
Rises, as sure as any gun,
 Next morning where he was afore?"
"Spoony!" replies a learned wight,
 "Your ignorance is truly risible;
He always travels back at night,
 And that's the reason he's invisible."

It was a penny Latinist, who said,
 In chaos there had been a battle
 Before the days of men and cattle,
 Though not set down in Holy Writ,
Because in Ovid he had read
 That was the time when *nihil fit.*
Such tales, (I hope that none have quizzed 'em,)
 Evince the march of penny wisdom,
 And might be told *ad infinitum,*
Had we just now the time to write 'em.

DIAMOND CUT DIAMOND.

A RECENT OCCURRENCE.

A FIRM there is, of civic fame,
   At all events of notoriety,
(Excuse my mentioning its name,)
   Which crams the public to satiety,
With rhyming puffs by shopmen bards,
And huge conspicuous placards,
Slung on the backs of men and boys,
   And hobble-de-hoys,
Plying all day their devious courses;
   Or stuck on the tall vans that flare
   Through every crowded thoroughfare,
To cozen asses and to frighten horses.

This firm's emporium or bazaar,
Near Aldgate pump, is known afar
   By catchpenny devices manifold,
By panes of glass worth many guineas,
And all that may attract the ninnies
Who think they're buying cheap, and find they're *sold.*

Two clowns, one day, before the shop,
   In rustic frocks and spatterdashes,
   Besmirched with stercoraceous splashes,
     Came to a stop;
Not to admire the flash habiliments,
Which a month's wear would turn to filaments;
   Not to indulge in talk domestic.
But to decide by imprecations,
And interchange of objurgations,
   Some unadjusted feud agrestic,

Their flashing eyes and gestures furious
Soon showed that words, howe'er injurious,
Would not interpret what their rage meant,
So they began a fist engagement;
And, in the very first attack,
One of the rustics, reeling back,
    Against the window fell slap dash.
    Zooks! what a crash!
'Twas obvious that the largest pane
(If we may speak in Yankee strain)
    Was sent to everlasting smash.

Away the first aggressor hurried,
    And presently was lost to sight;
Out rushed four shopmen, red and flurried,
    Who seized the window-breaking wight,
    Aghast and trembling with affright,
Dragged him into their shop or trap, and
Told their master what had happened.
" It cost ten pounds!" the latter roared;
    " Ten pounds, and you must pay them down,
Before your liberty 's restored.
    D' ye hear? hast got the money, clown?"

" Ten pounds!" cried Hodge, in blank dismay;
" Lord love you, I can never pay.
I've got ten shillings and some pence;
    ('Tis hard to make me such a loser,)
But if they 'll cover the offence,
    Take 'em and let me go, now do, sir."
" Blockhead! will such a mite atone?
    You must make good the whole disaster."
" I've nothing else, sir, of my own;
    What more I've got belongs to master."

" So you *have* money then ? how much ?"
" Why, sir, he sent me on a job,
    To cash a check for fifty pound ;
'Tis done, the note is in my fob.
    Wrapped in a paper, safe and sound ; ·
But that, you know, I mustn't touch ;
You wouldn't bring me to disgrace,
Wi' loss o' character and place ;
So don't ye ax me, sir, pray don't ;
Touch it I mustn't, and I won't."
" Your master, clown, is answerable
    For your misdeeds, whate'er they be ;
Down with the note upon the table,
    And we'll give change and set you free ;
If not, prepare to go to prison."
    " Dang it !" cried Hodge, with face of woe,
    " What *can* I do, sir, when you know
The money isn't mine, but his'n ?"
" Stuff !" quoth the magnate of the shop ;
    " Quick ! quick ! let the police be called,
And send him straight to jail."   " Stop ! stop !"
    Ejaculated Hodge, appalled,
And like a leaf of aspen shaking,
Such was his pitiable taking,
" Master, if I am missed, will say
I've robbed him, and have run away.
It can't be helped—what must be, must."
    So saying he fished up the note,
From the deep fob in which 'twas thrust,
    And twisted like a papillote,
Secured the change, and then departed,
Half frightened and half broken hearted,
Moaning and muttering, " I fegs !

How shall I ever tell my master
　About this terrible disaster ?
I'm ruined, sure as eggs is eggs."

Our cits, though chuckling with intense
Enjoyment at the clown's expense,
　Had little cause for mirth, if any.
For lo ! their banker's clerk appears
Next day, and whispers in their ears,
　"This fifty 's forged—not worth a penny !"

Such was the fact—our firm had lost,
Besides the broken window's cost,
Pounds forty at a single throw :
What had they in return to show
For such subtraction from their till ?
A piece of paper, value—*nil !*

Meanwhile the fighting clowns, whose roguery
　(They were colleagues) the plot had planned,
　By which the tradesmen were trepanned,
Changed their smock-frocks for stylish toggery,
To Margate steamed to take their pleasure,
And spent their forty pounds at leisure.
10

THE

POETICAL WORK

OF

JAMES SMITH.

LONDON LYRICS.

CHRISTMAS OUT OF TOWN.

FOR many a winter in Billiter-lane
My wife, Mrs. Brown, was not heard to complain ;
At Christmas the family met there to dine
On beef and plum-pudding, and turkey and chine.
Our bark has now taken a contrary heel,
My wife has found out that the sea is genteel.
To Brighton we duly go scampering down,
For nobody now spends his Christmas in Town.

Our register-stoves, and our crimson-baized doors,
Our weather-proof walls, and our carpeted floors,
Our casements well fitted to stem the North wind,
Our arm-chair and sofa, are all left behind.
We lodge on the Steine, in a bow-window'd box,
That beckons up-stairs every Zephyr that knocks ;
The sun hides his head, and the elements frown—
But nobody now spends his Christmas in Town.

In Billiter-lane, at this mirth-moving time,
The lamplighter brought us his annual rhyme,
The tricks of Grimaldi were sure to be seen,
We carved a twelfth-cake, and we drew king and queen
These pastimes gave oil to Time's roundabout wheel,
Before we began to be growing genteel :
'Twas all very well for a cockney or clown,
But nobody now spends his Christmas in Town.

At Brighton I'm stuck up in Donaldson's shop,
Or walk upon bricks till I'm ready to drop;
Throw stones at an anchor, look out for a skiff,
Or view the Chain-pier from the top of the cliff;
Till winds from all quarters oblige me to halt,
With an eye full of sand and a mouth full of salt.
Yet still I am suffering with folks of renown,
For nobody now spends his Christmas in Town.

In gallop the winds, at the full of the moon,
And puff up my carpet like Sadler's balloon;
My drawing-room rug is besprinkled with soot,
And there is not a lock in the house that will shut.
At Mahomet's steam-bath I lean on my cane,
And murmur in secret—" Oh, Billiter-lane !"
But would not express what I think for a crown,
For nobody now spends his Christmas in Town.

The Duke and the Earl are no cronies of mine,
His Majesty never invites me to dine ;
The Marquess won't speak, when we meet on the pie
Which makes me suspect that I'm *nobody* here.
If that be the case, why then welcome again
Twelfth-cake and snap-dragon in Billiter-lane.
Next winter I'll prove to my dear Mrs. Brown,
That *Nobody* now spends his Christmas in Town.

ST. JAMES'S PARK.

Twas June, and many a gossip wench,
    Child-freighted, trod the central Mall ;
I gained a white unpeopled bench,
    And gazed upon the long Canal.

Beside me, soon, in motley talk,
  Boys, nursemaids sat, a varying race;
At length two females crossed the walk,
  And occupied the vacant space.

In years they seem'd some forty-four,
  Of dwarfish stature, vulgar mien;
A bonnet of black silk each wore,
  And each a gown of bombazine:
And, while in loud and careless tones
  They dwelt upon their own concerns,
Ere long I learned that Mrs. Jones
  Was one, and one was Mrs. Burns.

They talked of little Jane and John,
  And hoped they'd come before 'twas dark,
Then wondered why, with pattens on,
  One might not walk across the Park:
They called it far to Camden-town,
  Yet hoped to reach it by-and-bye;
And thought it strange, since flour was down,
  That bread should still continue high.

They said, last Monday's heavy gales
  Had done a monstrous deal of ill;
Then tried to count the iron rails
  That wound up Constitution hill:
This 'larum sedulous to shun,
  I donn'd my gloves, to march away,
When, as I gazed upon the one,
  " Good Heavens!" I cried, " 'tis Nancy Gray."

'Twas Nancy, whom I led along
  The whitened and elastic floor,

Amid mirth's merry pancing throng,
    Just two-and-twenty years before.
Though sadly alter'd, I knew her,
    While she, 'twas obvious, knew me not;
But mildly said, "Good evening, sir,"
    And with her comrade left the spot.   -

"Is this," I cried, in grief profound,
    "The fair, with whom, eclipsing all,
I traversed Ranelagh's bright round,
    Or trod the mazes of Vauxhall?
And is this all that Time can do?
    Has Nature nothing else in store?
Is this, of lovely twenty-two,
    All that remains at forty-four?

"Could I to such a helpmate cling?
    Were such a wedded dowdy mine,
On yonder lamp-post would I swing,
    Or plunge in yonder Serpentine!"
I left the Park with eyes askance,
    But, ere I entered Cleveland-row,
Rude Reason thus threw in her lance,
    And dealt self-love a mortal blow.

"Time, at whose touch all mortals bow,
    From either sex his prey secures,
His scythe, while wounding Nancy's brow,
    Can scarce have smoothly swept o'er yours;
By her you plainly were not known;
    Then, while you mourn the alter'd hue
Of Nancy's face, suspect your own
    May be a *little* altered too."

THE UPAS IN MARYBONE LANE.

A TREE grew in Java, whose pestilent rind
A venom distilled of the deadliest kind;
The Dutch sent their felons its juices to draw,
And who returned safe, pleaded pardon by law.

Face-muffled the culprits crept into the vale,
Advancing from windward to 'scape the death-gale;
How few the reward of their victory earned!
For ninety-nine perished for one who returned.

Britannia this Upas-tree bought of Mynheer,
Removed it through Holland and planted it here;
'Tis now a stock plant, of the genus Wolf's bane,
And one of them blossoms in Marybone lane.

The house that surrounds it stands first in a row,
The doors, at right angles, swing open below;
And the children of misery daily steal in,
And the poison they draw we denominate *Gin*.

There enter the prude, and the reprobate boy,
The mother of grief, and the daughter of joy,
The serving-maid slim, and the serving-man stout,
They quickly steal in, and they slowly reel out.

Surcharged with the venom, some walk forth erect,
Apparently baffling its deadly effect;
But, sooner or later, the reckoning arrives,
And ninety-nine perish for one who survives.

They cautious advance, with slouchèd bonnet and hat,
They enter at this door, they go out at that ;
Some bear off their burden with riotous glee,
But most sink, in sleep, at the foot of the tree.

Tax, Chancellor Van, the Batavian to thwart,
This compound of crime, at a sovereign a quart ;
Let gin fetch, per bottle, the price of Champagne,
And hew down the Upas in Marybone-lane.

STAGE WEDLOCK.

FARREN, Thalia's dear delight,
Can I forget that fatal night
   Of grief, unstained by fiction,
(Even now the recollection damps)
When Wroughton led thee to the lamps
   In graceful valediction ?

This Derby prize by Hymen won,
Again the God made bold to run
   Beneath Thalia's steerage ;
Sent forth a second Earl to woo,
And captivating Brunton too,
   Exalted to the peerage.

Awhile no actress sought his shrine ;
When lovely Searle, in Columbine,
   Each heart held " cabined, cribbed in :"
Her dark-blue eye, and tresses loose,
Made the whole town dub Mother Goose
   Chef-d'œuvre of Tom Dibdin.

"Hail, feathered Conjuror!" I cried,
"September's dish, Saint Michael's pride,
  Theatric gold collector:
I pledge thee, bird, in Circe's cup!"—
But Heathcote, ring in hand, ripped up
  The Capitol's protector.

Thrice vanquished thus, on Thespian soil,
Heart-whole awhile, from Cupid's toil
  I caught a fleeting furlough;
Gay's Newgate Opera charmed me then,
But Polly sang her requiem when
  Fair Bolton changed to Thurlow.

These wounds some substitute might heal;
But what bold mortal bade O'Neil
  Renounce her tragic station?
Taste, talent, beauty to trepan—
By Heaven, I wonder how the man
  Escaped assassination!

I felt half bent to wing my way
With Werter, on whose table lay
  Emilia Galoti:
Stunned, like a skater by a fall,
I saw with unconcern Hughes Ball
  Elope with Mercandotti.

'Tis thus that prowling round Love's fold,
Hymen, by sufferance made bold,
  (Too bold for one of his age,)
Presumes behind the scenes to go,
Where only Cupid used to show
  His mythologic visage.

Would these bold suitors wield the fork,
And dip, as sailors dip for pork,
   Or urchins at a barrow,
First come, first take, one would not care:
But pick and choose was never fair
   At Eton or at Harrow.

Gain we no safeguard from the laws?
Contains the Marriage Act no clause
   To hush Saint Martin's steeple;
To bind the public's daughters sure,
And from stage larceny secure
   Us poor play-going people?

No! Eldon, all depends on thee:
Wards of thy Court let heroines be,
   Who to stage wealth have risen;
And then, if lovers ladders climb,
Contempt of Court will be their crime,
   The Fleet will be their prison.

DOCTOR GALL.

I SING of the organs and fibres
   That ramble about in the brains;
Avaunt! ye irreverent jibers,
   Or stay and be wise for your pains.
All heads were of yore on a level,
   One could not tell clever from dull,
Till I, like Le Sage's lame devil,
   Unroof'd with a touch every skull.
Oh, I am the mental dissector,
   I fathom the wits of you all,

Then come in a crowd to the lecture
   Of craniological Gall.

The passions, or active or passive,
   Exposed by my magical spells,
As busy as bees in a glass hive,
   Are seen in their separate cells.
Old Momus, who wanted a casement
   Whence all in the heart might be read,
Were he living, would stare with amazement
   To find what he wants in the head.

There's an organ for strains amoroso,
   Just under the edge of the wig,
An organ for writing but so-so,
   For driving a tilbury gig;
An organ for boxers, for stoics,
   For giving booksellers a lift,
For marching the zig-zag heroics,
   And editing Jonathan Swift.

I raise in match-making a rumpus,
   And Cupid his flame must impart
Henceforth with a rule and a compass,
   Instead of a bow and a dart.
"Dear Madam, your eye-brow is horrid;
   And Captain, too broad is your pate;
I see by that bump on your forehead
   You're shockingly dull *tête-à-tête*."

When practice has made my book plainer
   To manhood, to age, and to youth,
I'll build, like the genius Phanor,
   In London a palace of truth.

Then fibs, ah, beware how you tell 'em,
   Reflect how pellucid the skull,
Whose downright sincere cerebellum
   Must render all flattery null.

Your friend brings a play out at Drury,
   'Tis hooted and damned in the pit;
Your organ of friendship's all fury,
   But what says your organ of wit?
" Our laughter next time prithee stir, man,
   We don't pay our money to weep;
Your play must have come from the German,
   It set all the boxes asleep."

At first, all will be in a bustle;
   The eye will, from ignorance, swerve,
And some will abuse the wrong muscle,
   And some will adore the wrong nerve.
In love should your hearts then be sporting,
   Your heads on one level to bring,
You must go in your nightcaps a-courting,
   As if you were going to swing.

Yet some happy mortals, all virtue,
   Have sentiment just as they should,
Their occiput nought can do hurt to,
   Each organ's an organ of good;
Such couples angelic, when mated,
   To bid all concealment retire,
Should seek Hymen's altar bald-pated,
   And throw both their wigs in his fire.

My system, from great A to Izzard,
   You now, my good friends, may descry,

TABLE TALK.

Not Shakspeare's Bermudean wizard
  Was half so enchanting as I.
His magic a Tempest could smother,
  But mine the soul's hurricane clears,
By exposing your heads to each other,
  And setting those heads by the ears.

Oh, I am the mental dissector,
  I fathom the wits of you all;
So here is an end to the lecture
  Of craniological Gall.

TABLE TALK.

To weave a culinary clue,
When to eschew, and what to chew,
  Where shun, and where take rations,
I sing. Attend, ye diners-out,
And if my numbers please you, shout
  "Hear, hear!" in acclamations.

There are who treat you once a year,
To the same stupid set; good cheer
  Such hardship cannot soften.
To listen to the self same dunce,
At the same laden table, once
  Per annum 's once too often.

Rather than that, mix on my plate
With men I like the meat I hate—
  Colman with pig and treacle;
Luttrell with ven'son-pastry join,
Lord Normanby with orange wine,
  And rabbit-pie with Jekyll.

Add to George Lambe a sable snipe,
Conjoin with Captain Morris tripe
   By parsley-roots made denser ;
Mix Macintosh with mack'rel, with
Calves-head and bacon Sidney Smith,
   And mutton-broth with Spencer.

Shun sitting next the wight whose drone
Bores, *sotto voce*, you alone
   With flat colloquial pressure ;
Debarred from general talk, you droop
Beneath his buzz, from orient Soup
   To occidental Cheshire.

He who can only talk with one,
Should stay at home and talk with none—
   At all events, to strangers,
Like village epitaphs of yore,
He ought to cry " Long time I bore,"
   To warn them of their dangers.

There are whose kind inquiries scan
Your total kindred, man by man,
   Son, brother, cousin, joining,
They ask about your wife, who's dead,
And eulogize your uncle Ned,
   Who swung last week for coining.

When joined to such a son of prate,
His queries I anticipate,
   And thus my lee-way fetch up—
" Sir, all my relatives, I vow,
Are perfectly in health, and now
   I'd thank you for the ketchup !"

Others there are who but retail
Their breakfast journal, now grown stale,
   In print ere day was dawning;
When folks like these sit next to me,
They send me dinnerless to tea;
   One cannot chew while yawning.

Seat not good talkers one next one,
As Jacquier beards the Clarendon;
   Thus shrouded you undo 'em;
Rather confront them, face to face,
Like Holles-street and Harewood-place,
   And let the town run through 'em.

Poets are dangerous to sit nigh;
You waft their praises to the sky,
   And when you think you're stirring
Their gratitude, they bite you——(That's
The reason I object to cats;
   They scratch amid their purring.)

For those who ask you if you "malt,"
Who, "beg your pardon" for the salt,
   And ape our upper grandees,
By wondering folks can touch port wine;
That, reader, 's your affair, not mine;
   I never mess with dandies.

Relations mix not kindly; shun
Inviting brothers; sire and son
   Is not a wise selection:
Too intimate, they either jar
In converse, or the evening mar
   By mutual circumspection.

Lawyers are apt to think the view
That interests them must interest you;
　　Hence they appear at table
Or supereloquent, or dumb,
Fluent as nightingales, or mum,
　　As horses in a stable.

When men amuse their fellow guests
With Crank and Jones, or Justice Best's
　　Harangue in Dobbs and Ryal!
The host, beneath whose roof they sit, —
Must be a puny judge of wit,
　　Who grants them a new trial.

Shun technicals in each extreme;
Exclusive talk, whate'er the theme,
　　The proper boundary passes;
Nobles as much offend, whose clack 's
For ever running on Almack's,
　　As brokers on molasses.

I knew a man from glass to delf,
Who knew of nothing but himself,
　　Till checked by a vertigo;
The party who beheld him "floored,"
Bent o'er the liberated board,
　　And cried, "Hic jacet ego."

Some aim to tell a thing that hit
Where last they dined; what there was wit,
　　Here meets rebuffs and crosses.
Jokes are like trees; their place of birth
Best suits them; stuck in foreign earth,
　　They perish in the process.

Think, reader, of the few who groan
For any ailments save their own ;
   The world, from peer to peasant,
Is heedless of your cough or gout ;
Then pr'ythee, when you next dine out,
   Go armed with something pleasant.

Nay, even the very soil that nursed
The plant, will sometimes kill what erst
   It nurtured in full glory.
Like causes will not always move
To similar effects ; to prove
   The fact, I'll tell a story.

Close to that spot where Stuart turns
His back upon the clubs, and spurns
   The earth, a marble fixture,
We dined ; well matched, for pleasure met,
Wits, poets, peers, a jovial set
   In miscellaneous mixture.

Each card turned up a trump, the glee,
The catch went round, from eight to three,
   Decorum scorned to own us ;
We joked, we bantered, laughed, and roared,
Till high above the welkin soared,
   The helpmate of Tithonus.

Care kept aloof, each social soul
A brother hailed, Joy filled the bowl,
   And humor crowned the medley,
Till royal Charles, roused by the fun,
Looked toward Whitehall, and thought his son
   Was rioting with Sedley.

"Gad, John, this is a glorious joke—"
(Thus to our host his Highness spoke)—
  "The vicar with his Nappy
Would give an eye for this night's freak—
Suppose we meet again next week—"
  John bowed, and was too "happy."

The day arrived—'twas seven—we met:
Wits, poets, peers, the self-same set,
  Each hailed a joyous brother.
But in the blithe and débonnaire,
Saying, alas! is one affair,
  And doing is another.

Nature unkind, we turned to Art;
Heavens! how we labored to be smart;
  Zug sang a song in German:
We might as well have played at chess;
All dropped as dead-born from the press
  As last year's Spital sermon.

Ah! Merriment! when men entrap
Thy bells, and women steal thy cap,
  They think they have trepanned thee.
Delusive thought! aloof and dumb,
Thou wilt not at a bidding come,
  Though Royalty command thee.

The rich, who sigh for thee; the great,
Who court thy smiles with gilded plate,
  But clasp thy cloudy follies:
I've known thee turn, in Portman-square,
From Burgundy and Hock, to share
  A pint of Port at Dolly's.

Races at Ascot, tours in Wales,
White-bait at Greenwich ofttimes fails,
  To wake thee from thy slumbers.
Even now, so prone art thou to fly,
Ungrateful nymph! thou 'rt fighting shy
  Of these narcotic numbers.

THE POET OF FASHION.

His book is successful, he 's steeped in renown,
His lyric effusions have tickled the town ;
Dukes, dowagers, dandies, are eager to trace
The fountain of verse in the verse-maker's face ;
While, proud of Apollo, with peers *tête-à-tête*,
From Monday till Saturday dining off plate,
His heart full of hope, and his head full of gain,
The Poet of Fashion dines out in Park-lane.

Now lean-jointured widows, who seldom draw corks,
Whose tea-spoons do duty for knives and for forks,
Send forth, vellum-covered, a six o'clock card,
And get up a dinner to peep at the bard :
Veal, sweetbread, boiled chickens, and tongue, crown
      the cloth,
And soup *à la reine*, little better than broth :
While, past his meridian, but still with some heat,
The Poet of Fashion dines out in Sloane-street.

Enrolled in the tribe who subsist by their wits,
Remembered by starts, and forgotten by fits,
Now artists and actors the bardling engage,
To squib in the journals, and write for the stage.

Now soup à *la reine* bends the knee to ox-cheek,
And chickens and tongue bow to bubble and squeak—
While, still in translation employed by "The Row,"
The Poet of Fashion dines out in Soho.

Pushed down from Parnassus to Phlegethon's brink,
Tossed, torn, and trunk-lining, but still with some ink,
Now squab city misses their albums expand,
And woo the worn rhymer for "something off-hand;"
No longer with stilted effrontery fraught,
Bucklersbury now seeks what St. James's once sought,
And (O what a classical haunt for a bard!)
The Poet of Fashion dines out in Barge Yard.

NEXT-DOOR NEIGHBOURS.

My wife and I live, *comme il faut*,
At number Six in Crosby-row:
   So few our household labors,
We quickly turn from joints and pies,
To use two tongues and twice two eyes
   To meliorate our neighbours.

My eye-glass, thanks to Dolland's skill,
Sweeps up the lane to Mears's Mill,
   While, latticed in her chamber,
My wife peeps through her window-pane,
To note who ramble round the lane,
   And who the foot-stile clamber.

This morn the zig-zag man of meat
Trotted, tray-balanced, up the street—
   We saw him halt at Sydney's:

My wife asserts he left lamb there;
But I myself can all but swear
  'Twas mutton-chops and kidneys.

The man who goes about with urns
Is beckoned in by Betty Burns:
  The poor girl knows no better:
But Mrs. Burns should have more sense;
That broken tray is mere pretence—
  He brings the girl a letter.

Whether she goes up street for milk,
Or brings home sugar, pins, or silk,
  That silly wench for ever
Draws up, pretending at the stile
To rest herself, while all the while
  She waits for Captain Trevor.

The Captain, when he sees me, turns,
Seems not to notice Betty Burns,
  And round the pond betakes him,
Behind the stables of the Bear,
To get the back way in; but there
  My wife's back window rakes him.

There go the Freaks again—but hark!
I hear the gate-bell ring—'tis Bark,
  The glib apothecary,
Who in his mortar pounds the fame
Of every rumor-wounded dame,
  From Moll to Lady Mary.

"Well, Mr. Bark,"—"I've found her out."
"Who is she?"—"Not his wife."—"No doubt."
  "'Twas told me by his brother."

" Which brother ? Archibald ?"—" No, Fred.,
   An old connexion."—" So I said."
   "The woman 's—" " What ?"—" His mother."

" Who are the comers next to Blake's ?"
"At number Four ?"—" Yes."—" No great shakes :
   Sad junketings and wastings.
I've seen them play in ' Days of Yore,'
He acted Hastings in Jane Shore,
   And she Jane Shore in Hastings."

" Pray, Mr. Bark, what party drove
That dark-brown chariot to the Grove ?"
   " The Perry's, Ma'am, wet Quakers.
He married Mrs. Hartley Grant,
Whose father's uncle's mother's aunt
   Lived cook at Lady Dacre's."

But Sunday is the time, of course,
When Gossip's congregated force
   Pours from our central chapel :
Then hints and anecdotes increase,
And in the Mansion-house of Peace
   Dark Discord drops her apple.

Ope but a casement, turn a lock,
The whole row feels the electric shock,
   Springs tilt, their blinds up throwing.
And every ear and every eye
Darts to one centre, to descry
   Who 's coming or who 's going.

Thus occupied, in Crosby-row,
We covet not the Grange or Stowe ;
   Pent in by walls and palings,

Their lordly tenants can't, like us,
Drop in at tea-time to discuss
  Their neighbours' faults and failings.

THE IMAGE BOY.

WHOE'ER has trudged, on frequent feet,
From Charing Cross to Ludgate-street,
  That haunt of noise and wrangle,
Has seen, on journeying through the Strand,
A foreign Image-vender stand
  Near Somerset quadrangle.

His coal-black eye, his balanced walk,
His sable apron, white with chalk,
  His listless meditation,
His curly locks, his sallow cheeks,
His board of celebrated Greeks,
  Proclaim his trade and nation.

Not on that board, as erst, are seen
A tawdry troop; our gracious Queen
  With tresses like a carrot,
A milk-maid with a pea-green pail,
A poodle with a golden tail,
  John Wesley, and a parrot;——

No; far more classic is his stock;
With ducal Arthur, Milton, Locke,
  He bears, unconscious roamer,
Alcmena's Jove-begotten Son,
Cold Abelard's too tepid nun,
  And pass-supported Homer.

11

See yonder bust adorned with curls;
'Tis hers, the Queen who melted pearls
   Marc Antony to wheedle.
Her bark, her banquets, all are fled;
And Time, who cut her vital thread,
   Has only spared her Needle.

Stern Neptune, with his triple prong,
Childe Harold, peer of peerless song,
   So frolic Fortune wills it,
Stand next the Son of crazy Paul,
Who hugged the intrusive King of Gaul
   Upon a raft at Tilsit.

" Poor vagrant child of want and toil!
The sun that warms thy native soil
   Has ripened not thy knowledge;
'Tis obvious, from that vacant air,
Though Padua gave thee birth, thou ne'er
   Didst graduate in her College.

" 'Tis true thou nam'st thy motley freight;
But from what source their birth they date,
   Mythology or history,
Old records, or the dreams of youth,
Dark fable, or transparent truth,
   Is all to thee a mystery.

" Come tell me, Vagrant, in a breath,
Alcides' birth, his life, his death,
   Recount his dozen labours :
Homer thou know'st; but of the woes
Of Troy thou 'rt ignorant as those
   Dark Orange-boys thy neighbours."

THE IMAGE BOY.

'Twas thus, erect, I deigned to pour
My shower of lordly pity o'er
    The poor Italian wittol,
As men are apt to do to show
Their vantage-ground o'er those who know
    Just less than their own little.

When lo, methought Prometheus' flame
Waved o'er a bust of deathless fame,
    And woke to life Childe Harold:
The Bard aroused me from my dream
Of pity, alias self-esteem,
    And thus indignant carolled:

" O thou, who thus, in numbers pert
And petulant, presum'st to flirt
    With Memory's Nine Daughters:
Whose verse the next trade-winds that blow
Down narrow Paternoster-row
    Shall whelm in Lethe's waters:

" Slight is the difference I see
Between yon Paduan youth and thee;
    He moulds, of Paris plaster,
An urn by classic Chantrey's laws——
And thou a literary vase
    Of would-be alabaster.

" Were I to arbitrate betwixt
His terra cotta, plain or mixed,
    And thy earth-gendered sonnet,
Small cause has he th' award to dread :——
Thy images are in the head,
    And his, poor boy, are on it !"

THE LEES AND THE LAWSONS.

IF you call on the Lees, north of Bloomsbury-square,
They welcome you blandly, they proffer a chair,
　Decorously mild and well bred:
Intent on their music, their books, or their pen,
Employment absorbs their attention, and men
　Seem totally out of their head.

If you call on the Lawsons, in Bloomsbury-place,
No fabric of order you seem to deface,
　No sober arrangement to break:
They lounge on the sofa, their manners are odd,
Men drop in at luncheon, and give them a nod,
　Then run to the sherry and cake.

The house of the Lees has an orderly air,
It sets to its brethren of brick in the square
　A model from attic to basement:
The knocker is polished, the name is japanned,
The step, unpolluted, is sprinkled with sand,
　White blinds veil the drawing-room casement.

The house of the Lawsons is *toute autre chose*,
It certainly proffers no air of repose,
　For one of the girls always lingers
Athwart the verandah, alert as an ape,
To note to her sisters the forthcoming gape,
　Be it monkeys or Savoyard singers.

Whenever the Lees to the theatre stray,
The singers who sing, and the players who play,
　Attentive, untalkative, find 'em:

With sound to allure them, or sense to attract,
They rarely turn round, till the end of the act,
   To talk with the party behind 'em.

The Lawsons are bent on a different thing :
Miss Paton may warble, Miss Ayton may sing,
   To listeners tier above tier :
They heed not song, character, pathos, or plot,
But turn their heads back, to converse with a knot
   Of dandies who lounge in the rear.

In life's onward path it has happened to me
With many a Lawson and many a Lee,
   In parties to mix and to mingle :
And somehow, in spite of manœuvres and plans,
I've found that the Lees got united in banns,
   While most of the Lawsons keep single.

Coy Hymen is like the black maker of rum—
" De more massa call me de more I vont come,"
   He flies from the forward and bold : -
He gives to the coy what he keeps from the kind ;
The maidens who seek him, the maidens who find,
   Are cast in an opposite mould.

Ye female *gymnasians*, who strive joint by joint,
Come give to my Lawsons some lessons in point,
   (They can't from their own sex refuse 'em :)
Whenever you plan an athletic attack,
You know, from experience, to jump on man's back
   Is not the right road to his bosom.

MISCELLANEOUS PIECES.

COUNTRY COMMISSIONS.

Cousin Charles, please to send down to-morrow,
   At eight, by the Scarborough mail,
Claudine, or the Victim of Sorrow,
   Don Juan, two mops, and a pail.
As soon as you enter Hyde Park, it
   Must suit you to call in Gough-square;
And when you're in Leadenhall Market,
   Buy a rattle at Bartl'my Fair.

Do give the enclosed to George Colburn,
   The tinman—he's sure to be found—
He lives in Southampton-street, Holburn,
   Or else near the Islington Pound.
Papa wants a hamper of claret
   Like that which he smuggled from Tours,
Aunt Agatha wants a poll parrot—
   Perhaps you could let her have yours.

We are dying for Lord Byron's sonnet,
   Tell Jones I have sent him a pig,
Mamma wants a new sarcenet bonnet,
   The size of the head of our gig.

COUNTRY COMMISSIONS.

Could you match the enclosed bit of ribbon—
    Do buy Tom an ounce of rape-seed;
When you send the third volume of Gibbon,
    Do send Jack a velocipede.

Some shears that old Dobbin will well dock,
    A mouse-trap, a gold-headed cane,
A bottle of Steers' opedeldoc,
    Three ounces of alicampane,
Gold wire from Duke's Head, Little Britain,
    A purple tin kaleidescope,
A tea-tray, a tortoise-shell kitten,
    Rob Roy, and a long bit of soap.

Six ounces of Bohea from Twining's,
    A peg-top, a Parmesan cheese,
Some rose-coloured sarcenet for linings,
    A stew-pan, and Stevenson's Glees;
A song ending " Hey noni noni,"
    A chair with a cover of chintz,
A mummy dug up by Belzoni,
    A skein of white worsted from Flint's.

ANSWER.

Can I pocket St. Paul's like an apple,
    Take Waterloo bridge in my teeth,
Mount astride the Green Dragon, Whitechapel,
    And fight all the butchers beneath?
Can I eat Bank directors by dozens,
    Put the national debt in a dish?
If I cannot my dear country cousins,
    I cannot do half what you wish!

THE MAMMOTH.

Soon as the deluge ceased to pour
The flood of death from shore to shore,
   And verdure smiled again,
Hatched amidst elemental strife,
I sought the upper realms of life,
   The tyrant of the plain.

On India's shores my dwelling lay—
Gigantic, as I roamed for prey,
   All nature took to flight !
At my approach the lofty woods
Submissive bowed, the trembling floods
   Drew backward with affright.

Creation felt a general shock :
The screaming eagle sought the rock,
   The elephant was slain ;
Affrighted, men to caves retreat,
Tigers and leopards licked my feet,
   And owned my lordly reign.

Thus many moons my course I ran,
The general foe of beast and man,
   Till on one fatal day
The lion led the bestial train,
And I, alas ! was quickly slain,
   As gorged with food I lay.

With lightning's speed the rumour spread—
" Rejoice ! rejoice ! the Mammoth 's dead,"
   Resounds from shore to shore.

Pomona, Ceres, thrive again,
And, laughing, join the choral strain,
  "The Mammoth is no more."

In earth's deep caverns long immured,
My skeleton, from view secured,
  In dull oblivion lay;
Till late, with industry and toil,
A youth subdued the stubborn soil,
  And dragged me forth to day.

In London now my body's shown,
And while the crowd o'er every bone
  Incline the curious head,
They view my form with wondering eye,
And pleased in fancied safety, cry—
  "Thank Heaven, the monster's dead."

O mortals, blind to future ill,
My race yet lives, it prospers still—
  Nay, start not with surprise:
Behold, from Corsica's small isle,
Twin-born in cruelty and guile,
  A second Mammoth rise!

He seeks, on fortune's billows borne,
A land by revolution torn,
  A prey to civil hate:
And seizing on a lucky time
Of Gallic frenzy, Gallic crime,
  Assumes the regal state.

Batavian freedom floats in air,
The patriot Swiss, in deep despair,
  Deserts his native land;

While haughty Spain her monarch sees
Submissive wait, on bended knees,
   The tyrant's dread command.

All Europe o'er, the giant stalks,
Whole nations tremble as he walks,
   Extinct their martial fire ;
The Northern Bear lies down to rest,
The Prussian Eagle seeks her nest,
   The Austrian bands retire.

Yet, ah! a storm begins to lower,
Satiate with cruelty and power,
   At ease the monster lies ;
Lion of Britain, led by you,
If Europe's sons the fight renew,
   A second Mammoth dies.*

SONNETS IN IMITATION OF SHAKSPEARE.

ABSENCE and Presence, born of elder Night,
O'er common mortals hold a common sway ;
Absence alights when Presence takes her flight,
Presence presides when Absence is away.
O'er life's dull ocean, borne with steady sails,
Alike, as brother oft resembles brother ;
By cold indifference poised in equal scales,
The one may well pass current for the other.
But (thee once known) what heart can ever know,
Oblivion, weed that rots on Lethé's wharf ?

* This poem, admirably translated into French by M. Peltier, was
widely circulated upon the Continent.—

Presence dispensing joy, and Absence woe,
This soars a giant, and that droops a dwarf.
Oh! disproportioned size of joy and grief,
Absence, how endless long, and Presence brief!

Thou 'lt still survive, when I to time shall bow,
When my leaves scattered lie, thy rose will bloom;
Thou 'lt walk the earth, alert as thou art now,
When I am mould'ring in the silent tomb;
My face, my form, traced by the graver's tool,
Thou holdest: hold them then; and, with a sigh,
When shadowing night shall o'er the welkin rule,
Bethink thee, musing, of the days gone by.
Be not *too* happy, or my jealous sprite
Shall deem thy laughter light, thy spirits folly;
But, gazing on my portraiture, unite
Serene content with sober melancholy,
And cast, in thy beloved sobriety,
Some thoughts on him whose *all* thoughts dwelt on thee.

PHŒBE, OR MY GRANDMOTHER WEST.

Ah, Phœbe! how slily, love's arrow to barb,
You 've stolen down stairs in your grandmamma's garb!
Your ringlet-graced head, and your stomacher flat,
The cut of your cloak, and the bend of your hat,
Your flounce and your furbelow, all have confessed
Your masquerade likeness to Grandmamma West.

That necklace of coral I've seen all afloat
(Ere wrecked by old Time) on your grandmamma's throat;

Her hands, alike gazed on by dandies and boors,
I've seen her fold often as now you fold yours;
While crowds have around her at Ranelagh press'd,
Allured by the beauty of Grandmamma West.

Hold, Phœbe! thou archest of heart-stealing girls,
Thy hat, and thy cloak, and thy lace, and thy pearls,
May not be cast off, till thy painter shall trace
The raiment antique, and thy juvenile face,
With the ringlets and flounces that once gave a zest
To the now waning charms of your Grandmamma West.

'Tis done; now begone, and remember that Time,
By steps slow and sure is corroding your prime.
An æra shall come, spite of hopes and of fears,
When Phœbe shall be what she now but appears,
A tidy old woman arrayed in her best,
A counterfeit true of her Grandmamma West.

TIME AND LOVE.

An artist painted Time and Love;
Time with two pinions spread above,
    And Love without a feather;
Sir Harry patronized the plan,
And soon Sir Hal and Lady Ann
    In wedlock came together.

Copies of each the dame bespoke:
The artist, ere he drew a stroke,
    Reversed his old opinions,
And straightway to the fair one brings
Time in his turn devoid of wings,
    And Cupid with two pinions.

"What blunder's this?" the lady cries,
"No blunder, Madam," he replies,
  "I hope I'm not so stupid.
Each has his pinions in his day,
Time, before marriage, flies away,
  And, after marriage, Cupid."

PROVERBS.

My good Aunt Bridget, spite of age,
Versed in Valerian, Dock, and Sage,
  Well knew the virtues *of* herbs;
But Proverbs gain'd her chief applause,
"Child," she exclaim'd, "respect old saws,
  And pin your faith on Proverbs."

Thus taught, I dubb'd my lot secure;
And, playing long-rope, "slow and sure,"
  Conceived my movement clever.
When lo! an urchin by my side
Push'd me head foremost in, and cried
  "Keep Moving," "Now or Never."

At Melton next I join'd the hunt,
Of bogs and bushes bore the brunt.
  Nor once my courser held in;
But when I saw a yawning steep,
I thought of "Look before you leap,"
  And curb'd my eager gelding.

While doubtful thus I rein'd my roan,
Willing to save a fractured bone,
  Yet fearful of exposure:

11*

THE YEAR TWENTY-SIX.

A sportsman thus my spirit stirred—
" Delays are dangerous,"—I spurred
  My steed, and leaped the enclosure.

I ogled Jane, who heard me say,
That " Rome was not built in a day,"
  When lo! Sir Fleet O'Grady
Put this, my saw, to sea again,
And proved, by running off with Jane,
  " Faint heart ne'er won fair Lady."

Aware " New brooms sweep clean," I took
An untaught tyro for a cook,
  (The tale I tell a fact is;)
She spoilt my soup : but, when I chid,
She thus once more my work undid,
  " Perfection comes from Practice."

Thus, out of every adage hit,
And, finding that ancestral wit
  As changeful as the clime is :
From Proverbs, turning on my heel,
I now cull Wisdom from my seal,
  Whose motto's " Ne quid nimis."

THE YEAR TWENTY-SIX.

'Tis gone with its toys and its troubles,
  Its essays on cotton and corn,
Its laughing-stock company bubbles,
  Its Cherry-ripe—(music by Horn.)

'Tis gone, with its Catholic Question,
 Its Shiels, its O'Connells, and Brics:
Time, finding it light of digestion,
 Has swallow'd the Year Twenty-six.

I've penn'd a few private mementoes
 Of schemes that I meant to effect,
Which, sure as I hobble on ten toes,
 I vow'd I'd no longer neglect.
"My wits," I exclaim'd, "are receding,
 'Tis time I their energies fix:
I'll write the town something worth reading,
 To finish the Year Twenty-six."

My pamphlet, to tell Mr. Canning
 The Czar has an eye on the Turk;
My treatise, to show Mr. Manning
 The way to make currency work:
My essay, to prove to the nations
 (As sure as wax-candles have wicks)
Greek bonds are not Greek obligations—
 Were planned in the Year Twenty-six.

I sketched out a novel, where laughter
 Should scare evangelic Tremaine,
Shake Brambletye House off its rafter,
 And level Tor Hill with the plain.
Those volumes, as grave as my grandam,
 I swore with my book to transfix:
'Twas called the New Roderick Random,
 And meant for the Year Twenty-six.

My play had—I'd have the town know it—
 A part for Miss Elinor Tree;

At Drury I meant to bestow it
 On Price, the gigantic lessee.
Resolved the fourth act to diminish,
 ('Tis there, I suspect, the plot sticks,)
I solemnly swore that I'd finish
 The fifth, in the Year Twenty-six.

But somehow I thought the Haymarket
 Was better for hearing by half,
To people who live near the Park it
 Affords the best home for a laugh.
" There Liston," I muttered, " has taught 'em
 Mirth's balm in their bitters to mix :
I'll write such a part in the autumn
 For him—in the Year Twenty-six !"

I meant to complete my Italian—
 ('Tis done in a twelvemonth with ease,)
Nor longer, as mute as Pygmalion,
 Hang over the ivory keys.
I meant to learn music, much faster
 Than fellows at Eton learn tricks :
Vercellini might teach me to master
 The notes, in the Year Twenty-six.

'Tis past, with its corn and its cotton,
 Its shareholders broken and bit :
And where is my pamphlet ? forgotten.
 And where is my treatise ? unwrit.
My essay, my play, and my novel,
 Like so many Tumble-down Dicks,
All, all in inanity grovel—
 Alas ! for the Year Twenty-six.

My Haymarket farce is a bubble,
  My *Bocca Romana* moves stiff,
I've spared Vercellini all trouble,
  I do n't even know the bass cliff.
My brain has (supine anti-breeder)
  Neglected to hatch into chicks
Her offspring—Pray how, gentle reader,
  Thrive you for the Year Twenty-six?

George Whitfield, whom nobody mentions
  Now Irving has got into fame,
Has paved with abortive intentions
  A place too caloric to name.
I fear, if his masonry's real,
  That mine have Macadamized Styx:
So empty, cloud-capped, and ideal,
  My plans for the Year Twenty-six!

Past Year! if, to quash all evasions,
  Thou 'dst have me with granite repair,
On good terra firma foundations,
  My castles now nodding in air:
Bid Time from my brow steal his traces
  (As Bardolph abstracted the Pix),
Run back on his road a few paces,
  And make me — like thee—Twenty-six.

THE TABLET OF TRUTH.

SIT down, Mr. Clipstone, and take
  These hints, while my feelings are fresh;
My uncle, Sir Lionel Lake,
  Has journeyed the way of all flesh.

His heirs would in marble imprint
   His merits aloft o'er his pew --
Allow me the outline to hint—
   To finish, of course, rests with you.

And first, with a visage of woe,
   Carve two little cherubs of love,
Lamenting to lose one below
   They never will look on above.
And next, in smooth porphyry mould,
   (You cannot well cut them too small)
Two liliput goblets, to hold
   The tears that his widow lets fall.

Where charity seeks a supply
   He leaves not his equal behind :
I'm told there is not a dry eye
   In the School for the Indigent Blind.
Then chisel (not sunk in repose,
   But in *alto relief*, to endure,)
An orderly line of round O's.
   For the money he gave to the poor.

I league not in rhyme with the band
   Who elevate sound over sense :
Where Vanity bellows " expand,"
   Humility whispers " condense."
Then mark, with your mallet and blade,
   To paint the defunct to the life,
Four stars for his conduct in trade,
   And a blank for his love of his wife.

'Tis done—to complete a design,
   In brevity rivalling Greece,

Imprint me a black dotted line
  For the friends who lament his decease.
Thus lettered with merited praise,
  Ere long shall our travel-fraught youth
Turn back from the false Père la Chaise
  To gaze on my Tablet of Truth.

CLUB LAW.

DEAR TOM, since by a lucky knack,
Your white balls overtop the black,
  And counter-canvass smother,
Let me your mental garment darn,
As old Polonius spun a yarn
  To fair Ophelia's brother.

" Be thou familiar," should you see
At dinner an austere M.P.
  Just as his glass he's filling,
Accost him——whatsoe'er his rank —
With "Sir, I'd thank you for a frank,"
  And save your aunt a shilling.

" Give every man (of wealth) thine ear ;"
Smile when he smiles, his sallies cheer,
  Out his connexions ferret ;
Or roar his catch, or sing his psalm :
But, Thomas, " never dull thy palm"
  By shaking hands with Merit.

At a house-dinner show your fun—
Mount a horse-laugh, quiz, banter, pun,
  Be saucy as a squirrel ;

But if your foe possess a pair
Of Manton's polished pops, "beware
   Of entrance to a quarrel."

If a roast fillet deck the board,
With bacon, you can well afford
   To leave the viand *per se ;*
But if a haunch supplant the veal,
"Grapple" the joint "with hooks of steel,"
   And carve it without mercy.

"Apparel oft proclaims the man :"
Wear, then, the richest garb you can,
   Whilst in the club a dweller ;
And if men doubt your means and ways,
Reverse the *caveat emptor* phrase,
   And cast it to the seller.

"Take each man's censure" in good part ;—
Pliant humility 's an art
   That copper turns to siller.
"Be not a lender"—memories flit ;
"Nor borrower"—unless a wit
   From old Josephus Miller.

Place on the fender both your feet ;
When Boreas howls, complain of heat,
   And open all the windows ;
Ring for the waiter, bang the door,
And for your brethren care no more
   Than Tippoo cared for Hindoos.

Never to acquiesce be seen ;
To those who dwell on Edmund Kean,
   Talk of John Kemble's glories.

Dub all who do the civil, prigs ;
Revile Lord Melbourne to the Whigs,
   Sir Robert to the Tories.

And now, dear Tom, farewell ; the gale
" Sits in the shoulder of your sail,"—
   Defy disapprobation :
For, till committee-men begin
To ballot *out*, as well as *in*,
   You're safe in your location.

THE SWISS COTTAGE.

" YE gastric graces of Pall Mall,
Fish, soup, and paté, fare ye well,
   Give me some cot Helvetian,
Thither I fain my flight would wing,
Of clubs the abdicated king,
   An uncrown'd Dioclesian."

Scarce had I thus petitioned Fate,
When lo ! a card with lines so straight,
   Arachne seemed to rule 'em,
Wooed me to fair Pastora's shrine—
An invitation out to dine
   At Ivy Cottage, Fulham !

" 'Tis well !" I cried. " At Wilt's control
Here Temperance will pass the bowl,
   And Health rise up the winner,
Full well I know the classic spot—
Swiss is the scenery, Swiss the cot,
   And Swiss, no doubt the dinner.

THE SWISS COTTAGE.

" Deal table ; cloth as smooth as silk ;
Brown loaf ; an avalanche of milk ;
   At most a brace of rabbits ;
Cheese, hard enough to pose a shark ;
And water, ' clear as di'mond spark,'
   To suit my Hindoo habits.

" Six three-legg'd stools, of antique shapes :
Ripe figs ; a plate of purple grapes,
   As sweet as honeysuckles ;
A girl to wait, of buxom hue,
In dark-brown bodice, apron blue,
   Red hose, and silver buckles."

Nought rose to sever lip and cup :
I came. Had Fanny Kelly up
   The outside stair been skipping,
With three long plaits of braided hair,
'Twould seem the *ipse locus* where
   Macready pierced the pippin.

But soon the inside put to rout
The dreams engender'd by the out ;
   Chintz chairs with sofa paddings ;
Bright stoves, at war with humid damps ;
Pianos ; rosewood tables ; lamps,
   As brilliant as Aladdin's.

Fish, soup, and mutton, finely dress'd,
Adorned the board : a pleasant guest
   Was placed my right and left on ;
With dishes lateral, endued
With flavor to astonish Ude,
   Lucullus, or Lord Sefton.

The party, 'mid the sound of corks,
(Although the bread was white; the forks
   Were silver, not metallic,)
Seemed not to see the joke was this,
That, while the outside walls were Swiss,
   The feast was Anglo-Gallic.

So, as in eastern song is shown,
Some sable, antiquated crone,
   As wily as a bailiff,
Leads, blindfold, on his hands and knees,
Some youth, through alleys dark, to please
   Great Haroün the Caliph.

The bandage gone, a blaze of light
Salutes his now enchanted sight;
   He views a new creation:
Dim Bagdad totters to its fall,
A fairy palace smiles, and all
   Is bright illumination.

FIVE HUNDRED A YEAR.

THAT gilt middle path, which the poet of Rome
   Extolled as the only safe highway to bliss;
That "haven" which many a poet at home
   Assures us all Guinea-bound merchantmen miss;
      That blessed middle line,
      Which bard and divine
      In sonnet and sermon so sigh for, is mine;—
My uncle, a plain honest fat auctioneer,
Walked off, and bequeathed me Five Hundred a year.

I ne'er, if I live to the age of Old Parr,
    Can fail to remember how stared brother Bill,
Jack bullied, and Tom, who is now at the Bar,
    Drove post to a Proctor to knock up the will.
        They never could trace
        What beauty or grace
        Sir Christopher Catalogue saw in my face,
To cut off three youths, to his bosom so dear,
And deluge a fourth with Five Hundred a year !

The will, though law-beaten, stood firm as a rock,
    The probate was properly lodged at the Bank ;
Transferred to my name stood the spleen-moving stock,
    And I, in the West, bearded people of rank.
        No longer a clerk,
        I rode in the Park,
        Or lounged in Pall Mall till an hour after dark.
I entered, what seemed then, a happy career,
Possessed of a gig and Five Hundred a year.

Ere long, I began to be bored by a guest,
    A strange sort of harpy, who poisoned my feast :
He visits, in London, the folks who dwell West,
    But seldom cohabits with those who live East.
        Bar, door-chain, or key,
        Could not keep me free——
        As brisk as a bailiff in bolted *Ennui*.
" I'm come," he still cried, " to partake of your cheer,
I'm partial to folks of Five Hundred a year."

Meanwhile my three brothers, by prudence and care,
    Got onward in life, while I stuck by the wall ;
Bill opened a tea-shop in Bridgewater-square,
    And Jack, as a writer, grew rich in Bengal.

Tom made his impressions
Through Newgate transgressions,
And got half the business at Clerkenwell Sessions.
They marched in the van, while I lagged in the rear,
Condemned to *Ennui* and Five Hundred a year.

Too little encouraged to feel self-assured,
Too dull for retorts, and too timid for taunts;
By daughters and nieces I'm barely endured,
And mortally hated by uncles and aunts.
If e'er I entangle
A girl in an angle,
Up steps some Duenna, love's serpent to strangle;
"Come hither! don't talk to that fellow, my dear,
His income is only Five Hundred a year."

Without tact or talents to get into ton,
No calling to stick to, no trade to pursue:
Thus London, hard stepmother, leaves me alone,
With little to live on, and nothing to do.
Could I row a life-boat,
Make a boot or a coat,
Or serve in a silversmith's shop, and devote
My days to employment, my evenings to cheer,
I'd gladly give up my Five Hundred a year.

12

CHIGWELL;

OR, "PRÆTERITOS ANNOS."

SCHOOL that, in Burford's honoured time,
Reared me to youth's elastic prime
    From childhood's airy slumbers—
School at whose antique shrine I bow,
Sexagenarian pilgrim now,
    Accept a poet's numbers.

Those yew-trees never seem to grow:
The village stands in *statu quo*,
    Without a single new house.
But, heavens, how shrunk! how very small!
'Tis a mere step from Urmstone's wall,
    " Up town," to Morgan's brewhouse.

There, in yon rough-cast mansion, dwelt
Sage Denham, Galen's son, who dealt
    In squills and cream of tartar;
Fronting the room where now I dine,
Beneath thy undulating sign,
    Peak-bearded Charles the Martyr!

Pent in by beams of mouldering wood
The parish stocks stand where they stood—
    Did ever drunkard rue 'em?
I dive not in parochial law,
Yet this I know—I never saw
    Two legs protruded through 'em.

Here, to the right, rose hissing proofs
Of skill to solder horses' hoofs,
    Formed in the forge of Radley;

And there, the almshouses beyond,
Half-way before you gain the Pond,
   Lived wry-mouthed Martin Hadley.

Does Philby still exist?   Where now
Are Willis, Wilcox, Green, and Howe?
   Ann Wright, the smart and handy?
Hillman alone a respite steals
From Fate; and—*vice* Hadley—deals
   In tea and sugar-candy.

Can I my school-friend Belson track?
Where hides him Chamberlaine? where Black,
   Intended for the altar?
Does life-blood circulate in Bates?
Where are Jack Cumberlege and Yates?
   The Burrells, Charles and Walter?

There, at your ink-bespattered shrine,
Cornelius Nepos first was mine;
   Here fagged I hard at Plutarch:
Found Ovid's mighty pleasant ways,
While Plato's metaphysic maze
   Appeared like *Pluto*—too dark.

Here usher Ireland sat—and there
Stood Bolton, Cowal, Parker, Ware,
   Medley, the pert and witty,
And here—crack station, near the fire—
Sat Roberts, whose Haymarket sire
   Sold oil and spermaceti.

Yon pew, the gallery below,
Held Nancy, pride of Chigwell Row,
   Who set all hearts a dancing:

In bonnet white, divine brunette,
O'er Burnet's field I see thee yet,
    To Sunday church advancing.

Seek we the churchyard; there the yew
Shades many a swain whom once I knew,
    Now nameless and forgotten;
Here towers Sir Edward's marble bier,
Here lies stern Vickery, and here,
    My father's friend Tom Cotton.

The common herd serenely sleep,
Turf-bound, "in many a mouldering heap"
    Pent in by bands of osier;
While at the altar's feet is laid
The founder of the school, arrayed
    In mitre and in crosier.

'Tis nature's law: wave urges wave:
The coffined grandsire seeks the grave,
    The babe that feeds by suction,
Finds with his ancestor repose:
Life ebbs, and dissolution sows
    The seeds of reproduction.

World, in thy ever busy mart,
I've acted no unnoticed part—
    Would I resume it? oh no!
Four acts are done, the jest grows stale;
The waning lamps burn dim and pale,
    And reason asks—*Cui bono?*

I've met with no "affliction sore;"
But hold! methinks, "long time I bore;"
    Here ends my lucubration—

Content, with David's son, to know,
That all is vanity below,
    Tho' not quite all vexation.

CHIGWELL REVISITED.

DEPUTED by the tuneful Nine,
A pilgrim to an Eastern shrine,
    I once again out-sally;
Again to Chigwell wander back,
And, more excursive, aim to track
    Each neighbouring hill and valley.

Strange that a village should survive,
For ten years multiplied by five,
    The same in size and figure.
Knowing not plenty nor distress—
If foiled by fortune, why no less?
    If favoured, why no bigger?

Say, why has population got
Speed-bound upon this level spot,
    Undamaged by profusion?
A tyro, I the question ask—
Be thine, Miss Martineau, the task
    To tender the solution.

I pass the Vicar's white abode,
And, pondering, gain the upward road,
    By busy thoughts o'erladen,
To where "The pride of Chigwell-row"
Still lives—a handsome widow now,
    As erst a lovely maiden.

CHIGWELL REVISITED.

Here hills and dales and distant Thame,
And forest glens, green proof proclaim
   Of Nature's lavish bounty,
And dub thee, lofty region, still
Surrey's tall foe, the Richmond Hill
   Of this our eastern county.

Diverging from the road, the sod
I tread that once a boy I trod,
   With pace not quite so nimble—
But where 's the May-pole next the lane?
Who dared to banish from the plain
   That wreathed-encircled symbol?

ABRIDGE, her tank, and waterfall,
The path beneath Sir Eliab's wall,
   I once again am stepping;
Beyond that round we rarely stirred,
LOUGHTON we saw. but only heard
   Of Ongar and of Epping.

Seek we "the river's" grassy verge,
Where all were destined to immerge,
   Or willing or abhorrent;
I view the well-known "Mill-hole" still—
But time has dwindled to a rill
   What seemed, of yore, a torrent.

Here, fell destroyer, many a wound
The woodman's axe has dealt around;
   Lee Grove in death reposes.
Yet while her dryads seek their tombs,
The miller's moated garden blooms
   With all its wonted roses.

There, in yon copse, near Palmer's Gate,
Reclined, I mourned my hapless fate,
   Zerbino amoroso,
Glad to elope from both the schools,
" The world shut out," intent on Hoole's
" Orlando Furioso."

Twilight steals on : I wander back ;
The listless ploughman's homeward track,
   Again in thought I follow ;
Or sit the antique porch within,
Awed by the belfry's deafening din,
   And watch the wheeling swallow.

Chigwell, I cease thy charms to sing—
Time bears me elsewhere on his wing ;
   Perhaps, ere long, the poet,
Who now, in mental vigour bold,
Parades, erect, thy churchyard mould,
   May sleep, supine, below it.

So let it be : Time, take thy course ;
Let dotards with tenacious force
   Cling to this waning planet—
I'd rather soar to death's abode
On eagle wings, than " live a toad"
   Pent in a block of granite.

Grant me the happier lot of him,
Elate in hope, alert in limb,
   Who hurls Bellona's jav'lin ;
Fame's laurel ardent to entwine,
Dares death above the countermine,
   And meets him on the rav'lin.

I fear not, Fate, thy pendant shears—
There are who pray for length of years;
  To them, not me, allot 'em :
Life's cup is nectar at the brink,
Midway a palatable drink,
  And wormwood at the bottom.

THE EMPEROR ALEXANDER.

Air.—" Over the Water to Charley."

I've seen (lucky me !) what you all want to see—
  Good people, give ear to my sonnet—
I've gazed in the Ring on the Muscovy King,
  And I've peeped at the Oldenburg bonnet ;
At his sister's approach to get into her coach,
  Her brother steps forward to hand her,
What ecstacies throb in the hearts of the mob,
  With huzza for the great Alexander !

On bracelet and seal behold his profile
  At the shop too of Laurie and Whittle,
Nat Lee, hold your prate, Alexander the Great
  Is now Alexander the Little !
In Lord William's dell, near the Pulteney hotel,
  What multitudes every day wander !
They scamper like imps to indulge in a glimpse
  Of the mighty renowned Alexander.

Poor Madame De Stael is quite pushed to the wall,
  Chassé'd by the Czar and the Duchess,
And since his retreat, even Louis *dix-huit*
  Must walk on oblivion's crutches.

Clerks run from their quills, harberdashers their tills,
   John Bull is a great goosey gander;
Even Kean is forgot, we are all on the trot
   For a gaze upon great Alexander.

"Have you seen him 's" the talk, Piccadilly's the walk,
   I suppose since it is so, it must be,
And nobody thinks of that musical sphinx
   Catalani, or great Doctor Busby.
Anxiety burns every bosom by turns
   To flirt with this royal Philander,
And happy the wight who can utter at night—
   "This morning I saw Alexander."

He dresses with taste, he is small in the waist,
   I beheld him with Blucher and Platoff,
The Hetman appears with his cap on his ears,
   But the Emperor rides with his hat off:
He sits on his throne with a leg in each zone,
   No monarch on earth can be grander;
Half an hour after dark, the rails of the Park
   Are scaled to behold Alexander.

When the town was illumed, how his residence bloomed,
   With Lamps to the balcony fitted.
I'm told his Cossacks made eleven attacks
   To drink up the oil ere they lit it!
The Chronicle says that he laces in stays—
   Perhaps this is nothing but slander;
Since his stay is not long I will shorten my song
   With huzza for the great Alexander!

12*

THE GRETNA GREEN BLACKSMITH.

Air.—"The Sprig of Shillelah."

THOUGH my face is all smutty not fit to be seen,
I'm the tinkering parson of Gretna Green,
   With my rang, tang, hammer and nail.
To look like the ladies is always my plan,
So I roll up my sleeves as high as I can,
In spite of my vice, and though I am lame,
I make the sparks fly, and myself raise a flame,
   With my rang, tang, hammer and nail.

In chaises-and-four lovers fly to my cot,
With folly remembered, and prudence forgot,
   With a rang, tang, hammer and nail.
Down hill, helter-skelter they fearlessly move,
For who ever thinks of a hind wheel in love?
So, while the young lady her passion reveals,
I tack them together—then hammer the wheels,
   With my rang, tang, hammer and nail.

"Oh dear," says Miss Lucy, a delicate fright in,
"I was all over rust till they took me to Brighton,
   With my rang, tang, hammer and nail.
Indeed, Mr. Parson, you'll find me no fool,
I'm a great deal too old to be sent back to school;
Captain Shark of the Fourth is the man I adore,
My Pa is a bear, and my Ma is a bore,
   With their rang, tang, hammer and nail."

But, alas! ten to one, ere they got back to town,
My lady is up, and the carriage breaks down,
   With a rang, tang, hammer and nail.

Of tears my young Madam dissolves in a flood,
Her head in the clouds, and her feet in the mud,
Till both recollecting the cause of the evil,
Wish carriage, and marriage, and me at the devil,
 With my rang, tang, hammer and nail.

I can make a jack-chain, a pattern, a knife,
I forge heavy fetters for husband and wife,
 With my rang, tang, hammer and nail.
Here Venus and Vulcan their compact renew,
A partner for life or a tenpenny screw,
A wedlock, a padlock, I do not care which—
So the tinker of Gretna is sure to grow rich,
 With his rang, tang, hammer and nail.

MATRIMONIAL DUET.

Air.—" The Pretty Maid of Derby."

HE.

When we first were man and wife,
 And you swore to love for life,
We were quoted as a model, we were quite a show,
 Yes, we *tête-à-tête* were seen,
 Like King William and his Queen;
What a jewel of a wife was Mrs. John Prevôt!

SHE.

Ay, once I clave to thee, man,
 Like Baucis to Philemon,
Now, if I go to Brighton, you 're at Bath I know;
 Like the pair who tell the weather,
 We are never out together,
One at home, the other gadding, Mr. John Prevôt.

HE.

If a lion's to be seen,
Old Blucher—Mr. Kean,
You order out the carriage, and away you go
With that gossip, Mrs. Jones;
How you rattle o'er the stones,
You've no mercy on the horses, Mrs. John Prevôt.

SHE.

With Madeira, Port, and Sherry,
When you make what you call merry,
And sit in sober sadness, are you sober? No!
With that horrid Major Rock,
It is always twelve o'clock,
Ere you tumble up to coffee, Mr. John Prevôt.

BOTH.

Our vicar, Doctor Jervis,
When he read the marriage service,
United us for better and for worse—Heigh-ho!
Since the worse may turn to better,
And we cannot break our fetter.
Let us say no more about it, Mr. (Mrs.) John Prevôt.

OWEN OF LANARK.

WELCOME, welcome, mighty stranger,
To our transatlantic shore:
Anchored safe from seas of danger,
All our fears and doubts are o'er.
Sable Jews and flaxen Quakers
Imitate no more the shark;
Wealth lies planted out in acres—
Welcome, Owen of Lanark!

Parallelograms of virtue,
   Haunts from human frailty free,
Squares that vice can ne'er do hurt to,
   Circles of New Harmony :
Schemes that blossom while we view 'em,
   Swamp and prairie changed to park :
Meum melting into tuum—
   Wondrous Owen of Lanark !

All New York, in mind and body,
   Feels thy influence, and adores ;
Bitters, Sangaree, and Toddy
   Fly her fifteen hundred stores.
Big Ohio now looks bigger,
   Freedom fans the kindred spark :
Boss no longer scowls on nigger—
   Welcome, Owen of Lanark !

Lazarus lies down with Dives,
   Rich and poor no more are seen ;
Baltimore our common hive is ;
   Busy bees, and thou their Queen.
Uncle Ben lays down his rifle,
   While his Nephew—prone to bark—
Thanks his stars for "that 'ere trifle,"
   Mighty Owen of Lanark !

Failing schemers, retrograders,
   Lawyers fattening on strife,
Grim backwoodsmen, bankrupt traders,
   Squatters brandishing the knife :
Busy Banks their Cents up summing
   Many a Master, many a Clerk,
Drop their dollars at thy coming,
   Mighty Owen of Lanark !

THE TRITON OF THE MINNOWS.

Foe to titled Sirs and Madams,
  Prone Law's blunders to redress,
Washington nor Quincy Adams
  Ever saw thy like, I guess.
Let John Bull's polluted pages
  Dub thee staring, dub thee stark:
Solon of succeeding Ages,
  Welcome, Owen of Lanark!

Vast, I calculate, thy plan is,
  Born to soar where others creep;
Lofty as the Alleghanies,
  As the Mississippi deep.
As the German Brothers mingle,
  Prone to sing "hark follow hark,"
All our States, through dell and dingle,
  Hail thee, Owen of Lanark!

"I've an item," Boss and Peasant
  Feel quite mighty where you stray;
Competence is omnipresent,
  Poverty "slick right away."
See our bipeds, "like all natur,"
  Climbing up thy friendly ark,
Dub thee Sovereign Legislator,
  Welcome, Owen of Lanark!

THE TRITON OF THE MINNOWS.

"Why don't you strike out something new?"
Cried fair Euphemia, heavenly blue
    Of eye, as well as stocking!
"If shilly-shally long you stand,
You'll feel Time's enervating hand
    Your second cradle rocking."

"Ah, Madam! cease your bard to blame;
I view the pedestal of Fame,
    But at its base I falter:
On every step, terrific, stand
A troop of Poets, pen in hand,
    To scare me from her altar.

I first essayed to write in prose,
Plot, humor, character disclose,
    And ransack heaths and hovels:
But, when I sat me down to write,
I sighed to find that I had quite
    O'erlooked the Scottish Novels."

"Well," cried Euphemia, with a smile,
"Miss Austin's gone: assume her style;
    Turn playmate of Apollo—
But, hold! how heedless the remark!
Miss Austin's gone —but Mansfield Park
    And Emma scorn to follow."

A bolder flight I'd fain essay,
The Manners of the East portray,
    That field is rich and spacious:
Greece, Turkey, Egypt—what a scope!
There too I'm foiled—why will not Hope
    Un-write his Anastasius!

Rogers, in calm and even sense,
Byron, in ecstacy intense,
    Make my dim flame burn denser:
Shall I in Fashion's corps enlist,
A light gay epigrammatist?
    No!—there I'm marred by Spenser.

THE TRITON OF THE MINNOWS.

Thus " cribb'd and cabin'd"—" Poor indeed !"
I cantered on my winged steed
      Towards scenes of toil and tillage :
But there, alas ! my weary hack
Hit on another beaten track,
      Encountering Crabbe's Village.

Two pathways still to me belong,
Come, poignant Satire ! amorous Song !
      Beware, ye state empirics !—
Anticipated ! hideous bore !
I quite forgot Hibernian Moore,
      His Fudges, and his Lyrics.

Great Jove ! compassionate my lot !
On Campbell, Byron, Moore, and Scott,
      Point thy celestial cannon :
Sew Crabbe and Rogers in a sack.
Tie Hope and Spenser back to back,
      And souse them in the Shannon.

So shall I, with majestic tread,
My doughty predecessors dead,
      Up Pindus stretch my sinews :
And leave all lesser bards behind,
"The one-eyed monarch of the blind,"
      " The Triton of the Minnows."

THE HAUNCH OF VENISON.

AT Number One dwelt Captain Drew,
George Benson dwelt at Number Two,
   (The street we'll not now mention :)
The latter stunned the King's Bench bar,
The former being lamed in war,
   Sang small upon a pension.

Tom Blewit knew them both : than he
None deeper in the mystery
   Of culinary knowledge;
From turtle soup to Stilton cheese,
Apt student, taking his degrees
   In Mrs. Rundell's college.

Benson to dine invited Tom :
Proud of an invitation from
   A host who "spread" so nicely,
Tom answered, ere the ink was dry,
"Extremely happy—come on Fri-
   Day next, at six precisely."

Blewit, with expectation fraught,
Drove up at six, each savoury thought
   Ideal turbot rich in :
But, ere he reached the winning-post,
He saw a haunch of ven'son roast
   Down in the next-door kitchen.

"Hey! zounds! what's this? a haunch at Drews?
I must drop in; I can't refuse;
   To pass were downright treason :

To cut Ned Benson's not quite staunch;
But the provocative—a haunch!
    Zounds! it's the first this season.

" Ven'son, thou 'rt mine! I'll talk no more."
Then, rapping thrice at Benson's door,
    " John, I'm in such a hurry;
Do tell your master that my aunt
Is paralytic, quite aslant,
    I must be off for Surrey."

Now Tom at next door makes a din:
" Is Captain Drew at home?"—" Walk in."
    " Drew, how d'ye do?"—" What! Blewit!"
" Yes, I—you 've asked me, many a day,
To drop in, in a quiet way,
    So now I'm come to do it."

" I'm very glad you have," said Drew,
" I've nothing but an Irish stew"—
    Quoth Tom, (aside,) " No matter;
'Twont do—my stomach 's up to that—
'Twill lie by, till the lucid fat
    Comes quiv'ring on the platter."

" You see your dinner, Tom," Drew cried.
" No, but I don't though," Tom replied;
    " I smoked below."—" What?"—" Ven'son—
A haunch."—" Oh! true, it is not mine;
My neighbour has some friends to dine."
    " Your neighbour! who?"—" George Benson.

" His chimney smoked; the scene to change,
I let him have my kitchen range,
    While his was newly polished;

The ven'son you observed below .
Went home just half an hour ago ;
   I guess it's now demolished.

" Tom, why that look of doubtful dread ?
Come, help yourself to salt and bread,
   Don't sit with hands and knees up ;
But dine, for once, off Irish stew,
And read the ' Dog and Shadow' through,
   When next you open Æsop."

ODE TO SENTIMENT.

DAUGHTER of dulness ! canting dame !
   Thou night-mare on the breast of joy,
Whose drowsy morals, still the same,
   The stupid soothe, the gay annoy ;
Soft cradled in thy sluggish arms,
E'en footpads prate of guilt's alarms,
And pig-tailed sailors, sadly queer,
Affect the melting mood, and drop the pitying tear.

When first to tickle Britain's nose
   Hugh Kelly raised his leaden quill,
Thy poppies lent the wished repose,
   And bade the gaping town be still.
Poor *Comedy !* thine opiate lore
With patience many a day she bore,
Till Goldsmith all thy hopes dismay'd,
And drove thee from the stage by Tony Lumpkin's aid.

Scared by thy lanthorn visage, flee
   Thalia's offspring light and merry, .

Loud laughter, wit, and repartee,
   And leave us moralising Cherry.
They fly, and carry in their line,
Grimaldi, Goose, and Columbine,
To Sadler's Wells by Dibdin taken,
With him they vow to dwell, nor find themselves for-
    saken.

Soliloquy, with clamorous tongue,
   That brings the Lord knows what to view,
And, Affectation, pert and young,
   Swearing to love—the Lord knows who;
Still round the midnight caldron caper,
Warm Charity with Newland's paper,
And baby Bounty not unwilling
To give to mother dear her new *King George's* shilling.

O gently o'er the modern stage,
   Fair preacher, raise thy deafening din!
Not with the metaphoric rage
   That guides the sword of Harlequin,
(As erst thou didst the town amuse,)
With tender bailiffs, generous Jews,
Socratic soldiers, praying sailors,
Chaste harlots, lettered clowns, and duel-fighting tailors.

Forbear thy handkerchief of brine,
   Some gleams of merriment admit;
Be tears in moderation thine,
   To water, not to drown, the pit.
But if, with streaming eye askew,
Thou still wilt blubber five acts through,
Have pity on a son of rhyme,
Usurp the play—'tis your's—but spare the pantomime.

REJECTED ADDRESSES;

OR,

THE NEW THEATRUM POETARUM.

BY

JAMES SMITH AND HORACE SMITH.

" Fired that the House reject him!—'Sdeath, I 'll *print* it,
And shame the Fools!"

POPE.

" I think the ' Rejected Addresses' by far the best thing of the kind since ' The Rolliad,' and wish *you* had published them.   Tell the author ' I forgive him, were he twenty times over our satirist;' and think his imitations not at all inferior to the famous ones of Hawkins Browne."

Lord Byron to Mr. Murray, Oct. 19, 1812.

" I like the volume of ' Rejected Addresses' better and better."

Lord Byron to Mr. Murray, Oct. 23, 1812.

" I take the ' Rejected Addresses' to be the very best imitations (and often of difficult originals) that ever were made: and considering their great extent and variety, to indicate a talent, to which I do not know where to look for a parallel. Some few of them descend to the level of parodies ; but by far the greater part are of a much higher description."

Lord Jeffrey (in 1843), Note in Essays, iv. 470.

PREFACE.

On the 14th of August, 1812, the following advertisement appeared in most of the daily papers:—

"*Rebuilding of Drury-lane Theatre.*

"The Committee are desirous of promoting a free and fair competition for an Address to be spoken upon the opening of the Theatre, which will take place on the 10th of October next. They have, therefore, thought fit to announce to the public, that they will be glad to receive any such compositions, addressed to their Secretary, at the Treasury-office, in Drury-lane, on or before the 10th of September, sealed up, with a distinguishing word, number, or motto, on the cover, corresponding with the inscription on a separate sealed paper, containing the name of the author, which will not be opened unless containing the name of the successful candidate."

Upon the propriety of this plan, men's minds were, as they usually are upon matters of moment, much divided. Some thought it a fair promise of the future intention of the Committee to abolish that phalanx of authors who usurp the stage, to the exclusion of a large assortment of dramatic talent blushing unseen in the back-ground; while others contended, that the scheme would prevent men of real eminence from descending into an amphitheatre in which all Grub-street (that is to say, all London and Westminster) would be arrayed against them. The event has proved both parties to be in a degree right, and in a degree wrong. One hundred and twelve *Addresses* have been sent in, each sealed, and signed, and mottoed, "as per order," some written by men of great, some by men of little, and some by men of no talent.

[* To the First Edition published in October, 1812]

Many of the public prints have censured the taste of the Committee, in thus contracting for *Addresses* as they would for nails—by the gross; but it is surprising that none should have censured their *temerity.* One hundred and eleven of the *Addresses* must, of course, be unsuccessful: to each of the authors, thus infallibly classed with the *genus irritabile*, it would be very hard to deny six stanch friends, who consider his the best of all possible *Addresses*, and whose tongues will be as ready to laud him, as to hiss his adversary. These, with the potent aid of the bard himself, make seven foes per address; and thus will be created seven hundred and seventy seven implacable auditors, prepared to condemn the strains of Apollo himself—a band of adversaries which no prudent manager would think of exasperating.

But, leaving the Committee to encounter the responsibility they have incurred, the public have at least to thank them for ascertaining and establishing one point, which might otherwise have admitted of controversy. When it is considered that many amateur writers have been discouraged from becoming competitors, and that few, if any, of the professional authors can afford to write for nothing, and, of course, have not been candidates for the honorary prize of Drury-lane, we may confidently conclude that, as far as regards *number*, the present is undoubtedly the Augustan age of English poetry. Whether or not this distinction will be extended to the *quality* of its productions, must be decided at the tribunal of posterity; though the natural anxiety of our authors on this score ought to be considerably diminished when they reflect how few will, in all probability, be had up for judgment.

It is not necessary for the Editor to mention the manner in which he became possessed of this "fair sample of the present state of poetry in Great Britain." It was his first intention to publish the whole; but a little reflection convinced him that, by so doing, he might depress the good, without elevating the bad. He has therefore culled what had the appearance of flowers, from what possessed the reality of weeds, and is extremely sorry that, in. so doing, he has diminished his collection to twenty-one. Those which he has rejected may possibly make their appearance in a separate volume, or they may be admitted as volunteers in the files of some of the newspapers; or, at all events, they are sure of being received among the awkward squad of the Magazines. In general, they bear a close resemblance to each other; thirty of them contain extravagant compliments to the immortal Wellington and the indefatigable Whitbread; and, as the last-mentioned gentleman is said to dislike praise in the exact proportion in which he deserves it, these laudatory writers have probably been only building a wall against which they might run their own heads.

The Editor here begs leave to advance a few words in behalf of that useful and much abused bird the Phœnix; and in so doing, he is biassed by no partiality, as he assures the reader he not only never saw one, but (*mirabile dictu !*) never caged one, in a simile, in the whole course of his life. Not less than sixty-nine of the competitors have invoked the aid of this native of Arabia; but as, from their manner of using him when they caught him, he does not by any means appear to have been a native of Arabia *Felix*, the Editor has left the proprietors to treat with Mr. Polito, and refused to receive this *rara avis*, or black swan, into the collection. One exception occurs, in which the admirable treatment of this feathered incombustible entitles the author to great praise : that Address has been preserved, and in the ensuing pages takes the lead, to which its dignity entitles it.

Perhaps the reason why several of the subjoined productions of the MUSÆ LONDINENSES have failed of selection, may be discovered in their being penned in a metre unusual upon occasions of this sort, and in their not being written with that attention to stage effect, the want of which, like want of manners in the concerns of life, is more prejudicial than a deficiency of talent. There is an art of writing for the Theatre, technically called *touch and go*, which is indispensable when we consider the small quantum of patience which so motley an assemblage as a London audience can be expected to afford. All the contributors have been very exact in sending their initials and mottoes. Those belonging to the present collection have been carefully preserved, and each have been affixed to its respective poem. The letters that accompanied the Addresses having been honourably destroyed unopened, it is impossible to state the real authors with any certainty; but the ingenious reader, after comparing the initials with the motto, and both with the poem, may form his own conclusions.

The Editor does not anticipate any disapprobation from thus

13

giving publicity to a small portion of the *Rejected Addresses ;* for unless he is widely mistaken in assigning the respective authors, the fame of each individual is established on much too firm a basis to be shaken by so trifling and evanescent a publication as the present:

> ———————neque ego illi detrahere ausim
> Hærentem capiti multâ cum laude coronam.

Of the numerous pieces already sent to the Committee for performance, he has only availed himself of three vocal Travesties, which he has, selected, not for their merit, but simply for their brevity. Above one hundred spectacles, melodramas, operas, and pantomimes, have been transmitted, besides the two first acts of one legitimate comedy. Some of these evince considerable smartness of manual dialogue, and several repartees of chairs, tables, and other inanimate wits; but the authors seem to have forgotten that in the new Drury-lane the audience can hear as well as see. Of late our theatres have been so constructed, that John Bull has been compelled to have very long ears or none at all; to keep them dangling about his skull like discarded servants, while his eyes were gazing at pieballs and elephants, or else to stretch them out to an asinine length to catch the congenial sound of braying trumpets. An auricular revolution is, we trust, about to take place; and as many people have been much puzzled to define the meaning of this new era, of which we have heard so much, we venture to pronounce, that as far as regards Drury-lane Theatre, the new era means the reign of ears. If the past affords any pledge for the future, we may confiently expect from the Committee of that House every thing that can be accomplished by the union of taste and assiduity.

[" We have no conjecture to offer as to the anonymous author of this amusing little volume. He who is such a master of disguises may easily be supposed to have been successful in concealing himself, and, with the power of assuming so many styles, is not likely to be detected by his own. We should guess, however, that he had not written a great deal in his own character—that his natural style was neither very lofty nor very grave—and that he rather indulges a partiality for puns and verbal pleasantries. We marvel why he has shut out Campbell and Rogers from his theatre of living poets, and confidently expect to have our curiosity, in this and all other particulars, very speedily gratified, when the applause of the country shall induce him to take off his mask."]

LORD JEFFREY, *Edinburgh Review for Nov.* 1812.

PREFACE

TO

THE EIGHTEENTH EDITION.*

In the present publishing era, when books are like the multitudinous waves of the advancing sea, some of which make no impression whatever upon the sand, while the superficial traces left by others are destined to be perpetually obliterated by their successors, almost as soon as they are found, the authors of the *Rejected Addresses* may well feel flattered, after a lapse of twenty years, and the sale of seventeen large editions, in receiving an application to write a Preface to a new and more handsome impression. In diminution, however, of any overweening vanity which they might be disposed to indulge on this occasion, they cannot but admit the truth of the remark made by a particularly candid and good-natured friend, who kindly reminded them, that if their little work has hitherto floated upon the stream of time, while so many others of much greater weight and value have sunk to rise no more, it has been solely indebted for its buoyancy to that specific levity which enables feathers, straws, and similar trifles, to defer their submersion, until they have become thoroughly saturated with the waters of oblivion, when they quickly meet the fate which they had long before merited.

Our ingenuous and ingenious friend furthermore observed, that the demolition of Drury Lane Theatre by fire, its reconstruction under the auspices of the celebrated Mr. Whitbread,† the reward offered by the Committee for an opening address, and the public recitation of a poem composed expressly for the occasion by Lord Byron, one of the most popular writers of the age, formed

[* 12mo, 1833. The first published by Mr. Murray. The "Preface" was written by Horace Smith; the "Notes" to the Poems by James Smith.]
[† Samuel Whitbread, M.P. He died by his own hand in 1815.]

an extraordinary concurrence of circumstances which could not fail to insure the success of the *Rejected Addresses,* while it has subsequently served to fix them in the memory of the public, so far at least as a poor immortality of twenty years can be said to have effected that object. In fact, continued our impartial and affectionate monitor, your little work owes its present obscure existence entirely to the accidents that have surrounded and embalmed it,—even as flies, and other worthless insects, may long survive their natural date of extinction, if they chance to be preserved in amber, or any similar substance.

> The things we know, are neither rich nor rare—
> But wonder how the devil they get there!—Pope.

With the natural affection of parents for the offspring of their own brains, we ventured to hint that some portion of our success might perhaps be attributable to the manner in which the different imitations were executed; but our worthy friend protested that his sincere regard for us, as well as for the cause of truth, compelled him to reject our claim, and to pronounce that, when once the idea had been conceived, all the rest followed as a matter of course, and might have been executed by any other hands not less felicitously than by our own.

Willingly leaving this matter to the decision of the public, since we cannot be umpires in our own cause, we proceed to detail such circumstances attending the writing and publication of our little work, as may literally meet the wishes of the present proprietor of the copyright, who has applied to us for a gossiping Preface. Were we disposed to be grave and didactic, which is as foreign to our mood as it was twenty years ago, we might draw the attention of the reader, in a fine sententious paragraph, to the trifles upon which the fate of empires, as well as a four-and-sixpenny volume of parodies, occasionally hangs in trembling balance. No sooner was the idea of our work conceived, than it was about to be abandoned in embryo, from the apprehension that we had no time to mature and bring it forth, as it was indispensable that it should be written, printed, and published by the opening of Drury Lane Theatre, which would only allow us an interval of six weeks, and we had both of us other avocations that precluded us from the full command of even that limited period. Encouraged, however, by the conviction that the thought was a good one, and by the hope of making a lucky hit, we set to work *con amore*, our very hurry not improbably enabling us to strike out at a heat what we might have failed to produce so well, had we possessed time enough to hammer it into more careful and elaborate form.

Our first difficulty, that of selection, was by no means a light one. Some of our most eminent poets, such, for instance, as Rogers and Campbell, presented so much beauty, harmony, and proportion in their writings, both as to style and sentiment, that if we had attempted to caricature them, nobody would have recognised the likeness; and if we had endeavoured to give a servile copy of their manner, it would only have amounted, at best, to a tame and unamusing portrait, which it was not our object to present. Although fully aware that their names would, in the theatrical phrase, have conferred great strength upon our bill, we were reluctantly compelled to forego them, and to confine ourselves to writers whose style and habit of thought, being more marked and peculiar, was more capable of exaggeration and distortion. To avoid politics and personality, to imitate the turn of mind, as well as the phraseology of our originals, and, at all events, to raise a harmless laugh, were our main objects: in the attainment of which united aims, we were sometimes hurried into extravagance; by attaching much more importance to the last than to the two first. In no instance were we thus betrayed into a greater injustice than in the case of Mr. Wordsworth—the touching sentiment, profound wisdom, and copious harmony of whose loftier writings we left unnoticed, in the desire of burlesquing them; while we pounced upon his popular ballads, and exerted ourselves to push their simplicity into puerility and silliness. With pride and pleasure do we now claim to be ranked among the most ardent admirers of this true poet; and if he himself could see the state of his works, which are ever at our right hand, he would, perhaps, receive the manifest evidence they exhibit of constant reference, and delighted re-perusal, as some sort of *amende honorable* for the unfairness of which we were guilty, when we were less conversant with the higher inspirations of his muse. To Mr. Coleridge, and others of our originals, we must also do a tardy act of justice, by declaring that our burlesque of their peculiarities has never blinded us to those beauties and talents which are beyond the reach of all ridicule.

One of us* had written a genuine Address for the occasion, which was sent to the Committee, and shared the fate it merited, in being rejected. To swell the bulk, or rather to diminish the tenuity of our little work, we added it to the Imitations; and prefixing the initials of S. T. P. for the purpose of puzzling the critics, were not a little amused, in the sequel, by the many guesses and conjectures into which we had ensnared some of our readers. We could even enjoy the mysticism, qualified as it was by the poor compliment, that our carefully written Address exhibited no "very prominent trait of absurdity," when we saw it thus noticed in the *Edinburgh Review* for November 1812. "An Address by S. T. P. we can make nothing of; and professing our ignorance of the author designated by these letters, we can only add, that the Address, though a little affected, and not very full of meaning, has no very prominent trait of absurdity, that we can detect; and might have been adopted and spoken, so far as we can perceive, without any hazard of ridicule. In our simplicity we consider it as a very decent, mellifluous, occasional prologue: and do not understand how it has found its way into its present company."

Urged forward by hurry, and trusting to chance, two very bad coadjutors in any enterprise, we at length congratulated ourselves on having completed our task in time to have it printed and published by the opening of the theatre. But alas! our difficulties, so far from being surmounted, seemed only to be beginning. Strangers to the arcana of the bookseller's trade, and unacquainted with their almost invincible objection to single volumes of low price, especially when tendered by writers who have acquired no previous name, we little anticipated that they would refuse to publish our *Rejected Addresses*, even although we asked nothing for the copyright. Such, however, proved to be the case. Our manuscript was perused and returned to us by several of the most eminent publishers.† Well do we remember betaking our-

[* This was Horatio, the writer of the present Preface.]
[† The passage, as originally written, continued thus, "and among others, so difficult is it in forming a correct judgment in catering to the public taste, by the very bibliopolist who has now, after an interval of twenty [only seven] years, purchased the copyright from a brother bookseller and ventured upon the present edition." To this, on the proof-sheet, the late Mr. Murray appended the following note :—" I never saw or even had the MS. in my possession; but know-

selves to one of the craft in Bond-street, whom we found in a back parlour, with his gouty leg propped upon a cushion, in spite of which warning he diluted his luncheon with frequent glasses of Maderia. "What have you already written?" was his first question, an interrogatory to which we had been subjected in almost every instance. "Nothing by which we can be known." "Then I am afraid to undertake the publication." We presumed timidly to suggest that every writer must have a beginning, and that to refuse to publish for him until he had acquired a name, was to imitate the sapient mother who cautioned her son against going into the water until he could swim. "An old joke—a regular Joe!" exclaimed our companion, tossing off another bumper. "Still older than Joe Miller," was our reply; "for, if we mistake not, it is the very first anecdote in the facetiæ of Hierocles." "Ha, sirs!" resumed the bibliopolist, "you are learned, are you? So, soh!—Well, leave your manuscript with me; I will look it over to-night, and give you an answer to-morrow." Punctual as the clock we presented ourselves at his door on the following morning, when our papers were returned to us with the observation—"These trifles are really not deficient in smartness; they are well, vastly well for beginners; but they will never do—never. They would not pay for advertising, and without it I should not sell fifty copies."

This was discouraging enough. If the most experienced publishers feared to be out of pocket by the work, it was manifest, *à fortiori*, that its writers ran a risk of being still more heavy losers, should they undertake the publication on their own account. We had no objection to raise a laugh at the expense of others; but to do it at our own cost, uncertain as we were to what extent we might be involved, had never entered into our contemplation. In this dilemma, our *Addresses*, now in every sense rejected, might probably have never seen the light, had not some good angel whispered us to betake ourselves to Mr. John Miller, a dramatic publisher, then residing in Bow-street, Covent Garden. No sooner had this gentleman looked over our manuscript, than he immediately offered to take upon himself all the

ing that Mr. Smith was brother-in-law to Mr. Cadell, I took it for granted that the MS. had been previously offered to him and declined." Mr. H. Smith consequently drew his pen through the passage.]

risk of publication, and to give us half the profits, *should there be any* ; a liberal proposition with which we gladly closed. So rapid and decided was its success, at which none were more unfeignedly astonished than its authors, that Mr. Miller advised us to collect some *Imitations of Horace*, which had appeared anonymously in the *Monthly Mirror*,* offering to publish them upon the same terms. We did so accordingly; and as new editions of the *Rejected Addresses* were called for in quick succession, we were shortly enabled to sell our half copyright in the two works to Mr. Miller, for one thousand pounds!! We have entered into this unimportant detail, not to gratify any vanity of our own, but to encourage such literary beginners as may be placed in similar circumstances; as well as to impress upon publishers the propriety of giving more consideration to the possible merit of the works submitted to them, than to the mere magic of a name.

To the credit of the *genus irritabile* be it recorded, that not one of those whom we had parodied or burlesqued ever betrayed the least soreness on the occasion, or refused to join in the laugh that we had occasioned. With most of them we subsequently formed acquaintanceship; while some honoured us with an intimacy which still continues, where it has not been severed by the rude hand of Death. Alas! it is painful to reflect, that of the twelve writers whom we presumed to imitate, five are now no more; the list of the deceased being unhappily swelled by the most illustrious of all, the *clarum et venerabile nomen* of Sir Walter Scott! From that distinguished writer, whose transcendent talents were only to be equalled by his virtues and his amiability, we received favours and notice, both public and private, which it will be difficult to forget, because we had not the smallest claim upon his kindness. "I certainly must have written this myself!" said that fine-tempered man to one of the authors, pointing to the description of the Fire, "Although I forget upon what occasion." Lydia White,† a literary lady who was prone to feed the lions of the day, invited one of us to dinner; but, recollecting afterwards

[* Between 1807 and 1810. The *Monthly Mirror* was edited by Edward Du Bois, author of " My Pocket-Book," and by Thomas Hill ; the original Paul Pry ; and the Hull of Mr. Theodore Hook's novel of " Gilbert Gurney."]

[† Miss Lydia White, celebrated for her lively wit and for her blue-stocking parties, unrivalled, it is said, in " the soft realm of *blue* May Fair." She died in 1827, and is mentioned in the Diaries of Scott and Byron.]

that William Spencer formed one of the party, wrote to the latter to put him off; telling him that a man was to be at her table whom "he would not like to meet." "Pray who is this whom I should not like to meet?" inquired the poet. "Of" answered the lady, "one of those men who have made that shameful attack upon you!" "The very man upon earth I should like to know!" rejoined the lively and careless bard. The two individuals accordingly met, and have continued fast friends ever since. Lord Byron, too, wrote thus to Mr. Murray from Italy— "Tell him I forgive him, were he twenty times over our satirist."

It may not be amiss to notice, in this place, one criticism of a Leicestershire clergyman, which may be pronounced unique: "I do not see why they should have been rejected," observed the matter-of-fact annotator; "I think some of them very good!" Upon the whole, few have been the instances, in the acrimonious history of literature, where a malicious pleasantry like the *Rejected Addresses*—which the parties ridiculed might well consider more annoying than a direct satire—instead of being met by querulous bitterness or petulant retaliation, has procured for its authors the acquaintance, or conciliated the good-will, of those whom they had the most audaciously burlesqued.

In commenting on a work, however trifling, which has survived the lapse of twenty years, an author may almost claim the privileged garrulity of age; yet even in a professedly gossiping Preface, we begin to fear that we are exceeding our commission, and abusing the patience of the reader. If we are doing so, we might urge extenuating circumstances, which will explain, though they may not excuse, our diffuseness. To one of us the totally unexpected success of this little work proved an important event, since it mainly decided him, some years afterwards, to embark in the literary career which the continued favour of that novel-reading world has rendered both pleasant and profitable to him. This is the first, as it will probably be the last, occasion upon which we shall ever intrude ourselves personally on the public notice; and we trust that our now doing so will stand excused by the reasons we have adduced. For the portraits prefixed to this edition we are in no way responsible. At the sale of the late Mr. Harlowe's effects, the drawing from

13*

which they are engraved was purchased by Mr. Murray; who, conceiving probably that we had no interest in the matter— since they were not likenesses of our present heads, but of those which we possessed twenty years ago—has thought proper to give them publicity, without consulting their now rather anti- quated originals.

LONDON, *March*, 1833.

I.

LOYAL EFFUSION.

BY W. T. F.

" Quicquid dicunt, laudo : id rursum si negant,
Laudo id quoque."   TERENCE.

HAIL, glorious edifice, stupendous work !
God bless the Regent and the Duke of York !
   Ye Muses ! by whose aid I cried down Fox,
Grant me in Drury Lane a private box,
Where I may loll, cry Bravo ! and profess
The boundless powers of England's glorious press ,
While Afric's sons exclaim, from shore to shore,
" Quashee ma boo !"——the slave-trade is no more !
   In fair Arabia (happy once, now stony,
Since ruined by that arch apostate Boney,)
A Phœnix late was caught : the Arab host
Long ponder'd——part would boil it, part would roast
But while they ponder, up the pot-lid flies,
Fledged, beak'd, and claw'd, alive they see him rise
To heaven, and caw defiance in the skies.
So Drury, first in roasting flames consumed,
Then by old renters to hot water doom'd,
By Wyatt's[1] trowel patted, plump and sleek,
Soars without wings, and caws without a beak.
Gallia's stern despot shall in vain advance
From Paris, the metropolis of France ;
By this day month the monster shall not gain
A foot of land in Portugal or Spain.

See Wellington in Salamanca's field
Forces his favourite general to yield,
Breaks through his lines, and leaves his boasted Marmont
    mont
Expiring on the plain without his arm on;
Madrid he enters at the cannon's mouth,
And then the villages still further south.
Base Buonaparte, fill'd with deadly ire,
Sets, one by one, our playhouses on fire.
Some years ago he pounced with deadly glee on
The Opera House, then burnt down the Pantheon;
Nay, still unsated, in a coat of flames,
Next at Millbank he cross'd the river Thames;
Thy hatch, O Halfpenny![2] pass'd in a trice,
Boil'd some black pitch, and burnt down Astley's twice;
Then buzzing on through ether with a vile hum,
Turn'd to the left hand, fronting the Asylum,
And burnt the Royal Circus in a hurry—
('Twas call'd the Circus then, but now the Surrey).
    Who burnt (confound his soul!) the houses twain
Of Covent Garden and of Drury Lane?[3]
Who, while the British squadron lay off Cork
(God bless the Regent and the Duke of York!)
With a foul earthquake ravaged the Caraccas,
And raised the price of dry goods and tobaccos?
Who makes the quartern loaf and Luddites rise?
Who fills the butchers' shops with large blue flies?
Who thought in flames St. James's court to pinch?[4]
Who burnt the wardrobe of poor Lady Finch?—
Why he, who, forging for this isle a yoke,
Reminds me of a line I lately spoke,
"The tree of freedom is the British oak."
    Bless every man possess'd of aught to give;
Long may Long Tylney Wellesley Long Pole live;[5]

God bless the Army, bless their coats of scarlet,
God bless the Navy, bless the Princess Charlotte;
God bless the guards, though worsted Gallia scoff,
God bless their pig-tails, though they 're now cut off;
And, oh ! in Downing Street should Old Nick revel,
England's prime minister, then bless the devil!

II.

THE BABY'S DEBUT.

"Thy lisping prattle and thy mincing gait,
All thy false mimic fooleries I hate :
For thou art Folly's counterfeit, and she
Who is right foolish hath the better plea :
Nature's true Idiot I prefer to thee."

CUMBERLAND.

[*Spoken in the character of Nancy Lake, a girl eight years of age, who is drawn upon the stage in a child's chaise by Samuel Hughes, her uncle's porter.*]

My brother Jack was nine in May,[1]
And I was eight on New-year's-day ;
    So in Kate Wilson's shop
Papa (he's my papa and Jack's)
Bought me, last week, a doll of wax,
    And brother Jack a top.

Jack 's in the pouts, and this it is,——
He thinks mine came to more than his ;
    So to my drawer he goes,
Takes out the doll, and, O, my stars !
He pokes her head between the bars,
    And melts off half her nose !

Quite cross, a bit of string I beg,
And tie it to his peg-top's peg,
    And bang, with might and main,

THE BABY'S DEBUT.

Its head against the parlour-door :
Off flies the head, and hits the floor,
    And breaks a window-pane.

This made him cry with rage and spite :
Well, let him cry, it serves him right.
    A pretty thing, forsooth !
If he 's to melt, all scalding hot,
Half my doll's nose, and I am not
    To draw his peg-top's tooth !

Aunt Hannah heard the window break,
And cried, " O naughty Nancy Lake,
    Thus to distress your aunt :
No Drury Lane for you to-day !"
And while papa said, " Pooh, she may !"
    Mamma said, " No, she sha'n't !"

Well, after many a sad reproach,
They got into a hackney coach,
    And trotted down the street.
I saw them go : one horse was blind,
The tails of both hung down behind,
    Their shoes were on their feet.

The chaise in which poor brother Bill
Used to be drawn to Pentonville,
    Stood in the lumber-room :
I wiped the dust from off the top,
While Molly mopp'd it with a mop,
    And brushed it with a broom.

My uncle's porter, Samuel Hughes,
Came in at six to black the shoes,
    (I always talk to Sam :)

So what does he, but takes, and drags
Me in the chaise along the flags,
    And leaves me where I am.

My father's walls are made of brick,
But not so tall and not so thick
    As these ; and, goodness me !
My father's beams are made of wood,
But never, never half so good
    As those that now I see.

What a large floor ! 'tis like a town !
The carpet, when they lay it down,
    Won't hide it I 'll be bound ;
And there's a row of lamps !——my eye !
How they do blaze ! I wonder why
    They keep them on the ground.

At first I caught hold of the wing,
And kept away ; but Mr. Thing-
    um bob, the prompter man,
Gave with his hand my chaise a shove,
And said, " Go on, my pretty love ;
    Speak to 'em, little Nan.

" You 've only got to curtsey, whisp-
er, hold your chin up, laugh, and lisp,
    And then you 're sure to take :
I 've known the day when brats, not quite
Thirteen, got fifty pounds a night ;[3]
    Then why not Nancy Lake ? "

But while I 'm speaking, where 's papa?
And where 's my aunt? and where 's mamma?
    Where 's Jack ? O, there they sit !

They smile, they nod; I 'll go my ways,
And order 'round poor Billy's chaise,
    To join them in the pit.

And now, good gentlefolks, I go
To join mamma, and see the show;
    So, bidding you adieu,
I curtsey, like a pretty miss,
And if you 'll blow to me a kiss,
    I 'll blow a kiss to you.

                [Blows a kiss, and exit.]

III.

AN ADDRESS

WITHOUT A PHŒNIX.[1]

BY S. T. P.

"This was looked for at your hand, and this was balked."
What You Will.

WHAT stately vision mocks my waking sense?
Hence, dear delusion, sweet enchantment, hence!
Ha! is it real?——can my doubts be vain?
It is, it is, and Drury lives again!
Around each grateful veteran attends,
Eager to rush and gratulate his friends,
Friends whose kind looks, retraced with proud delight,
Endear the past, and make the future bright:
Yes, generous patrons, your returning smile
Blesses our toils, and consecrates our pile.

When last we met, Fate's unrelenting hand
Already grasped the devastating brand;
Slow crept the silent flame, ensnared its prize,
Then burst resistless to the astonished skies.
The glowing walls disrobed of scenic pride,
In trembling conflict stemmed the burning tide,
Till crackling, blazing, rocking to its fall,
Down rushed the thundering roof and buried all!

Where late the sister Muses sweetly sung,
And raptured thousands on their music hung,

Where Wit and Wisdom shone, by Beauty graced,
Sat lonely Silence, empress of the waste;
And still had reigned—but he, whose voice can raise
More magic wonders than Amphion's lays,
Bade jarring bands with friendly zeal engage
To rear the prostrate glories of the stage.
Up leaped the Muses at the potent spell,
And Drury's genius saw his temple swell;
Worthy, we hope, the British Drama's cause,
Worthy of British arts, and *your* applause.

Guided by you, our earnest aims presume
To renovate the drama with the dome;
The scenes of Shakespeare and our bards of old,
With due observance splendidly unfold,
Yet raise and foster with parental hand
The living talent of our native land.
O! may we still, to sense and nature true,
Delight the many, nor offend the few.
Though varying tastes our changeful Drama claim,
Still be its moral tendency the same,
To win by precept, by example warn,
To brand the front of Vice with pointed scorn,
And Virtue's smiling brows with votive wreaths adorn.

IV.

CUI BONO?

BY LORD B.

I.

SATED with home, of wife, of children tired,
The restless soul is driven abroad to roam ; [1]
Sated abroad, all seen yet nought admired,
The restless soul is driven to ramble home ;
Sated with both, beneath new Drury's dome
The fiend Ennui awhile consents to pine,
There growls, and curses, like a deadly Gnome,
Scorning to view fantastic Columbine,
Viewing with scorn and hate the nonsense of the Nine. [2]

II.

Ye reckless dupes, who hither wend your way
To gaze on puppets in a painted dome,
Pursuing pastimes glittering to betray,
Like falling stars in life's eternal gloom,
What seek ye here ?   Joy's evanescent bloom ?
Woe 's me ! the brightest wreaths she ever gave
Are but as flowers that decorate a tomb.
Man's heart, the mournful urn o'er which they wave,
Is sacred to despair, its pedestal the grave.

III.

Has life so little store of real woes,
That here ye wend to taste fictitious grief?

Or is it that from truth such anguish flows,
Ye court the lying drama for relief?
Long shall ye find the pang, the respite brief:
Or if one tolerable page appears
In folly's volume, 'tis the actor's leaf,
Who dries his own by drawing others' tears,
And, raising present mirth, makes glad his future years.

IV.

Albeit, how like young Betty doth he flee!
Light as the moat that danceth in the beam,
He liveth only in man's present e'e;
His life a flash, his memory a dream,
Oblivious down he drops in Lethe's stream.
Yet what are they, the learned and the great?
Awhile of longer wonderment the theme!
Who shall presume to prophesy *their* date,
Where nought is certain, save the uncertainty of fate?

V.

This goodly pile, upheaved by Wyatt's toil,
Perchance than Holland's edifice [3] more fleet,
Again red Lemnos' artisan may spoil;
The fire-alarm and midnight drum may beat,
And all bestrewed ysmoking at your feet!
Start ye? perchance Death's angel may be sent,
Ere from the flaming temple ye retreat;
And ye who met, on revel idlesse bent,
May find, in pleasure's fane, your grave and monument.

VI.

Your debts mount high—ye plunge in deeper waste;
The tradesman duns—no warning voice ye hear;
The plaintiff sues—to public shows ye haste;
The bailiff threats—ye feel no idle fear.

Who can arrest your prodigal career?
Who can keep down the levity of youth?
What sound can startle age's stubborn ear?
Who can redeem from wretchedness and ruth
Men true to falsehood's voice, false to the voice of truth?

VII.

To thee, blest saint! who doffed thy skin to make
The Smithfield rabble leap from theirs with joy,
We dedicate the pile—arise! awake!——
Knock down the Muses, wit and sense destroy,
Clear our new stage from reason's dull alloy,
Charm hobbling age, and tickle capering youth
With cleaver, marrow-bone, and Tunbridge toy;
While, vibrating in unbelieving tooth,[4]
Harps twang in Drury's walls, and make her boards a
          booth.

VIII.

For what is Hamlet, but a hare in March?
And what is Brutus, but a croaking owl?
And what is Rolla?   Cupid steeped in starch,
Orlando's helmet in Augustin's cowl.
Shakespeare, how true thine adage, " fair is foul!"
To him whose soul is with fruition fraught,
The song of Braham is an Irish howl,
Thinking is but an idle waste of thought,
And nought is everything, and everything is nought.

IX.

Sons of Parnassus! whom I view above,
Not laurel-crown'd, but clad in rusty black;
Not spurring Pegasus through Tempè's grove,
But pacing Grub-street on a jaded hack:

What reams of foolscap, while your brains ye rack,
Ye mar to make again! for sure, ere long,
Condemn'd to tread the bard's time-sanction'd track,
Ye all shall join the bailiff-haunted throng,
And reproduce, in rags, the rags ye blot in song.

X.

So fares the follower in the Muses' train;
He toils to starve, and only lives in death;
We slight him, till our patronage is vain,
Then round his skeleton a garland wreathe,
And o'er his bones an empty requiem breathe—
Oh! with what tragic horror would he start,
(Could he be conjured from the grave beneath)
To find the stage again a Thespian cart,
And elephants and colts down trampling Shakespeare's
        art.

XI.

Hence, pedant Nature! with thy Grecian rules!
Centaurs (not fabulous) those rules efface;
Back, sister Muses, to your native schools;
Here booted grooms usurp Apollo's place,
Hoofs shame the boards that Garrick used to grace,
The play of limbs succeeds the play of wit,
Man yields the drama to the Hou'yn'm race,
His prompter spurs, his licenser the bit,
The stage a stable-yard, a jockey-club the pit.

XII.

Is it for these ye rear this proud abode?
Is it for these your superstition seeks
To build a temple worthy of a god,
To laud a monkey, or to worship leeks!

Then be the stage, to recompense your freaks,
A motley chaos, jumbling age and ranks,
Where Punch, the lignum-vitæ Roscius, squeaks,
And Wisdom weeps, and Folly plays his pranks,
And moody Madness laughs and hugs the chain he clanks.

THE SECRETARY OF THE MANAGING COMMITTEE OF DRURY-LANE PLAYHOUSE.

SIR,

To the gewgaw fetters of *rhyme* (invented by the monks to enslave the people) I have a rooted objection. I have therefore written an address for your Theatre in plain, homespun, yeoman's *prose;* in the doing whereof I hope I am swayed by nothing but an *independent* wish to open the eyes of this gulled people, to prevent a repetition of the dramatic *bamboozling* they have hitherto laboured under. If you like what I have done, and mean to make use of it, I do n't want any such *aristocratic* reward as a piece of plate with two griffins sprawling upon it, or a *dog* and a *jackass* fighting for a ha'p'worth of *gilt gingerbread*, or any such Bartholomew-fair nonsense. All I ask is that the door-keepers of your playhouse may take all the *sets of my Register'* now on hand, and *force* every body who enters your doors to buy one, giving afterwards a debtor and creditor account of what they have received, *post-paid*, and in due course remitting me the money and unsold Registers, *carriage-paid.*

I am, &c.

W. C.

14

A HAMPSHIRE FARMER.

——————" Rabida qui concitus irâ
Implevit pariter ternis latratibus auras,
Et sparsit virides spumis albentibus agros."—OVID.

MOST THINKING PEOPLE,

WHEN persons address an audience from the stage, it is
usual, either in words or gesture, to say, " Ladies and
Gentlemen, your servant." If I were base enough,
mean enough, paltry enough, and *brute beast* enough,
to follow that fashion, I should tell two lies in a breath.
In the first place, you are *not* Ladies and Gentlemen,
but I hope something better, that is to say, honest men
and women; and in the next place, if you were ever so
much ladies, and ever so much gentlemen, I am not,
nor ever will be, your humble servant. You see me
here, *most thinking people*, by mere chance. I have
not been within the doors of a playhouse before for
these ten years; nor, till that abominable custom of
taking money at the doors is discontinued, will I ever
sanction a theatre with my presence. The stage-door is
the only gate of *freedom* in the whole edifice, and
through that I made my way from Bagshaw's* in
Brydges Street, to accost you. Look about you. Are
you not all comfortable ? Nay, never slink, mun;
speak out, if you are dissatisfied, and tell me so before I
leave town. You are now, (thanks to *Mr. Whitbread*),
got into a large, comfortable house. Not into a *gim-
crack palace ;* not into a *Solomon's temple ;* not into a
frost-work of Brobdignag filigree; but into a plain,

honest, homely, industrious, wholesome, *brown brick playhouse.* You have been struggling for independence and elbow-room these three years : and who gave it you? Who helped you out of Lilliput? Who routed you from a rat-hole, five inches by four, to perch you in a palace? Again and again I answer, *Mr. Whitbread.* You might have sweltered in that place with the Greek name till doomsday, and neither *Lord Castlereagh, Mr. Canning,* no, nor the *Marquess Wellesley,* would have turned a trowel to help you out! Remember that. Never forget that. Read it to your children, and to your children's children! And now, *most thinking people,* cast your eyes over my head to what the builder, (I beg his pardon, the architect,) calls the *proscenium.* No motto, no slang, no popish Latin, to keep the people in the dark. No *veluti in speculum.* Nothing in the dead languages, properly so called, for they ought to die, ay and be *damned* to boot! The Covent Garden manager tried that, and a pretty business he made of it! When a man says *veluti in speculum,* he is called a man of letters. Very well, and is not a man who cries O. P. a man of letters too? You ran your O. P. against his *veluti in speculum,* and pray which beat? I prophesied that, though I never told any body. I take it for granted, that every intelligent man, woman, and child, to whom I address myself, has stood severally and respectively in Little Russell Street, and cast their, his, her, and its eyes on the outside of this building before they paid their money to view the inside. Look at the brick-work, *English Audience!* Look at the brick-work! All plain and smooth like a quakers' meeting. None of your Egyptian pyramids, to entomb subscribers' capitals. No overgrown colonnades of stone,[4] like an alderman's gouty legs in white cotton stockings, fit only to use as rammers for paving Tottenham Court Road.   This house is neither after the model of a temple in Athens, no, nor a *temple* in *Moorfields*, but it is built to act English plays in ; and, provided you have good scenery, dresses, and decorations, I daresay you would n't break your hearts if the outside was as plain as the pikestaff I used to carry when I was a sergeant. *Apropos*, as t e French valets say, who cut their masters' throats`—*apropos*, a word about dresses.   You must, many of you, have seen what I have read a description of, Kemble and Mrs. Siddons in Macbeth, with more gold and silver plastered on their doublets than would have kept an honest family in butcher's meat and flannel from year's end to year's end!   I am informed, (now mind, I do not vouch for the fact), but I am informed that all such extravagant idleness is to be done away with here.   Lady Macbeth is to have a plain quilted petticoat, a cotton gown, and a *mob cap* (as the court parasites call it;—it will be well for them, if, one of these days, they do n't wear a mob cap—I mean a *white cap*, with a *mob* to look at them) ; and Macbeth is to appear in an honest yeoman's drab coat, and a pair of black calamanco breeches.   Not *Sala*manca ; no, nor *Talavera* neither, my most Noble Marquess ; but plain, honest, black calamanco stuff breeches.   This is right ; this is as it should be.   *Most thinking people*, I have heard you much abused.   There is not a compound in the language but is strung fifty in a rope, like onions, by the Morning Post, and hurled in your teeth.   You are called the mob, and when they have made you out to be the mob, you are called the *scum* of the people, and the *dregs* of the people.   I should like to know how you can be both.   Take a basin of broth—not *cheap soup*, Mr. *Wilberforce*—not soup for the poor, at a penny a quart, as your mixture of horses' legs, brick-dust, and old shoes, was denominated—but plain, wholesome, patriotic beef or mutton broth; take this, examine it, and you will find—mind, I do n't vouch for the fact, but I am told—you will find the dregs at the bottom, and the scum at the top. I will endeavour to explain this to you: England is a large *earthenware pipkin;* John Bull is the *beef* thrown into it; taxes are the *hot water* he boils in; rotten boroughs are the *fuel* that blazes under this same pipkin; parliament is the *ladle* that stirs the hodge-podge, and sometimes ———. But, hold! I do n't wish to pay *Mr. Newman*⁶ a second visit. I leave you better off than you have been this many a day: you have a good house over your head; you have beat the French in Spain; the harvest has turned out well; the comet keeps its distance;⁷ and red slippers are hawked about Constantinople for next to nothing; and for all this, *again and again* I tell you, you are indebted to *Mr. Whitbread! ! !*

VI.

THE LIVING LUSTRES.

BY T. M. T...

"Jam te juvaverit
Viros relinquere,
Doctæque conjugis
Sinu quiescere."
Sir T. More.

I.

O WHY should our dull retrospective addresses
　Fall damp as wet blankets on Drury Lane fire?
Away with blue devils, away with distresses,
　And give the gay spirit to sparkling desire!

II.

Let artists decide on the beauties of Drury,
　The richest to me is when woman is there;
The question of houses I leave to the jury;
　The fairest to me is the house of the fair.

III.

When woman's soft smile all our senses bewilders,
　And gilds, while it carves, her dear form on the heart,
What need has New Drury of carvers and gilders?
　With Nature so bounteous, why call upon Art?

IV.

How well would our actors attend to their duties,
　Our house save in oil, and our authors in wit,
In lieu of yon lamps, if a row of young beauties
　Glanced light from their eyes between us and the pit!

V.

The apples that grew on the fruit-tree of knowledge
  By woman were pluck'd, and she still wears the prize,
To tempt us in theatre, senate, or college—
  I mean the love-apples that bloom in the eyes.

VI.

There too is the lash which, all statutes controlling,
  Still governs the slaves that are made by the fair;
For man is the pupil, who, while her eye's rolling,
  Is lifted to rapture, or sunk in despair.

VII.

Bloom, Theatre, bloom, in the roseate blushes
  Of beauty illumed by a love-breathing smile!
And flourish, ye pillars,' as green as the rushes
  That pillow the nymphs of the Emerald Isle!

VIII.

For dear is the Emerald Isle of the ocean,
  Whose daughters are fair as the foam of the wave,
Whose sons, unaccustomed to rebel commotion,
  Tho' joyous, are sober—tho' peaceful, are brave.

IX.

The shamrock their olive, sworn foe to a quarrel,
  Protects from the thunder and lightning of rows;
Their sprig of shillelagh is nothing but laurel,
  Which flourishes rapidly over their brows.

X.

O! soon shall they burst the tyrannical shackles
  Which each panting bosom indignantly names,
Until not one goose at the capital cackles
  Against the grand question of Catholic claims.

XI.

And then shall each Paddy, who once on the Liffy
    Perchance held the helm of some mackerel-hoy,
Hold the helm of the state, and dispense in a jiffy
    More fishes than ever he caught when a boy.

XII.

And those who now quit their hods, shovels, and barrows,
    In crowds to the bar of some ale-house to flock,
When bred to *our* bar shall be Gibbses and Garrows,
    Assume the silk gown, and discard the smock-frock.

XIII.

For Erin surpasses the daughters of Neptune,
    As Dian outshines each encircling star ;
And the spheres of the heavens could never have kept tune
    Till set to the music of Erin-go-bragh !

VII.

THE REBUILDING.

BY R. S.

—————— "Per audaces nova dithyrambos
Verba devolvit, numerisque fertur
Lege solutis." HORAT.

[Spoken by a Glendoveer.]

I AM a blessed Glendoveer:[1]
'Tis mine to speak, and yours to hear.
Midnight, yet not a nose
From Tower-hill to Piccadilly snored!
Midnight, yet not a nose
From Indra drew the essence of repose!
See with what crimson fury,
By Indra fann'd, the god of fire ascends the walls of
Drury!

Tops of houses, blue with lead,
Bend beneath the landlord's tread.
Master and 'prentice, serving-man and lord,
Nailor and tailor,
Grazier and brazier,
Through streets and alleys pour'd—
All, all abroad to gaze,
And wonder at the blaze.
Thick calf, fat foot, and slim knee,
Mounted on roof and chimney,[2]
The mighty roast, the mighty stew

14*

To see;
As if the dismal view
Were but to them a Brentford jubilee.
Vainly, all-radiant Surya, sire of Phaeton
(By Greeks call'd Apollo')
Hollow
Sounds from thy harp proceed;
Combustible as reed,
The tongue of Vulcan licks thy wooden legs.:
From Drury's top, dissever'd from thy pegs,
Thou tumblest,
Humblest,
Where late thy bright effulgence shone on high ;-
While, by thy somerset, excited, fly
Ten million
Billion
Sparks from the pit, to gem the sable sky.

Now come the men of fire to quench the fires :
To Russell Street see Globe and Atlas run,
Hope gallops first, and second Sun ;
On flying heel,
See Hand-in-Hand
O'ertake the band !
View with what glowing wheel
He nicks
Phœnix !
While Albion scampers from Bridge Street, Black-
friars ——
Drury Lane !   Drury Lane !
Drury Lane !   Drury Lane !
They shout and they bellow again and again.
All, all in vain !

Water turns steam ;
Each blazing beam
Hisses defiance to the eddying spout ;
It seems but too plain that nothing can put it out !
Drury Lane ! Drury Lane
See, Drury Lane expires.

Pent in by smoke-dried beams, twelve moons or more,
Shorn of his ray,
Surya in durance lay :
The workmen heard him shout,
But thought it would not pay,
To dig him out.
When lo ! terrific Yamen, lord of hell,
Solemn as lead,
Judge of the dead,
Sworn foe to witticism,
By men call'd criticism,
Came passing by that way :
Rise ! cried the fiend, behold a sight of gladness !
Behold the rival theatre !
I 've set O. P. at her,
Who, like a bull-dog bold,
Growls and fastens on his hold.
The many-headed rabble roar in madness ;
Thy rival staggers : come and spy her
Deep in the mud as thou art in the mire.
So saying, in his arms he caught the beaming one,
And crossing Russell Street,
He placed him on his feet
'Neath Covent Garden dome. Sudden a sound,
As of the bricklayers of Babel, rose :
Horns, rattles, drums, tin trumpets, sheets of copper,
Punches and slaps, thwacks of all sorts and sizes,

From the knobb'd bludgeon to the taper switch,[5]
Ran echoing round the walls ; paper placards
Blotted the lamps, boots brown with mud the benches ;
A sea of heads roll'd roaring in the pit ;
On paper wings O. P.'s
Reclin'd in lettered ease ;
While shout and scoff,
Ya ! ya ! off ! off !
Like thunderbolt on Surya's ear-drum fell,
And seemed to paint
The savage oddities of Saint
Bartholomew in hell.

Tears dimm'd the god of light—
" Bear me back, Yamen, from this hideous sight;
Bear me back, Yamen, I grow sick,
Oh ! bury me again in brick ;
Shall I on New Drury tremble,
To be O. P.'d like Kemble ?
No,
Better remain by rubbish guarded,
Than thus hubbubish groan placarded ;
Bear me back, Yamen, bear me quick,
And bury me again in brick."
Obedient Yamen
Answered " Amen,"
And did
As he was bid.

There lay the buried god, and Time
Seemed to decree eternity of lime ;
But pity, like a dew-drop, gently prest
Almighty Veeshnoo's' adamantine breast :

He, the preserver, ardent still
To do whate'er he says he will,
From South-hill wing'd his way,
To raise the drooping lord of day.
All earthly spells the busy one o'erpower'd;
He treats with men of all conditions,
Poets and players, tradesmen, and musicians;
Nay, even ventures
To attack the renters,
Old and new:
A list he gets
Of claims and debts,
And deems nought done, while aught remains to do.

Yamen beheld, and wither'd at the sight;
Long had he aim'd the sunbeam to control,
For light was hateful to his soul:
"Go on!" cried the hellish one, yellow with spite;
"Go on!" cried the hellish one, yellow with spleen,
"Thy toils of the morning, like Ithaca's queen,
I'll toil to undo every night."

Ye sons of song, rejoice!
Veeshnoo has stilled the jarring elements,
The spheres hymn music;
Again the god of day
Peeps forth with trembling ray,
Wakes, from their humid caves, the sleeping Nine,
And pours at intervals a strain divine.
"I have an iron yet in the fire," cried Yamen;
"The vollied flame rides in my breath,
My blast is elemental death;
This hand shall tear your paper bonds to pieces;
Ingross your deeds, assignments, leases,

My breath shall every line erase
Soon as I blow the blaze."

The lawyers are met at the Crown and Anchor,
And Yamen's visage grows blanker and blanker;
The lawyers are met at the Anchor and Crown,
And Yamen's cheek is a russety brown:
Veeshnoo, now thy work proceeds;
The solicitor reads,
And, merit of merit!
Red wax and green ferret
Are fixed at the foot of the deeds!

Yamen beheld and shiver'd;
His finger and thumb were cramp'd;
His ear by the flea in 't was bitten,
When he saw by the lawyer's clerk written,
Sealed and delivered,
Being first duly stamped.

" Now for my turn!" the demon cries, and blows
A blast of sulphur from his mouth and nose.
Ah! bootless aim! the critic fiend,
Sagacious Yamen, judge of hell,
Is judged in his turn;
Parchment won't burn!
His schemes of vengeance are dissolved in air,
Parchment won't tear!!

Is it not written in the Himakoot book,
(That mighty Baly from Kehama took)
" Who blows on pounce
Must the Swerga renounce?"
It is! it is! Yamen, thine hour is nigh;

Like as an eagle claws an asp,
Veeshnoo has caught him in his mighty grasp,
And hurl'd him, in spite of his shrieks and his squalls,
Whizzing aloft, like the Temple fountain,
Three times as high as Meru mountain,
Which is
Ninety-nine times as high as St. Paul's.

Descending, he twisted like Levy the Jew,
Who a durable grave meant
To dig in the pavement
Of Monument-yard:
To earth by the laws of attraction he flew,
And he fell, and he fell
To the regions of hell;
Nine centuries bounced he from cavern to rock,
And his head, as he tumbled, went nickety-nock,
Like a pebble in Carisbrook well.

Now Veeshnoo turn'd round to a capering varlet,
Array'd in blue and white and scarlet,
And cried, "Oh! brown of slipper as of hat!
Lend me, Harlequin, thy bat!"
He seized the wooden sword, and smote the earth;
When lo! upstarting into birth
A fabric, gorgeous to behold,
Outshone in elegance the old,
And Veeshnoo saw, and cried, "Hail, playhouse mine!"
Then, bending his head, to Surya he said:
" Soon as thy maiden sister Di
Caps with her copper lid the dark blue sky,
And through the fissures of her clouded fan
Peeps at the naughty monster man,

REJECTED ADDRESSES.

Go mount yon edifice,
And show thy steady face
In renovated pride,
More bright, more glorious than before!"
But ah! coy Surya still felt a twinge,
Still smarted from his former singe;
And to Veeshnoo replied,
In a tone rather gruff,
" No, thank you! one tumble 's enough!"

DRURY'S DIRGE.

BY LAURA MATILDA.[1]

"You praise our sires : but though they wrote with force
Their rhymes were vicious, and their diction coarse :
We want their *strength*, agreed ; but we atone
For that, and more, by *sweetness* all our own."—GIFFORD.

I.

BALMY Zephyrs, lightly flitting,
   Shade me with your azure wing;
On Parnassus' summit sitting,
   Aid me, Clio, while I sing.

II.

Softly slept the dome of Drury
   O'er the empyreal crest,
When Alecto's sister-fury
   Softly slumb'ring sunk to rest.

III.

Lo ! from Lemnos limping lamely,
   Lags the lowly Lord of Fire,
Cytherea yielding tamely
   To the Cyclops dark and dire.

IV.

Clouds of amber, dreams of gladness,
   Dulcet joys and sports of youth,
Soon must yield to haughty sadness ;
   Mercy holds the veil to Truth.

V.

See Erostratus the second
    Fires again Diana's fane;
By the Fates from Orcus beckon'd,
    Clouds envelope Drury Lane.

VI.

Lurid smoke and frank suspicion
    Hand in hand reluctant dance:
While the God fulfils his mission,
    Chivalry, resign thy lance.

VII.

Hark! the engines blandly thunder,
    Fleecy clouds dishevell'd lie,
And the firemen, mute with wonder,
    On the son of Saturn cry.

VIII.

See the bird of Ammon sailing,
    Perches on the engine's peak,
And, the Eagle firemen hailing,
    Soothes them with its bickering beak.

IX.

Juno saw, and mad with malice,
    Lost the prize that Paris gave:
Jealousy's ensanguined chalice,
    Mantling pours the orient wave.

X.

Pan beheld Patroclus dying,
    Nox to Niobe was turn'd;
From Busiris Bacchus flying,
    Saw his Semele inurn'd.

XI.

Thus fell Drury's lofty glory,
    Levell'd with the shuddering stones;
Mars, with tresses black and gory,
    Drinks the dew of pearly groans.

XII.

Hark! what soft Eolian numbers
    Gem the blushes of the morn!
Break, Amphion, break your slumbers,
    Nature's ringlets deck the thorn.

XIII.

Ha! I hear the strain erratic
    Dimly glance from pole to pole;
Raptures sweet and dreams ecstatic
    Fire my everlasting soul.

XIV.

Where is Cupid's crimson motion?
    Billowy ecstasy of woe,
Bear me straight, meandering ocean,
    Where the stagnant torrents flow.

XV.

Blood in every vein is gushing,
    Vixen vengeance lulls my heart;
See, the Gorgon gang is rushing!
    Never, never let us part!

IX.

A TALE OF DRURY LANE.

BY W. S.

"Thus he went on, stringing one extravagance upon another, in the style his books of chivalry had taught him, and imitating, as near as he could, their very phrase."—DON QUIXOTE.[1]

[To be spoken by Mr. Kemble, in a suit of the Black Prince's armour, borrowed from the Tower.]

SURVEY this shield, all bossy bright—
These cuisses twain behold!
Look on my form in armour dight
Of steel inlaid with gold;
My knees are stiff in iron buckles,
Stiff spikes of steel protect my knuckles.
These once belonged to sable prince,
Who never did in battle wince;
With valour tart as pungent quince,
    He slew the vaunting Gaul.
Rest there awhile, my bearded lance,
While from green curtain I advance
To yon foot-lights, no trivial dance,[2]
And tell the town what sad mischance
    Did Drury Lane befall.

The Night.

On fair Augusta's towers and trees
Flitted the silent midnight breeze,
Curling the foliage as it past
Which from the moon-tipp'd plumage ca~

A spangled light, like dancing spray,
Then re-assumed its still array;
When, as night's lamp unclouded hung,
And down its full effulgence flung,
It shed such soft and balmy power
That cot and castle, hall and bower,
And spire and dome, and turret height,
Appeared to slumber in the light.
From Henry's chapel, Rufus' hall,
To Savoy, Temple, and St. Paul;
From Knightsbridge, Pancras, Camden Town,
To Redriffe, Shadwell, Horsleydown,
No voice was heard, no eye unclosed,
But all in deepest sleep reposed.
They might have thought, who gazed around
Amid a silence so profound,
 It made the senses thrill,
That 'twas no place inhabited,
But some vast city of the dead—
 All was so hushed and still.

The Burning.

As Chaos, which, by heavenly doom,
Had slept in everlasting gloom,
Started with terror and surprise
When light first flashed upon her eyes—
So London's sons in nightcap woke,
 In bed-gown woke her dames;
For shouts were heard 'mid fire and smoke,
And twice ten hundred voices spoke—
 "The playhouse is in flames!"
And, lo! where Catherine Street extends,
A fiery tail its lustre lends
 To every window-pane;

Blushes each spout in Martlet Court,
And Barbican, moth-eaten fort,
And Covent garden kennels sport,
 A bright ensanguined drain;
Meux's new Brewhouse shows the light,
Rowland Hill's Chapel, and the height
 Where Patent Shot they sell;
The Tennis Court, so fair and tall,
Partakes the ray, with Surgeons' Hall,
The Ticket-Porters' House of Call.
Old Bedlam, close by London Wall,
Wright's shrimp and oyster shop withal,
 And Richardson's Hotel.
Nor these alone, but far and wide,
Across red Thames's gleaming tide,
To distant fields, the blaze was borne,
And daisy white and hoary thorn
In borrow'd lustre seem'd to sham
The rose or red sweet Wil-li-am.
To those who on the hills around
Beheld the flames from Drury's mound,
 As from a lofty altar rise,
It seem'd that nations did conspire
To offer to the God of fire
 Some vast stupendous sacrifice!
The summon'd firemen woke at call,
And hied them to their stations all:
Starting from short and broken snooze,
Each sought his pond'rous hobnail'd shoes,
But first his worsted hosen plied,
Plush breeches next, in crimson dyed,
 His nether bulk embraced;
Then jacket thick, of red or blue,

A TALE OF DRURY LANE.

Whose massy shoulder gave to view
The badge of each respective crew,
 In tin or copper traced.
The engines thunder'd through the street,
Fire-hook, pipe, bucket, all complete,
And torches glared, and clattering feet
 Along the pavement paced.
And one, the leader of the band,
From Charing Cross along the Strand,
Like stag by beagles hunted hard,
Ran till he stopp'd at Vin'gar Yard.[5]
The burning badge his shoulder bore,
The belt and oil-skin hat he wore,
The cane he had, his men to bang,
Show'd foreman of the British gang—
His name was Higginbottom. Now
 'Tis meet that I should tell you how
 The others came in view:
The Hand-in-Hand-the race began,[6]
Then came the Phœnix and the Sun,
Th' Exchange, where old insurers run,
 The Eagle, where the new:
With these came Rumford, Bumford, Cole,
Robins from Hockley in the Hole,
Lawson and Dawson, cheek by jowl,
 Crump from St. Giles's Pound:
Whitford and Mitford joined the train,
Huggins and Muggins from Chick Lane,
And Clutterbuck, who got a sprain
 Before the plug was found.
Hobson and Jobson did not sleep,
But ah! no trophy could they reap,
For both were in the Donjon Keep
 Of Bridewell's gloomy mound!

E'en Higginbottom now was posed,
For sadder scene was ne'er disclosed ;
Without, within, in hideous show,
Devouring flames resistless glow,
And blazing rafters downward go,
And never halloo " Heads below !"
  Nor notice give at all.
The firemen terrified are slow
To bid the pumping torrent flow,
  For fear the roof should fall.
Back, Robins, back! Crump, stand aloof !
Whitford, keep near the walls !
Huggins, regard your own behoof,
For, lo! the blazing rocking roof
Down, down, in thunder falls !
An awful pause succeeds the stroke,
And o'er the ruins volumed smoke,
Rolling around its pitchy shroud,
Conceal'd them from th' astonish'd crowd.
At length the mist awhile was clear'd,
When, lo ! amid the wreck uprear'd,
Gradual a moving head appear'd,
  And Eagle firemen knew
'Twas Joseph Muggins, name revered,
  The foreman of their crew,
Loud shouted all in signs of woe,
" A Muggins ! to the rescue, ho !"
  And pour'd the hissing tide :
Meanwhile the Muggins fought amain,
And strove and struggled all in vain,
For, rallying but to fall again,
  He totter'd, sunk, and died !
Did none attempt, before he fell,
To succour one they loved so well ?

Yes, Higginbottom did aspire
(His fireman's soul was all on fire),
   His brother chief to save;
But ah! his reckless generous ire
   Served but to share his grave!
'Mid blazing beams and scalding streams,
Through fire and smoke he dauntless broke,
   Where Muggins broke before.
But sulphry stench and boiling drench
Destroying sight o'erwhelm'd him quite,
   He sunk to rise no more.
Still o'er his head, while Fate he braved,
His whizzing water-pipe he waved;
" Whitford and Mitford, ply your pumps,
" You, Clutterbuck, come, stir your stumps,
" Why are you in such doleful dumps?
" A fireman, and afraid of bumps!—
" What are they fear'd on? fools! 'od rot 'em!"
Were the last words of Higginbottom.

The Revival.

Peace to his soul! new prospects bloom,
And toil rebuilds what fires consume!
Eat we and drink we, be our ditty,
" Joy to the managing committee!"
Eat we and drink we, join to rum
Roast beef and pudding of the plum;
Forth from thy nook, John Horner, come,
With bread of ginger brown thy thumb,
   For this is Drury's gay day;
Roll, roll thy hoop, and twirl thy tops,
And buy, to glad thy smiling chops,
Crisp parliament with lollypops,
   And fingers of the Lady.

15

REJECTED ADDRESSES.

Didst mark, how toil'd the busy train,
From morn to eve, till Drury Lane
Leap'd like a roebuck from the plain?
Ropes rose and sunk, and rose again,
 And nimble workmen trod;
To realise bold Wyatt's plan
Rush'd many a howling Irishman;
Loud clatter'd many a porter-can,
And many a ragamuffin clan
 With trowel and with hod.

Drury revives! her rounded pate
Is blue, is heavenly blue with slate;
She "wings the midway air" elate,
 As magpie, crow, or chough;
White paint her modish visage smears,
Yellow and pointed are her ears,
No pendant portico appears
Dangling beneath, for Whitbread's shears[7]
 Have cut the bauble off.

Yes, she exalts her stately head;
And, but that solid bulk outspread,
Opposed you on your onward tread,
And posts and pillars warranted
That all was true that Wyatt said,
You might have deem'd her walls so thick
Were not composed of stone or brick,
But all a phantom, all a trick,
Of brain disturb'd and fancy sick,
So high she soars, so vast, so quick!

X.

JOHNSON'S GHOST.

[Ghost of Dr. Johnson rises from trap-door P. S., and Ghost of Boswell from trap-door O. P. The latter bows respectfully to the House, and obsequiously to the Doctor's Ghost, and retires.]

DOCTOR'S GHOST *loquitur.*

THAT which was organised by the moral ability of one has been executed by the physical efforts of many, and DRURY LANE THEATRE is now complete. Of that part behind the curtain, which has not yet been destined to glow beneath the brush of the varnisher, or viprate to the hammer of the carpenter, little is thought by the public, and little need be said by the committee. Truth, however, is not to be sacrificed for the accommodation of either; and he who should pronounce that our edifice has received its final embellishment would be disseminating falsehood without incurring favour, and risking the disgrace of detection without participating the advantage of success.

Professions lavishly effused and parsimoniously verified are alike inconsistent with the precepts of innate rectitude and the practice of external policy: let it not then be conjectured, that because we are unassuming, we are imbecile; that forbearance is any indication of despondency, or humility of demerit. He that is the most assured of success will make the fewest appeals to favour, and where nothing is claimed that is undue, nothing that is due will be withheld. A swelling opening is too often succeeded by an insignificant conclusion. Parturient mountains have ere now produced muscipular abortions; and the auditor who compares incipient grandeur with final vulgarity is reminded of the pious hawkers of Constantinople, who solemnly perambulate her streets, exclaiming, " In the name of the Prophet—figs !"

Of many who think themselves wise, and of some who are thought wise by others, the exertions are directed to the revival of mouldering and obscure dramas; to endeavours to exalt that which is now rare only because it was always worthless, and whose deterioration, while it condemned it to living obscurity, by a strange obliquity of moral perception constitutes its title to posthumous renown. To embody the flying colours of folly, to arrest evanescence, to give to bubbles the globular consistency as well as form, to exhibit on the stage the piebald denizen of the stable, and the half-reasoning parent of combs, to display the brisk locomotion of Columbine, or the tortuous attitudinising of Punch;—these are the occupations of others, whose ambition, limited to the applause of unintellectual fatuity, is too innocuous for the application of satire, and too humble for the incitement of jealousy.

Our refectory will be found to contain every species of fruit, from the cooling nectarine and luscious peach to the puny pippin and the noxious nut. There Indolence may repose, and Inebriety revel; and the spruce apprentice, rushing in at second account, may there chatter with impunity; debarred, by a barrier of brick and mortar, from marring that scenic interest in others, which nature and education have disqualified him from comprehending himself.

Permanent stage-doors we have none. That which is

permanent cannot be removed, for, if removed, it soon ceases to be permanent.. What stationary absurdity can vie with the ligneous barricado, which, decorated with frappant and tintinnabulant appendages, now serves as the entrance of the lowly cottage, and now as the exit of a lady's bedchamber; at one time, insinuating plastic Harlequin into a butcher's shop, and, at another, yawning as a flood-gate, to precipitate the Cyprians of St. Giles's into the embraces of Macheath. To elude this glaring absurdity, to give each respective mansion the door which the carpenter would doubtless have given, we vary our portal with the varying scene, passing from deal to mahogany, and from mahogany to oak, as the opposite claims of cottage, palace, or castle, may appear to require.

Amid the general hum of gratulation which flatters us in front, it is fit that some regard should be paid to the murmurs of despondence that assail us in the rear. They, as I have elsewhere expressed it, "who live to please," should not have their own pleasures entirely overlooked. The children of Thespis are general in their censures of the architect, in having placed the locality of exit at such a distance from the oily irradiators which now dazzle the eyes of him who addresses you. I am, cries the Queen of Terrors, robbed of my fair proportions. When the king-killing Thane hints to the breathless auditory the murders he means to, perpetrate, in the castle of Macduff, "ere his purpose cool;" so vast is the interval he has to travel before he can escape from the stage, that his purpose has even time to freeze. Your condition, cries the Muse of Smiles, is hard, but it is cygnet's down in comparison with mine. The peerless peer of capers and congees' has laid it down as a rule, that the best good thing uttered by the

morning visitor should conduct him rapidly to the door-
way, last impressions vying in durability with first.
But when, on this boarded elongation, it falls to my lot
to say a good thing, to ejaculate, "keep moving," or
to chant, "*hic hoc horum genitivo*," many are the
moments that must elapse, ere I can hide myself from
public vision in the recesses of O. P. or P. S.

To objections like these, captiously urged and queru-
lously maintained, it is time that equity should conclu-
sively reply.　Deviation from scenic propriety has only
to vituperate itself for the consequences it generates.
Let the actor consider the line of exit as that line beyond
which he should not soar in quest of spurious applause:
let him reflect, that in proportion as he advances to the
lamps, he recedes from nature; that the truncheon of
Hotspur acquires no additional charm from encountering
the cheek of beauty in the stage-box, and that the bra-
vura of Mandane may produce effect, although the
throat of her who warbles it should not overhang the
orchestra.　The Jove of the modern critical Olympus,
Lord Mayor of the theatric sky,[2] has, *ex cathedrâ*,
asserted, that a natural actor looks upon the audience
part of the theatre as the third side of the chamber he
inhabits.　Surely, of the third wall thus fancifully
erected, our actors should, by ridicule or reason, be
withheld from knocking their heads against the stucco.

Time forcibly reminds me, that all things which have
a limit must be brought to a conclusion.　Let me, ere
that conclusion arrives, recall to your recollection, that
the pillars which rise on either side of me, blooming in
virid antiquity, like two massy evergreens, had yet
slumbered in their native quarry, but for the ardent
exertions of the individual who called them into life: to
his never-slumbering talents you are indebted for what-

ever pleasure this haunt of the Muses is calculated to afford. If, in defiance of chaotic malevolence, the destroyer of the temple of Diana yet survives in the name of Erostratus, surely we may confidently predict, that the rebuilder of the temple of Apollo will stand recorded to distant posterity in that of—SAMUEL WHITBREAD.

XI.

THE BEAUTIFUL INCENDIARY.

BY THE HON. W. S.

Formosam resonare doces Amaryllida sylvas.—VIRGIL.

Scene draws, and discovers a Lady asleep on a couch.

Enter PHILANDER.

PHILANDER

I.

SOBRIETY, cease to be sober,[1]
  Cease Labour, to dig and to delve ;
All hail to this tenth of October,
  One thousand eight hundred and twelve ![2]
Ha ! whom do my peepers remark ?
  'Tis Hebe with Jupiter's jug ;
O no, 'tis the pride of the Park,
  Fair Lady Elizabeth Mugg.

II.

Why, beautiful nymph, do you close
  The curtain that fringes your eye ?
Why veil in the clouds of repose
  The sun that should brighten our sky !
Perhaps jealous Venus has oiled
  Your hair with some opiate drug,
Not choosing her charms should be foiled
  By Lady Elizabeth Mugg.

III.

But ah! why awaken the blaze
  Those bright-burning glasses contain,
Whose lens with concentrated rays
  Proved fatal to old Drury Lane?
'Twas all accidental, they cry—
  Away with the flimsy humbug!
'Twas fired by a flash from the eye
  Of Lady Elizabeth Mugg.

IV.

Thy glance can in us raise a flame,
  Then why should old Drury be free?
Our doom and its doom are the same,
  Both subject to beauty's decree.
No candles the workmen consumed,
  When deep in the ruins they dug;
Thy flash still their progress illumed,
  Sweet Lady Elizabeth Mugg.

V.

Thy face a rich fire-place displays:
  The mantel-piece marble—thy brows;
Thine eyes are the bright beaming blaze;
  Thy bib, which no trespass allows,
The fender's tall barrier marks;
  Thy tippet's the fire-quelling rug,
Which serves to extinguish the sparks
  Of Lady Elizabeth Mugg.

VI.

The Countess a lily appears,
  Whose tresses the pearl-drops emboss;
The Marchioness, blooming in years,
  A rose-bud enveloped in moss;

15*

But thou art the sweet passion-flower,
   For who would not slavery hug,
To pass but one exquisite hour,
   In the arms of Elizabeth Mugg?

VII.

When at court, or some Dowager's rout,
   Her diamond aigrette meets our view,
She looks like a glow-worm dressed out,
   Or tulips bespangled with dew.
Her two lips denied to man's suit,
   Are shared with her favourite Pug;
What lord would not change with the brute,
   To live with Elizabeth Mugg?

VIII.

Could the stage be a large vis-à-vis,
   Reserved for the polished and great,
Where each happy lover might see
   The nymph he adores tête-à-tête;
No longer I 'd gaze on the ground,
   And the load of despondency lug,
For I 'd book myself all the year round,
   To ride with the sweet Lady Mugg.

IX.

Yes, she in herself is a host,
   And if she were here all alone,
Our house might nocturnally boast
   A bumper of fashion and ton.
Again should it burst in a blaze,
   In vain would they ply Congreve's plug,[3]
For nought could extinguish the rays
   From the glance of divine Lady Mugg.

X.

O could I as Harlequin frisk,
　And thou be my Columbine fair,
My wand should with one magic whisk
　Transport us to Hanover Square:
St. George's should lend us its shrine,
　The parson his shoulders might shrug,
But a license should force him to join
　My hand in the hand of my Mugg.

IX.

Court-plaster the weapons should tip,
　By Cupid shot down from above,
Which, cut into spots for thy lip,
　Should still barb the arrows of love.
The God who from others flies quick,
　With us should be slow as a slug;
As close as a leech he should stick
　To me and Elizabeth Mugg.

X.

For time would, with us, 'stead of sand,
　Put filings of steel in his glass,
To dry up the blots of his hand,
　And spangle life's page as they pass.
Since all flesh is grass ere 'tis hay,⁴
　O may I in clover live snug,
And when old Time mows me away,
　Be stacked with defunct Lady Mugg!

XII.

FIRE AND ALE.

BY M. G. L.

Omnia transformat sese in miracula rerum.—VIRGIL.

My palate is parched with Pierian thirst,
    Away to Parnassus I'm beckoned ;
List, warriors and dames, while my lay is rehearsed,
I sing of the singe of Miss Drury the first,
    And the birth of Miss Drury the second.

The Fire King, one day, rather amorous felt ;
    He mounted his hot copper filly ;
His breeches and boots were of tin, and the belt
Was made of cast iron, for fear it should melt
    With the heat of the copper colt's belly.

Sure never was skin half so scalding as his !
    When an infant 'twas equally horrid ;
For the water, when he was baptized, gave a fizz,
And bubbled and simmer'd and started off, whizz !
    As soon as it sprinkled its forehead.

O ! then there was glitter and fire in each eye,
    For two living coals were the symbols ;
His teeth were calcined, and his tongue was so dry,
It rattled against them, as though you should try
    To play the piano in thimbles.

From his nostrils a lava sulphureous flows,
　　Which scorches wherever it lingers;
A snivelling fellow he's call'd by his foes,
For he can't ra'se his paw up to blow his red nose,
　　For fear it should blister his fingers.

His wig is of flames curling over his head,
　　Well powder'd with white smoking ashes;
He drinks gunpowder tea, melted sugar of lead,
Cream of tartar, and dines on hot spice gingerbread,
　　Which black from the oven he gnashes.

Each fire-nymph his kiss from her countenance shields,
　　'Twould soon set her cheek bone a frying;
He spit in the Tenter-Ground near Spital-fields,
And the hole that it burnt, and the chalk that it yields,
　　Make a capital lime-kiln for drying.

When he open'd his mouth, out there issued a blast,
　　(Nota bene, I do not mean swearing,)
But the noise that it made, and the heat that it cast,
I 've heard it from those who have seen it, surpass'd
　　A shot manufactory flaring.

He blazed, and he blazed, as he gallop'd to snatch
　　His bride, little dreaming of danger;
His whip was a torch, and his spur was a match,
And over the horse's left eye was a patch,
　　To keep it from burning the manger.

And who is the housemaid he means to enthral
　　In his cinder-producing alliance?
'Tis Drury-Lane Playhouse, so wide, and so tall,
Who, like other combustible ladies, must fall,
　　If she cannot set sparks at defiance.

On his warming-pan kneepan he clattering roll'd,
    And the housemaid his hand would have taken,
But his hand, like his passion, was too hot to hold,
And she soon let it go, but her new ring of gold
    All melted, like butter or bacon!

Oh! then she look'd sour, and indeed well she might,
    For Vinegar Yard was before her;
But, spite of her shrieks, the ignipotent knight,
Enrobing the maid in a flame of gas light,
    To the skies in a sky-rocket bore her.

Look! look! 'tis the Ale King, so stately and starch,
    Whose votaries scorn to be sober;
He pops from his vat, like a cedar or larch;
Brown-stout is his doublet, he hops in his march,
    And froths at the mouth in October.

His spear is a spigot, his shield is a bung;
    He taps where the housemaid no more is,
When lo! at his magical bidding, upsprung
A second Miss Drury, tall, tidy and young,
    And sported *in loco sororis.*

Back, lurid in air, for a second regale,
    The Cinder King, hot with desire,
To Bridges Street hied; but the Monarch of Ale,
With uplifted spigot and faucet, and pail,
    Thus chided the Monarch of Fire:

" Vile tyrant, beware of the ferment I brew;
    I rule the roast here, dash the wig o' me!
If, spite of your marriage with Old Drury, you
Come here with your tinderbox, courting the New,
    I'll have you indicted for bigamy!"

XIII.

PLAYHOUSE MUSINGS.

BY S. T. C.

Ille velut fidis arcana sodalibus olim
Credebat libris: neque si male cesserat, usquam
Decurrens alio, neque si bene. HOR.

My pensive Public, wherefore look you sad?
I had a grandmother, she kept a donkey
To carry to the mart her crockery ware,
And when that donkey look'd me in the face,
His face was sad! and you are sad, my Public!

   Joy should be yours: this tenth day of October
Again assembles us in Drury Lane.
Long wept my eye to see the timber planks
That hid our ruins; many a day I cried,
Ah me! I fear they never will rebuild it!
Till on one eve, one joyful Monday eve,
As along Charles Street I prepared to walk,
Just at the corner, by the pastrycook's,
I heard a trowel tick against a brick.
I look'd me up, and straight a parapet
Uprose at least seven inches o'er the planks.
Joy to thee, Drury! to myself I said:
'He of Backfriars' Road, who hymned thy downfall
In loud Hosannahs, and who prophesied
That flames, like those from prostrate Solyma,

Would scorch the hand that ventured to rebuild thee,
Has proved a lying prophet.   From that hour,
As leisure offer'd, close to Mr. Spring's
Box-office door, I've stood and eyed the builders.
They had a plan to render less their labours;
Workmen in olden times would mount a ladder
With ho lded heads, but these stretched forth a pole
From the wall's pinnacle, they placed a pulley
Athwart the pole, a rope athwart the pulley;
To this a basket dangled; mortar and bricks
Thus freighted, swung securely to the top,
And in the empty basket workmen twain
Precipitate, unhurt, accosted earth.

Oh! 'twas a goodly sound, to hear the people
Who watch'd the work, express their various thoughts!
While some believed it never would be finish'd,
Some, on the contrary, believed it would.

I've heard our front that faces Drury Lane
Much criticised; they say 'tis vulgar brick-work,
A mimic manufactory of floor-cloth.
One of the morning papers wish'd that front
Cemented like the front in Brydges Street;
As now it looks, they call it Wyatt's Mermaid,
A handsome woman with a fish's tail.

White is the steeple of St. Bride's in Fleet Street:
The Albion (as its name denotes) is white;
Morgan and Saunders' shop for chairs and tables
Gleams like a snow-ball in the setting sun;
White is Whitehall.   But not St. Bride's in Fleet
          Street,

The spotless Albion, Morgan, no, nor Saunders,
Nor white Whitehall, is white as Drury's face.

    ²Oh, Mr. Whitbread! fie upon you, sir!
I think you should have built a colonnade;
When tender Beauty, looking for her coach,
Protrudes her gloveless hand, perceives the shower
And draws the tippet closer round her throat,
Perchance her coach stands half a dozen off,
And, ere she mounts the step, the oozing mud
Soaks through her pale kid slipper.   On the morrow,
She coughs at breakfast, and her gruff papa
Cries, "There you go! this comes of playhouses!"
To build no portico is penny wise:
Heaven grant it prove not in the end pound foolish!

    Hail to thee, Drury! Queen of Theatres!
What is the Regency in Tottenham Street,
The Royal Amphitheatre of Arts,
Astley's, Olympic, or the Sans Pareil,
Compared with thee? Yet when I view thee push'd
Back from the narrow street that christened thee,
I know not why they call thee Drury Lane.

    Amid the freaks that modern fashion sanctions,
It grieves me much to see live animals
Brought on the stage.   Grimaldi has his rabbit,
Laurent his cat, and Bradbury his pig;
Fie on such tricks! Johnson, the machinist
Of former Drury, imitated life
Quite to the life.   The Elephant in Blue Beard,
Stuff'd by his hand, wound round his lithe proboscis,
As spruce as he who roar'd in Padmanaba.³
Nought born on earth should die.   On hackney stands

I reverence the coachman who cries " Gee,"
And spares the lash.   When I behold a spider
Prey on a fly, a magpie on a worm,
Or view a butcher with horn-handled knife
Slaughter a tender lamb as dead as mutton,
Indeed, indeed, I'm very, very sick!
                              [*Exit hastily.*

XIV.

DRURY LANE HUSTINGS.

A New Halfpenny Ballad.

BY A PIC-NIC POET.

This is the very age of promise: To promise is most courtly and fashionable. Performance is a kind of will or testament, which argues a great sickness in his judgment that makes it.—TIMON OF ATHENS.

[To be sung by MR. JOHNSTONE *in the character of* LOOKEY M'TWOLTER.]

I.

MR. JACK, your address, says the Prompter to me,
So I gave him my card—no, that a'nt it, says he ;
'Tis your public address.   Oh ! says I, never fear,
If address you are bother'd for, only look here.

[Puts on hat affectedly.
Tol de rol lol, &c.

II.

With Drury's for sartin we 'll never have done,
We 've built up another, and yet there 's but one ;
The old one was best, yet I 'd say, if I durst,
The new one is better—the last is the first.

Tol de rol, &c.

III.

These pillars are call'd by a Frenchified word,
A something that's jumbled of antique and verd ;
The boxes may show us some verdant antiques,
Some old harridans who beplaster their cheeks.

Tol de rol, &c.

IV.

Only look how high Tragedy, Comedy, stick,
Lest their rivals, the horses, should give them a kick !
If you will not descend when our authors beseech ye,
You 'll stop there for life, for I 'm sure they can 't
    reach ye.
                        Tol de rol, &c.

V.

Each one shilling god within the reach o. a nod is,
And plain are the charms of each gallery goddess—
You, Brandy-faced Moll, don't be looking askew,
When I talked of a goddess I didn't mean you.
                        Tol de rol, &c.

VI.

Our stage is so prettily fashion'd for viewing,
The whole house can see what the whole house is doing :
'Tis just like the Hustings, we kick up a bother ;
But saying is one thing, and doing's another.
                        Tol de rol, &c.

VII.

We 've many new houses, and some of them rum ones,
But the newest of all is the new House of Commons ;
'Tis a rickety sort of a bantling, I 'm told,
It will die of old age when it 's seven years old.
                        Tol de rol, &c.

VIII.

As I don't know on whom the election will fall,
I move in return for returning them all ;
But for fear Mr. Speaker my meaning should miss,
The house that I wish 'em to sit in is this.
                        Tol de rol, &c.

IX.

Let us cheer our great Commoner, but for whose aid
We all should have gone with short commons to bed;
And since he has saved all the fat from the fire,
I move that the house be call'd Whitbread's Entire.'

Tol de rol, &c.

ARCHITECTURAL ATOMS.

TRANSLATED BY DR. B.

Lege, Dick, Lege!—JOSEPH ANDREWS.

To be recited by the Translator's Son.

AWAY, fond dupes! who, smit with sacred lore,
Mosaic dreams in Genesis explore,
Doat with Copernicus, or darkling stray
With Newton, Ptomley, or Tycho Brahe!
To you I sing not, for I sing of truth,
Primeval systems, and creation's youth;
Such as of old, with magic wisdom fraught,
Inspired LUCRETIUS to the Latians taught.

I sing how casual bricks, in airy climb,
Encounter'd casual cow-hair, casual lime;
How rafters, borne through wondering clouds elate,
Kiss'd in their slope blue elemental slate,
Clasp'd solid beams in chance-directed fury,
And gave to birth our renovated Drury.

Thee, son of Jove! whose sceptre was confess'd,
Where fair Æolia springs from Tethys' breast;
Thence on Olympus, 'mid celestials placed,
GOD OF THE WINDS, and Ether's boundless waste—
Thee I invoke! Oh *puff* my bold design,   [line;
Prompt the bright thought, and swell th' harmonious

Uphold my pinions, and my verse inspire
With Winsor's [1] patent gas, or wind of fire,
In whose pure blaze thy embryo form enroll'd,
The dark enlightens, and enchafes the cold.

But, while I court thy gifts, be mine to shun
The deprecated prize Ulysses won ;
Who, sailing homeward from the breezy shore,
The prison'd winds in skins of parchment bore.
Speeds the fleet bark till o'er the billows green
The azure heights of Ithaca are seen ;
But while with favouring gales her way she wins,
His curious comrades ope the mystic skins ;
When, lo ! the rescued winds, with boisterous sweep,
Roar to the clouds and lash the rocking deep ;
Heaves the smote vessel in the howling blast,
Splits the stretch'd sail, and cracks the tottering mast.
Launch'd on a plank, the buoyant hero rides,
Where ebon Afric stems the sable tides,
While his duck'd comrades o'er the ocean fly,
And sleep not in the whole skins they untie.

So, when to raise the wind some lawyer tries,
Mysterious skins of parchment meet our eyes ;
On speeds the smiling suit—" Pleas of our Lord
The King" shine sable on the wide record ;
Nods the prunella'd bar, attorneys smile,
And syren jurors flatter to beguile ;
Till stript—nonsuited—he is doomed to toss
In legal shipwreck and redeemless loss !
Lucky, if, like Ulysses, he can keep,
His head above the waters of the deep.

Æolian monarch ! Emperor of Puffs !
We modern sailors dread not thy rebuffs ;

See to thy golden shore promiscuous come
Quacks for the lame, the blind, the deaf, the dumb;
Fools are their bankers——a prolific line,
And every mortal malady 's a mine.
Each sly Sangrado, with his poisonous pill,
Flies to the printer's devil with his bill,
Whose Midas touch can gild his ass's ears,
And load a knave with folly's rich arrears.
And lo ! a second miracle is thine,
For sloe-juice water stands transformed to wine.
Where Day and Martin's patent blacking roll'd,
Burst from the vase Pactolian streams of gold ;
Laugh the sly wizards, glorying in their stealth,
Quit the black art, and loll in lazy wealth.
See Britain's Algerines, the lottery fry,
Win annual tribute by the annual lie !
Aided by thee——but whither do I stray ?——
Court, city, borough, own thy sovereign sway ;
An age of puffs an age of gold succeeds,
And windy bubbles are the spawn it breeds.

If such thy power, O hear the Muse's prayer !
Swell thy loud lungs and wave thy wings of air ;
Spread, viewless giant, all thy arms of mist
Like windmill-sails to bring the poet grist ;
As erst thy roaring son, with eddying gale,
Whirl'd Orithyia from her native vale——
So, while Lucretian wonders I rehearse,
Augusta's sons shall patronise my verse.

I sing of ATOMS, whose creative brain,
With eddying impulse, built new Drury Lane ;
Not to the labours of subservient man,
To no young Wyatt appertains the plan——

We mortals stalk, like horses in a mill,
Impassive media of atomic will;
Ye stare! then Truth's broad talisman discern—
'Tis demonstration speaks—attend, and learn!

From floating elements in Chaos hurl'd,
Self-form'd of atoms, sprang the infant world:
No great *First Cause* inspired the happy plot,
But all was matter—and no matter what.
Atoms, attracted by some law occult,
Settling in spheres, the globe was the result;
Pure child of *Chance*, which still directs the ball,
As rotatory atoms rise or fall.
In ether launch'd, the peopled bubble floats,
A mass of particles and confluent motes,
So nicely poised, that if one atom flings
Its weight away, aloft the planet springs,
And wings its course through realms of boundless space,
Outstripping comets in eccentric race.
Add but one atom more, it sinks outright
Down to the realms of Tartarus and night.
What waters melt or scorching fires consume,
In different forms their being re-assume:
Hence can no change arise, except in name,
For weight and substance ever are the same.

Thus with the flames that from old Drury rise
Its elements primeval sought the skies;
There pendulous to wait the happy hour
When new attractions should restore their power:
So, in this procreant theatre elate,
Echoes unborn their future life await:
Here embryo sounds in ether lie conceal'd,
Like words in northern atmosphere congeal'd.

16

Here many a fœtus laugh and half encore
Clings to the roof, or creeps along the floor;
By puffs concipient some in ether flit,
And soar in bravos from the thundering pit:
Some forth on ticket-nights' from tradesmen break,
To mar the actor they design to make;
While some this mortal life abortive miss,
Crush'd by a groan, or strangled by a hiss.
So, when " Dog's-meat" re-echoes through the streets,
Rush sympathetic dogs from their retreats,
Beam with bright blaze their supplicating eyes,
Sink their hind-legs, ascend their joyful cries;
Each, wild with hope, and maddening to prevail,
Points the pleased ear, and wags the expectant tail.

Ye fallen bricks! in Drury's fire calcined,
Since doom'd to slumber, couch'd upon the wind,
Sweet was the hour, when, tempted by your freaks,
Congenial trowels smooth'd your yellow cheeks.
Float dulcet serenades upon the ear,
Bends every atom from its ruddy sphere,
Twinkles each eye, and, peeping from its veil,
Marks in the adverse crowd its destined male.
The oblong beauties clap their hands of grit,
And brick-dust titterings on the breezes flit;
Then down they rush in amatory race,
Their dusty bridegrooms eager to embrace.
Some choose old lovers, some decide for new,
But each, when fix'd, is to her station true.
Thus various bricks are made, as tastes invite—
The red, the gray, the dingy, or the white.

Perhaps some half-baked rover, frank and free,
To alien beauty bends the lawless knee.

But of unhallow'd fascinations sick,
Soon quits his Cyprian for his married brick ;
The Dido atom calls and scolds in vain,
No crisp Æneas soothes the widow's pain.

So in Cheapside, what time Aurora peeps,
A mingled noise of dustmen, milk, and sweeps,
Falls on the housemaid's ear : amazed she stands,
Then opes the door with cinder-sabled hands,
And "Matches" calls. The dustman, bubbled flat,
Thinks 'tis for him, and doffs his fan-tail'd hat ;
The milkman, whom her second cries assail,
With sudden sink unyokes the clinking pail ;
Now louder grown, by turns she screams and weeps—
Alas! her screaming only brings the sweeps.
Sweeps but put out—she wants to raise a flame,
And calls for matches, but 'tis all the same.
Atoms and housemaids! mark the moral true—
If once ye go astray, no *match* for you!

As atoms in one mass united mix,
So bricks attraction feel for kindred bricks :
Some in the cellar view, perchance, on high,
Fair chimney chums on beds of mortar lie :
Enamour'd of the sympathetic clod,
Leaps the red bridegroom to the labourer's hod :
And up the ladder bears the workman, taught
To think he bears the bricks—mistaken thought!
A proof behold : if near the top they find
The nymphs or broken-corner'd or unkind,
Back to the base, "resulting with a bound,"[3]
They bear their bleeding carriers to the ground!

So legends tell along the lofty hill
Paced the twin heroes, gallant Jack and Jill ;

On trudged the Gemini to reach the rail
That shields the well's top from the expectant pail,
When, ah! Jack falls; and, rolling in the rear,
Jill feels the attraction of his kindred sphere;
Head over heels begins his toppling track,
Throws sympathetic somersets with Jack,
And at the mountain's base bobs plump against him, whack!

Ye living atoms, who unconscious sit,
Jumbled by chance in gallery, box, and pit,
For you no Peter opes the fabled door,
No churlish Charon plies the shadowy oar;
Breathe but a space, and Boreas' casual sweep
Shall bear your scatter'd corses o'er the deep,
To gorge the greedy elements, and mix
With water, marl, and clay, and stones, and sticks;
While, charged with fancied souls, sticks, stones, and clay,
Shall take your seats, and hiss or clap the play.

O happy age! when convert Christians read
No sacred writings but the Pagan creed—
O happy age! when, spurning Newton's dreams,
Our poets' sons recite Lucretian themes,
Abjure the idle systems of their youth,
And turn again to atoms and to truth;—
O happier still! when England's dauntless dames,
Awed by no chaste alarms, no latent shames,
The bard's fourth book unblushingly peruse,
And learn the rampant lessons of the stews!

All hail, Lucretius! renovated sage!
Unfold the modest mystics of thy page;
Return no more to thy sepulchral shelf,
But live, kind bard—that I may live myself.

XVI.

THEATRICAL ALARM-BELL.

BY THE EDITOR OF THE M. P.

"Bounce, Jupiter, bounce!"—O'HARA.

LADIES AND GENTLEMEN,

As it is now the universally-admitted, and indeed pretty-generally-suspected, aim of Mr. Whitbread and the infamous, bloodthirsty, and, in fact, illiberal faction to which he belongs, to burn to the ground this free and happy Protestant city, and establish himself in St. James's Palace, his fellow committeemen have thought it their duty to watch the principles of a theatre built under his auspices. The information they have received from an undoubted authority—particularly from an old fruit-woman who had turned king's evidence, and whose name, for obvious reasons, we forbear to mention, though we have had it some weeks in our possession—has induced them to introduce various reforms—not such reforms as the vile factions clamour for, meaning thereby revolution, but such reforms as are necessary to preserve the glorious constitution of the only free, happy, and prosperous country now left upon the face of the earth. From the valuable and authentic source above alluded to, we have learnt that a sanguinary plot has been formed by some united Irishmen, combined with a gang of Luddites, and a special committee sent over by the Pope at the instigation of the beastly Corsican fiend, for destroying all the loyal part of the audience on the anniversary of that deeply-to-be-abhorred-and-highly-to-be-blamed stratagem, the Gunpowder Plot, which falls this year on Thursday the fifth of November. The whole is under the direction of a delegated committee of O. P's whose treasonable exploits at Covent Garden you all recollect, and all of whom would have been hung from the chandeliers at that time, but for the mistaken lenity of government. At a given signal, a well-known O. P. was to cry out from the gallery, " Nosey ! Music !" whereupon all the O. P.'s were to produce from their inside pockets a long pair of shears, edged with felt, to prevent their making any noise, manufactured expressly. by a wretch at Birmingham, one of Mr. Brougham's evidences, and now in custody. With these they were to cut off the heads of all the loyal N. P.'s in the house, without distinction of sex or age. At the signal, similarly given, of "Throw him over !" which it now appears always alluded to the overthrow of our never-sufficiently-enough - to-be-deeply-and-universally-to - be-venerated constitution, all the heads of the N. P.'s were to be thrown at the fiddler, to prevent their appearing in evidence, or perhaps as a false and illiberal insinuation that they have no heads of their own. All that we know of the further designs of these incendiaries is, that they are by-a-great-deal-too-much-too-horrible-to-be-mentioned.

The manager has acted with his usual promptitude on this trying occasion. He has contracted for 300 tons of gunpowder, which are at this moment placed in a small barrel under the pit; and a descendant of Guy Faux, assisted by Col. Congreve, has undertaken to blow up the house, when necessary, in so novel and ingenious a manner, that every O. P. shall be annihilated, while not a whisker of the N. P.'s shall be singed. This strikingly displays the advantages of loyalty and attachment to government. Several other hints have been taken from the theatrical regulations of the not-a-bit-the-less-on-that-account-to-be-universally-execrated monster Bonaparte. A park of artillery, provided with chain-shot, is to be stationed on the stage, and play upon the audience, in case of any indication of misplaced applause or popular discontent (which accounts for the large space between the curtain and the lamps); and the public will participate our satisfaction in learning that the indecorous custom of standing up with the hat on is to be abolished, as the Bow-street officers are provided with daggers, and have orders to stab all such persons to the heart, and send their bodies to Surgeons' Hall. Gentlemen who cough are only to be slightly wounded. Fruit-women bawling "Bill of the Play!" are to be forthwith shot, for which purpose soldiers will be stationed in the slips, and ball-cartridge is to be served out with the lemonade. If any of the spectators happen to sneeze or spit, they are to be transported for life; and any person who is so tall as to prevent another seeing, is to be dragged out and sent on board the tender, or, by an instrument to be taken out of the pocket of Procrustes, to be forthwith cut shorter, either at the head or foot, according as his own convenience may dictate.

Thus, ladies and gentlemen, have the committee, through my medium, set forth the not-in-a-hurry-to-be-paralleled plan they have adopted for preserving order and decorum within the walls of their magnificent edifice. Nor have they, while attentive to their own concerns, by any means overlooked those of the cities of London and Westminster. Finding on enumeration,

that they have with a with-two-hands-and-one-tongue-
to-be-applauded liberality contracted for more gunpow-
der than they want, they have parted with the surplus
to the mattock-carrying and hustings-hammering high-
bailiff of Westminster, who has, with his own shovel,
dug a large hole in the front of the parish-church of
St. Paul, Covent Garden, that, upon the least symptom
of ill-breeding in the mob at the general election, the
whole of the market may be blown into the air.   This,
ladies and gentlemen, may at first make provisions *rise*,
but we pledge the credit of our theatre that they will
soon *fall* again, and people be supplied, as usual, with
vegetables, in the in-general-strewed-with-cabbage-stalks-
but-on-Saturday-night-lighted-up-with-lamps market of
Covent Garden.

 I should expatiate more largely on the other advan-
tages of the glorious constitution of these by-the-whole-
of-Europe-envied realms, but I am called away to take
an account of the ladies, and other artificial flowers of a
fashionable rout, of which a full and particular account
will hereafter appear.   For the present, my fashionable
intelligence is scanty, on account of the opening of
Drury Lane; and the ladies and gentlemen who honour
me will not be surprised to find nothing under my usual
head ! !

XVII.

THE THEATRE.

BY THE REV. G. C.

" Nil intentatum nostri liquére poetæ,
Nec minimum meruére decus, vestigia Græca
Ausi deserere, et celebrare domestica facta."   Hor.

A PREFACE OF APOLOGIES.[1]

IF the following poem should be fortunate enough to be selected for the opening address, a few words of explanation may be deemed necessary, on my part, to avert invidious misrepresentation. The animadversion I have thought it right to make on the noise created by tuning the orchestra, will, I hope, give no lasting remorse to any of the gentlemen employed in the band. It is to be desired that they would keep their instruments ready tuned, and strike off at once. This would be an accommodation to many well-meaning persons who frequent the theatre, who, not being blest with the ear of St. Cecilia, mistake the tuning for the overture, and think the latter concluded before it is begun.

> *" ————one fiddle will*
> *Give, half ashamed, a tiny flourish still,"*

was originally written "one hautboy will;" but, having providentially been informed, when this poem was on the point of being sent off, that there is but one hautboy in the band, I averted the storm of popular and managerial indignation from the head of its blower : as it now stands,

16*

" one fiddle" among many, the faulty individual, will, I hope, escape detection. The story of the flying play-bill is calculated to expose a practice much too common, of pinning play-bills to the cushions insecurely, and frequently, I fear, not pinning them at all. If these lines save one play-bill only from the fate I have recorded, I shall not deem my labour ill employed. The concluding episode of Patrick Jennings glances at the boorish fashion of wearing the hat in the one-shilling gallery. Had Jennings thrust his between his feet at the commencement of the play, he might have leaned forward with impunity, and the catastrophe I relate would not have occurred. The line of handkerchiefs formed to enable him to recover his loss, is purposely so crossed in texture and materials as to mislead the reader in respect to the real owner of any one of them. For, in the statistical view of life and manners which I occasionally present, my clerical profession has taught me how extremely improper it would be, by any allusion, however slight, to give any uneasiness, however trivial, to any individual, however foolish or wicked.

G. C.

THE THEATRE.

'Tis sweet to view, from half-past five to six,
Our long wax-candles, with short cotton wicks,
Touch'd by the lamplighter's Promethean art,
Start into light, and make the lighter start;
To see red Phœbus through the gallery-pane
Tinge with his beam the beams of Drury Lane;
While gradual parties fill our widen'd pit,
And gape, and gaze, and wonder, ere they sit.

At first, while vacant seats give choice and ease,
Distant or near, they settle where they please:
But when the multitude contracts the span,
And seats are rare, they settle where they can.

Now the full benches to late-comers doom
No room for standing, miscall'd *standing room.*

Hark! the check-taker moody silence breaks,
And bawling "Pit full!" gives the check he takes;
Yet onward still the gathering numbers cram,
Contending crowders shout the frequent damn,
And all is bustle, squeeze, row, jabbering, and jam.

See to their desks Apollo's sons repair—
Swift rides the rosin o'er the horse's hair !
In unison their various tones to tune,
Murmurs the hautboy, growls the hoarse bassoon ;
In soft vibration sighs the whispering lute,
Tang goes the harpsichord, too-too the flute,
Brays the loud trumpet, squeaks the fiddle sharp,
Winds the French-horn, and twangs the tingling harp ;
Till, like great Jove, the leader, figuring in,
Attunes to order the chaotic din.
Now all seems hush'd—but, no, one fiddle will
Give, half-ashamed, a tiny flourish still.
Foil'd in his crash, the leader of the clan
Reproves with frowns the dilatory man :
Then on his candlestick thrice taps his bow,
Nods a new signal, and away they go.

Perchance, while pit and gallery cry, " Hats off !"
And awed Consumption checks his chided cough,
Some giggling daughter of the Queen of Love
Drops, reft of pin, her play-bill from above :
Like Icarus, while laughing galleries clap,
Soars, ducks, and dives in air the printed scrap ;
But, wiser far than he, combustion fears,
And, as it flies, eludes the chandeliers ;
Till, sinking gradual, with repeated twirl,
It settles, curling, on a fiddler's curl ;
Who from his powder'd pate the intruder strikes,
And, from mere malice, sticks it on the spikes.

Say, why these Babel strains from Babel tongues ?
Who 's that calls " Silence !" with such leathern lungs ?
He who, in quest of quiet, " Silence !" hoots,
Is apt to make the hubbub he imputes.

What various swains our motley walls contain !—
Fashion from Moorfields, honour from Chick Lane;
Bankers from Paper Buildings here resort,
Bankrupts from Golden Square and Riches Court;
From the Haymarket canting rogues in grain,
Gulls from the Poultry, sots from Water Lane;
The lottery-cormorant, the auction-shark,
The full-price master, and the half-price clerk;
Boys who long linger at the gallery-door,
With pence twice five—they want but twopence more;
Till some Samaritan the twopence spares,
And sends them jumping up the gallery-stairs.

Critics we boast who ne'er their malice balk,
But talk their minds—we wish they'd mind their talk;
Big-worded bullies, who by quarrels live—
Who give the lie, and tell the lie they give;
Jews from St. Mary Axe,[2] for jobs so wary,
That for old clothes they'd even axe St. Mary;
And bucks with pockets empty as their pate,
Lax in their gaiters, laxer in their gait;
Who oft, when we our house lock up, carouse
With tippling tipstaves in a lock-up house.

Yet here, as elsewhere, Chance can joy bestow,
For scowling Fortune seem'd to threaten woe.

John Richard William Alexander Dwyer
Was footman to Justinian Stubbs, Esquire;
But when John Dwyer listed in the Blues,
Emanuel Jennings polish'd Stubbs's shoes.
Emanuel Jennings brought his youngest boy
Up as a corn-cutter—a safe employ;
In Holy-well Str.et, St. Pancras, he was bred

(At number twenty-seven, it is said),
Facing the pump, and near the Granby's Head:
He would have bound him to some shop in town,
But with a premium he could not come down.
Pat was the urchin's name—a red-hair'd youth,
Fonder of purl and skittle grounds than truth.

Silence, ye gods! to keep your tongues in awe,
The Muse shall tell an accident she saw.

Pat Jennings in the upper gallery sat,
But, leaning forward, Jennings lost his hat:
Down from the gallery the beaver flew,
And spurn'd the one to settle in the two.
How shall he act ? Pay at the gallery-door
Two shillings for what cost, when new, but four ?
Or till half-price, to save his shilling, wait,
And gain his hat again at half-past eight ?
Now, while his fears anticipate a thief,
John Mullens whispers, "Take my handkerchief."
"Thank you," cries Pat; "but one won't make a line."
"Take mine," cried Wilson ; and cried Stokes, "Take
　　　mine."
A motley cable soon Pat Jennings ties,
Where Spitalfields with real India vies.
Like Iris' bow, down darts the painted clue,
Starr'd, striped, and spotted, yellow, red, and blue,
Old calico, torn silk, and muslin new.
George Green below, with palpitating hand,
Loops the last 'kerchief to the beaver's band—
Upsoars the prize ! The youth with joy unfeign'd,
Regain'd the felt, and felt what he regain'd :
While to the applauding galleries grateful Pat
Made a low bow, and touch'd the ransom'd hat.

TO THE MANAGING COMMITTEE OF THE NEW DRURY LANE THEATRE.

GENTLEMEN,

Happening to be wool-gathering at the foot of Mount Parnassus, I was suddenly seized with a violent travestie in the head. The first symptoms I felt were several triple rhymes floating about my brain, accompanied by a singing in my throat, which quickly communicated itself to the ears of every body about me, and made me a burthen to my friends and a torment to Dr. Apollo; three of whose favourite servants—that is to say, Macbeth, his butcher; Mrs. Haller, his cook; and George Barnwell, his book-keeper—I waylaid in one of my fits of insanity, and mauled after a very frightful fashion. In this woeful crisis, I accidentally heard of your invaluable New Patent Hissing Pit, which cures every disorder incident to Grub Street. I send you inclosed a more detailed specimen of my case: if you could mould it into the shape of an address, to be said or sung on the first night of your performance, I have no doubt that I should feel the immediate effects of your invaluable New Patent Hissing Pit, of which they tell me one hiss is a dose.

I am, &c.,
MOMUS MEDLAR.

CASE No. I.

MACBETH.

[Enter Macbeth in a red nightcap. Page following with a torch.]

Go, boy, and thy good mistress tell
    (She knows that my purpose is cruel),
I 'd thank her to tingle her bell
    As soon as she 's heated my gruel.
Go, get thee to bed and repose—
    To sit up so late is a scandal;
But ere you have ta'en off your clothes,
    Be sure that you put out that candle.
              Ri fol de rol tol de rol lol.

My stars, in the air here 's a knife!—
    I 'm sure it can not be a hum;
I 'll catch at the handle, add's life!
    And then I shall not cut my thumb.
I 've got him!—no, at him again!
    Come, come, I 'm not fond of these jokes;
This must be some blade of the brain—
    Those witches are given to hoax.

I 've one in my pocket, I know,
    My wife left on purpose behind her;
She bought this of Teddy-high-ho,
    The poor Caledonian grinder.

I see thee again! o'er thy middle
  Large drops of red blood now are spill'd,
Just as much as to say, diddle diddle,
  Good Duncan, pray come and be kill'd.

It leads to his chamber, I swear;
  I tremble and quake every joint—
No dog at the scent of a hare
  Ever yet made a cleverer point.
Ah, no! 'twas a dagger of straw—
  Give me blinkers, to save me from starting;
The knife that I thought that I saw
  Was nought but my eye, Betty Martin.

Now o'er this terrestrial hive
  A life paralytic is spread;
For while the one half is alive,
  The other is sleepy and dead.
King Duncan, in grand majesty,
  Has got my state-bed for a snooze;
I 've lent him my slippers, so I
  May certainly stand in his shoes.

Blow softly, ye murmuring gales!
  Ye, feet, rouse no echo in walking!
For though a dead man tells no tales,
  Dead walls are much given to talking,
This knife shall be in at the death -
  I 'll stick him, then off safely get!
Cries the world, this could not be Macbeth,
  For he 'd ne'er stick at any thing yet.

Hark, hark! 'tis the signal, by goles!
  It sounds like a funeral knell;

REJECTED ADDRESSES.

O, hear it not, Duncan ! it tolls
  To call thee to heaven or hell.
Or if you to heaven won't fly,
  But rather prefer Pluto's ether.
Only wait a few years till I die,
  And we 'll go to the devil together.
Ri fol de rol, &c.

CASE No. II.

THE STRANGER.[1]

WHO has e'er been at Drury must needs know the
    Stranger,
A wailing old Methodist, gloomy and wan,
A husband suspicious—his wife acted Ranger,
She took to her heels, and left poor Hypocon.
Her martial gallant swore that truth was a libel,
That marriage was thraldom, elopement no sin;
Quoth she, I remember the words of my Bible—
My spouse is a Stranger, and I'll take him in.
    With my sentimentalibus lachrymæ roar'em,
     And pathos and bathos delightful to see;
     And chop and change ribs, à-la-mode Germanorum,
     And high diddle ho diddle, pop tweedle dee.

To keep up her dignity no longer rich enough,
Where was her plate?—why, 'twas laid on the shelf:
Her land fuller's earth, and her great riches kitchen-
    stuff—
Dressing the dinner instead of herself.
No longer permitted in diamonds to sparkle,
Now plain Mrs. Haller, of servants the dread,
With a heart full of grief, and a pan full of charcoal,
She lighted the company up to their bed.

Incensed at her flight, her poor Hubby in dudgeon
Roam'd after his rib in a gig and a pout,

Till, tired with his journey the peevish curmudgeon
Sat down and blubber'd just like a church-spout.
One day on a bench as dejected and sad he laid,
Hearing a squash, he cried, Damn it, what 's that ?
'Twas a child of the count's, in whose service lived
        Adelaide,
Soused in the river, and squall'd like a cat.

Having drawn his young excellence up to the bank, it
Appear'd that himself was all dripping, I swear ;
No wonder he soon became dry as a blanket,
Exposed as he was to the count's *son* and *heir*,
Dear sir, quoth the count, in reward of your valour,
To shew that my gratitude is not mere talk,
You shall eat a beefsteak with my cook, Mrs. Haller,
Cut from the rump with her own knife and fork.

Behold, now the count gave the Stranger a dinner,
With gunpowder-tea, which you know brings a ball,
And, thin as he was, that he might not grow thinner,
He made of the Stranger no stranger at all.
At dinner fair Adelaide brought up a chicken—
A bird that she never had met with before ;
But, seeing him, scream'd, and was carried off kicking,
And he bang'd his nob 'gainst the opposite door.

To finish my tale without roundaboutation,
Young master and missee besieged their papa ;
They sung a quartetto in grand blubberation—
The Stranger cried Oh ! Mrs. Haller cried Ah !
Though pathos and sentiment largely are dealt in,
I have no good moral to give in exchange ;

For though she, as a cook, might be given to melting,
The Stranger's behaviour was certainly strange,
  With this sentimentalibus lachrymæ roar 'em,
  And pathos and bathos delightful to see,
  And chop and change ribs, à-la-mode Germanorum,
  And high diddle ho diddle, pop tweedle dee.

GEORGE BARNWELL.

GEORGE BARNWELL stood at the shop-door,
A customer hoping to find, sir ;
His apron was hanging before,
But the tail of his coat was behind, sir.
A lady, so painted and smart,
Cried, Sir, I've exhausted my stock o' late ;
I've got nothing left but a groat—
Could you give me four penn'orth of chocolate ?
        Rum ti, &c.

Her face was rouged up to the eyes,
Which made her look prouder and prouder ;
His hair stood on end with surprise,
And hers with pomatum and powder.
The business was soon understood ;
The lady, who wish'd to be more rich,
Cries, Sweet sir, my name is Milwood,
And I lodge at the Gunner's in Shoreditch.
        Rum ti, &c.

Now nightly he stole out, good lack !
And into her lodging would pop, sir ;
And often forgot to come back,
Leaving master to shut up the shop, sir.

Her beauty his wits did bereave—
Determined to be quite the crack O,
He lounged at the Adam and Eve,
And call'd for his gin and tobacco.
    Rum ti, &c.

And now—for the truth must be told,
Though none of a 'prentice should speak ill—
He stole from the till all the gold,
And ate the lump-sugar and treacle.
In vain did his master exclaim,
Dear George, do n't engage with that dragon;
She 'll lead you to sorrow and shame,
And leave you the devil a rag on
    Your rum ti, &c.

In vain he entreats and implores
The weak and incurable ninny,
So kicks him at last out of doors,
And Georgy soon spends his last guinea.
His uncle, whose generous purse
Had often relieved him, as I know,
Now finding him grow worse and worse,
Refused to come down with the rhino.
    Rum ti, &c.

Cried Milwood, whose cruel heart's core
Was so flinty that nothing could shock it,
If ye mean to come here any more,
Pray come with some cash in your pocket:
Make Nunky surrender his dibs,
Rub his pate with a pair of lead towels,
Or stick a knife into his ribs—
I 'll warrant he 'll then shew some bowels.
    Rum ti. &c.

A pistol he got from his love—
'Twas loaded with powder and bullet;
He trudged off to Camberwell Grove,
But wanted the courage to pull it.
There's Nunky as fat as a hog,
While I am as lean as a lizard;
Here's at you, you stingy old dog!—
And he whips a long knife in his gizard.
     Rum ti, &c.

All of you who attend to my song,
A terrible end of the farce shall see,
If you join in the inquisitive throng
That follow'd poor George to Marshalsea.
If Milwood were here, dash my wigs,
Quoth he, I would pummel and lam her well;
Had I stuck to my prunes and figs,
I ne'er had stuck Nunky at Camberwell.
     Rum ti, &c.

Their bodies were never cut down;
For granny relates with amazement,
A witch bore 'em over the town,
And hung them on Thorowgood's casement.
The neighbours, I've heard the folks say,
The miracle noisily brag on;
And the shop is, to this very day,
The sign of the George and the Dragon.
     Rum ti, &c.

XXI.

PUNCH'S APOTHEOSIS.

BY T. H.

"Rhymes the rudders are of verses,
With which, like ships, they steer their courses."
HUDIBRAS.

Scene draws, and discovers PUNCH *on a throne, surrounded by* LEAR, LADY MACBETH, MACBETH, OTHELLO, GEORGE BARNWELL, HAMLET, GHOST, MACHEATH, JULIET, FRIAR, APOTHECARY, ROMEO, *and* FALSTAFF.——PUNCH *descends and addresses them in the following*

RECITATIVE.

As manager of horses Mr. Merryman is,
So I with you am master of the ceremonies—
These grand rejoicings. Let me see, how name ye 'em ?—
Oh, in Greek lingo 'tis E-pi-thalamium.
October's tenth it is : toss up each hat to-day,
And celebrate with shouts our opening Saturday !
On this great night, 'tis settled by our manager,
That we, to please great Johnny Bull, should plan a
     jeer,
Dance a bang-up theatrical cotillion,
And put on tuneful Pegasus a pillion ;
That every soul, whether or not a cough he has,
May kick like Harlequin, and sing like Orpheus.
So come, ye pupils of Sir John Gallini,[1]
Spin up a teetotum like Angiolini :[2]

17

That John and Mrs. Bull, from ale and tea-houses,
May shout huzza for Punch's Apotheosis!

They dance and sing.

AIR—*" Sure such a day."*   TOM THUMB.

LEAR.

Dance, Regan! dance, with Cordelia and Goneril—
Down the middle, up again, poussette, and cross;
Stop, Cordelia! do not tread upon her heel,
Regan feeds on coltsfoot, and kicks like a horse.
See, she twists her mutton fists like Molyneux or Beel-
    zebub,
And t' other's clack, who pats her back, is louder far
    than hell's hubbub.
They tweak my nose and round it goes—I fear they 'll
    break the ridge of it,
Or leave it all just like Vauxhall, with only half the
    bridge of it.[3]

OMNES.

Round let us bound, for this is Punch's holyday,
Glory to Tomfoolery, huzza! huzza!

LADY MACBETH.

I kill'd the king; my husband is a heavy dunce;
He left the grooms unmassacred, then massacred the
    stud.
One loves long gloves; for mittens, like king's evidence,
Let truth with the fingers out, and won't hide blood.

MACBETH.

When spoonys on two knees implore the aid of sorcery,
To suit their wicked purposes they quickly put the laws
    awry;

With Adam I in wife may vie, for none could tell the
    use of her,
Except to cheapen golden pippins hawk'd about by
    Lucifer.

OMNES.

Round let us bound, for this is Punch's holyday,
Glory to Tomfoolery, huzza! huzza!

OTHELLO.

Wife, come to life, forgive what your black lover did,
Spit the feathers from your mouth, and munch roast
    beef;
Iago he may go and be toss'd in the coverlet
That smother'd you, because you pawn'd my handker-
    chief.

GEORGE BARNWELL.

Why, neger, so eager about your rib immaculate?
Milwood shews for hanging us they 've got an ugly
    knack o' late;
If on beauty 'stead of duty but one peeper bent he sees,
Satan waits with Dolly baits to hook in us apprentices.

OMNES.

Round let us bound, for this is Punch's holyday,
Glory to Tomfoolery, huzza! huzza!

HAMLET.

I'm Hamlet in camlet, my ap and peri-helia
The moon can fix, which lunatics makes sharp or flat.
I stuck by ill luck, enamour'd of Ophelia,
Old Polony, like a sausage, and exclaim'd, "Rat, rat!"

GHOST.

Let Gertrude sup the poison'd cup—no more I'll be an
    actor in
Such sorry food, but drink home-brew'd of Whitbread's
    manufacturing.

MACHEATH.

I'll Polly it, and folly it, and dance it quite the dandy O;
But as for tunes, I have but one, and that is Drops of
    Brandy O.

OMNES.

Round let us bound, for this is Punch's holyday,
Glory to Tomfoolery, huzza! huzza!

JULIET.

I'm Juliet Capulet, who took a dose of hellebore—
A hell-of-a-bore I found it to put on a pall.

FRIAR.

And I am the friar, who so corpulent a belly bore.

APOTHECARY.

And that is why poor skinny I have none at all.

ROMEO.

I'm the resurrection-man, of buried bodies amorous.

FALSTAFF.

I'm fagg'd to death, and out of breath, and am for quiet
    clamorous;

For though my paunch is round and stanch, I ne'er
    begin to feel it ere I
Feel that I have no stomach left for entertainment mili-
    tary.

OMNES.

Round let us bound, for this is Punch's holiday,
Glory to Tomfoolery, huzza! huzza!

                               [*Exeunt dancing.*

NOTES

TO

THE REJECTED ADDRESSES.

NOTES TO THE REJECTED ADDRESSES.

I.—LOYAL EFFUSION.

BY W. T. F. [WILLIAM THOMAS FITZGERALD.]

[Mr. Fitzgerald died 9th July, 1829, aged 70.]

"The first piece, under the name of the loyal Mr. Fitzgerald, though as good we suppose as the original, is not very interesting. Whether it be very like Mr. Fitzgerald or not, however, it must be allowed that the vulgarity, servility, and gross absurdity of the newspaper scribblers is well rendered."—JEFFREY, *Edinburgh Review.*

WILLIAM THOMAS FITZGERALD. The annotator's first personal knowledge of this gentleman was at Harry Greville's Pic-Nic Theatre, in Tottenham-street, where he personated Zanga in a wig too small for his head. The second time of seeing him was at the table of old Lord Dudley, who familiarly called him Fitz, but forgot to name him in his will. The Viscount's son (recently deceased), however, liberally supplied the omission by a donation of five thousand pounds. The third and last time of encountering him was at an anniversary dinner of the Literary Fund, at the Freemasons' Tavern. Both parties, as two of the stewards, met their brethren in a small room about half an hour before dinner. The lampooner, out of delicacy, kept aloof from the poet. The latter, however, made up to him, when the following dialogue took place:

Fitzgerald (with good humor). "Mr. ——, I mean to recite after-dinner."

Mr. ——. "Do you?"

Fitzgerald. "Yes: you'll have more of 'God bless the Regent and the Duke of York!'"

The whole of this imitation, after a lapse of twenty years, appears to the Authors too personal and sarcastic; but they may shelter themselves under a very broad mantle :

> " Let hoarse Fitzgerald bawl
> His creaking couplets in a tavern-hall."—*Byron.*

Fitzgerald actually sent in an address to the committee on the 31st of August, 1812. It was published among the other *Genuine Rejected Addresses*, in one volume, in that year. The following is an extract :——

> " The troubled shade of Garrick, hovering near,
> Dropt on the burning pile a pitying tear."

What a pity that, like Sterne's recording angel, it did not succeed in blotting the fire out forever! That failing, why not adopt Gulliver's remedy?

1. [Mr. B. Wyatt, architect of Drury Lane Theatre, son of James Wyatt, architect of the Pantheon.]

2. In plain English, the Halfpenny-hatch, then a footway through fields; but now, as the same bards sing elsewhere——

> " St. George's Fields are fields no more,
> The trowel supersedes the plough :
> Swamps, huge and inundate of yore,
> Are changed to civic villas now."

3. [Covent Garden Theatre was burnt down 20th September, 1808; Drury Lane Theatre 24th February, 1809.]

4. [The east end of St. James's Palace was destroyed by fire, 21st January, 1809. The wardrobe of Lady Charlotte Finch (alluded to in the next line) was burnt in the fire.]

5. [The Honourable William Wellesley Pole, now (1852) Earl of Mornington, married, 14th March, 1812, Catherine, daughter and heir of Sir James Tylney Long, Bart.; upon which occasion he assumed the additional names of Tylney and Long.]

II.—THE BABY'S DEBUT.

BY W. W.   [WILLIAM WORDSWORTH.]

[Mr. Wordsworth died 23d April, 1850, in his eighty-second year.]

" The Author does not, in this instance, attempt to copy any of the higher attributes of Mr. Wordsworth's poetry; but has succeeded perfectly in the imitation of his mawkish affectations of childish simplicity and nursery stammering. We hope it will make him ashamed of his *Alice Fell*, and the greater part of his last volumes—of which it is by no means a parody, but a very fair, and indeed we think a flattering, imitation."—JEFFREY, *Edinburgh Review*.

1. Jack and Nancy, as it was afterwards remarked to the Authors, are here made to come into the world at periods not sufficiently remote. The writers were then bachelors. One of them [James], unfortunately, still continues so, as he has thus recorded in his niece's album :

> "Should I seek Hymen's tie,
>   As a poet I die—
> Ye Benedicks, mourn my distresses!
>   For what little fame
>   Is annexed to my name
> Is derived from *Rejected Addresses*."

The blunder, notwithstanding, remains unrectified. The reader of poetry is always dissatisfied with emendations : they sound discordantly upon the ear, like a modern song, by Bishop or Braham, introduced in *Love in a Village*.

2. This alludes to the Young Betty mania. The writer was in the stage-box at the height of this young gentleman's popularity. One of the other occupants offered, in a loud voice, to prove that young Betty did not understand Shakespeare. " Silence !" was the cry ; but he still proceeded. " Turn him out !" was the next ejaculation. He still vociferated, " He does not understand Shakespeare ;" and was consequently shouldered into the lobby. " I 'll prove it to you," said the critic to the door-keeper. " Prove what, sir ?" " That he does not understand Shakespeare." This was Molière's housemaid with a vengeance !

Young Betty may now [1833] be seen walking about town—a portly personage, aged about forty—clad in a furred and frogged surtout; probably muttering to himself (as he has been at college), " O mihi præteritos !" &c. [He is still alive, 1852. Master Betty, or " The young Roscius," was born in 1791, and made his first appearance on a London stage as Achmet in " Barbarossa," at Covent Garden Theatre, on the first of December, 1804. He was, therefore, " not quite thirteen." He lasted two seasons.]

III.—AN ADDRESS WITHOUT A PHŒNIX.

BY S. T. P.

For an account of this anonymous gentleman, see Preface.

1. [A "Phœnix" was perhaps excusable. The first Theatre in Drury Lane was called "The Cock-pit or Phœnix Theatre." Whitbread himself wrote an address, it is said, for the occasion; like the others, it had of course a Phœnix. "But Whitbread," said Sheridan, "made more of the bird than any of them; he entered into particulars, and described its wings, beak, tail, &c.; in short, it was a *poulterer's* description of a Phœnix."]

IV.—CUI BONO?

BY LORD B. [LORD BYRON.]

[Lord Byron died 19th April, 1824, in his thirty-seventh year.]

" The author has succeeded better in copying the melody and misanthropic sentiments of *Childe Harold*, than the nervous and impetuous diction in which his noble biographer has embodied them. The attempt, however, indicates very considerable power; and the flow of the verse and the construction of the poetical period are imitated with no ordinary skill."—JEFFREY, *Edinburgh Review.*

1. This would seem to show that poet and prophet are synonymous, the noble bard having afterwards returned to England, and again quitted it, under domestic circumstances painfully notorious. His good-humored forgiveness of the Authors has already been alluded to in the preface. Nothing of this illustrious poet, however trivial, can be otherwise than interesting. "We knew him well." At Mr. Murray's dinner-table the annotator met him and Sir John Malcolm. Lord Byron talked of intending to travel in Persia. "What must I do when I set off?" said he to Sir John. "Cut off your buttons!" "My buttons! what, these metal ones?" "Yes; the Persians are in the main very honest fellows; but if you go thus bedizened, you will infallibly be murdered for your buttons!" At a dinner at Monk

Lewis's chambers in the Albany, Lord Byron expressed to the writer his determination not to go there again, adding, "I never will dine with a middle-aged man who fills up his table with young ensigns, and has looking-glass panels to his book-cases." Lord Byron, when one of the Drury-lane Committee of Management, challenged the writer to sing alternately (like the swains in Virgil) the praises of Mrs. Mardyn, the actress, who, by the bye, was hissed off the stage for an imputed intimacy of which she was quite innocent.

The contest ran as follows:

> "Wake, muse of fire, your ardent lyre,
>   Pour forth your amorous ditty,
> But first profound, in duty bound,
>   Applaud the new committee;
> Their scenic art from Thespis' cart
>   All jaded nags discarding,
> To London drove this queen of love,
>   Enchanting Mrs. Mardyn.
>
> Though tides of love around her rove,
>   I fear she'll choose Pactolus—
> In that bright surge bards ne'er immerge,
>   So I must e'en swim solus.
> 'Out, out, alas!' ill-fated gas,
>   That shin'st round Covent Garden,
> Thy ray how flat, compared with that
>   From eye of Mrs. Mardyn!"

And so on. The reader has, no doubt, already discovered "which is the justice, and which is the thief."

Lord Byron at that time wore a very narrow cravat of white sarsnet, with the shirt-collar falling over; a black coat and waistcoat, and very broad white trousers, to hide his lame foot—these were of Russia duck in the morning and jean in the evening. His watch-chain had a number of small gold seals appended to it, and was looped up to a button of his waistcoat. His face was void of colour; he wore no whiskers. His eyes were grey, fringed with long black lashes; and his air was imposing, but rather supercilious. He undervalued David Hume; denying his claim to genius on account of his bulk, and calling him, from the Heroic Epistle,

> "The fattest hog in Epicurus' sty."

One of this extraordinary man's allegations was, that "fat is an oily dropsy." To stave off its visitation, he frequently chewed tobacco in lieu of dinner, alleging that it absorbed the gastric juice of the stomach, and prevented hunger. "Pass your hand down my side," said his lordship to the writer; "can you count my ribs?" "Every one of them." "I am delighted to hear you say so. I called last week on Lady —— ; 'Ah, Lord Byron,' said she, 'how fat you grow!' But you know Lady —— is fond of saying spiteful things!" Let this gossip be summed up with the words of Lord Chesterfield, in his character of Bolingbroke : "Upon the whole, on a survey of this extraordinary character, what can we say, but 'Alas, poor human nature!'"

His favourite Pope's description of man is applicable to Byron individually :

> "Chaos of thought and passion all confused,
> Still by himself abused or disabused ;
> Created part to rise and part to fall,
> Great lord of all things, yet a slave to all :
> Sole judge of truth, in endless error hurled—
> The glory, jest, and riddle of the world."

The writer never heard him allude to his deformed foot except upon one occasion, when, entering the green-room of Drury-lane, he found Lord Byron alone, the younger Byrne and Miss Smith the dancer having just left him, after an angry conference about a *pas seul*. "Had you been a here a minute sooner," said Lord B., "you would have heard a question about dancing referred to me ;—me! (looking mournfully downward) whom fate from my birth has prohibited from taking a single step."

2. [The first stanza (see Preface) was written by James Smith; the remainder by Horace.]

3. "Holland's edifice." The late theatre was built by Holland the architect. The writer visited it on the night of its opening [April 21, 1794]. The performances were *Macbeth* and the *Virgin Unmasked*. Between the play and the farce, an excellent epilogue, written by George Colman, was excellently spoken by Miss Farren. It referred to the iron curtain which was, in the event of fire, to be let down between the stage and the audience, and which accordingly descended, by way of experiment, leaving Miss Farren between the lamps and the curtain. The fair speaker informed the audience, that should the fire break out on the stage (where it usually originates), it would thus be kept from the spectators; adding, with great solemnity—

> "No! we assure our generous benefactors
> 'Twill only burn the scenery and the actors."

A tank of water was afterwards exhibited, in the course of the epilogue, in which a wherry was rowed by a real live man, the band playing—

" And did you not hear of a jolly young waterman ?"

Miss Farren reciting—

" Sit still, there 's nothing in it,
We 'll undertake to drown you in a single minute."

" O vain thought !" as Othello says. Notwithstanding the boast in the epilogue—

" Blow, wind—come rack, in ages yet unborn,
Our castle's strength shall laugh a siege to scorn"—

the theatre fell a victim to the flames within fifteen years from the prognostic ! These preparations against fire always presuppose presence of mind and promptness in those who are to put them into action. They remind one of the dialogue in Morton's *Speed the Plough*, between Sir Able Handy and his son Bob :

" *Bob.* Zounds, the castle's on fire !
Sir A. Yes.
Bob. Where 's your patent liquid for extinguishing fire ?
Sir A. It is not mixed.
Bob. Then where 's your patent fire-escape ?
Sir A. It is not fixed.
Bob. You are never at a loss ?
Sir A. Never.
Bob. Then what do you mean to do ?
Sir A. I don't know."

4. A rather obscure mode of expression for *Jews*'-harp ; which some etymologists allege, by the way, to be a corruption of *Jaws*'-harp. No connection, therefore, with King David.

V.—HAMPSHIRE FARMER'S ADDRESS.

BY W. C. [WILLIAM COBBETT.]

[Mr. Cobbett died 18th June, 1835, aged seventy-three.]

1. [The Weekly Register, which he kept up without the failure of a single week from its first publication till his death—a period of above thirty-three years.]

2. Bagshaw.   At that time the publisher of Cobbett's Register.

3. The old Lyceum Theatre, pulled down by Mr. Arnold. That since destroyed by fire [16th Feb., 1830], was erected on its site.   [The Drury Lane Company performed at the Lyceum till the house was rebuilt.]

4. [The present colonnade in Little Russell Street formed no part of the original design ; and was erected only a few years back.]

5. An allusion to a murder then recently committed on Barnes Terrace.   [The murder (22d July, 1812) of the Count and Countess D'Antraigues (distantly related to the Bourbons) by a servant out of livery of the name of Laurence—an Italian or Piedmontese ; who made away with himself immediately after.]

6. At that time keeper of Newgate.   The present superintendent (1833) is styled governor !

7. A portentous one that made its appearance in the year 1811 ; in the midst of the war,

" With fear of change perplexing nations."

VI.—THE LIVING LUSTRES.

BY T. M.   [THOMAS MOORE.]

[Mr. Moore died 26th February, 1852, in his seventy-third year.]

" *The Living Lustres* appears to us a very fair imitation of the fantastic verses which that ingenious person, Mr. Moore, indites when he is merely gallant, and, resisting the lures of voluptuousness, is not enough in earnest to be tender."—JEFFREY, *Edinburgh Review.*

1. This alludes to two massive pillars of verd antique which then flanked the proscenium, but which have since been removed. Their colour reminds the bard of the Emerald Isle, and this causes him (*more suo*) to fly off at a tangent, and Hibernicise the rest of the poem.

VII.—THE REBUILDING.

BY R. S. [ROBERT SOUTHEY.]

[Mr. Southey died March 13, 1843, in his sixty-ninth year.]

" *The Rebuilding* is in the name of Mr. Southey, and is one of the best in the collection. It is in the style of the Kehama of that multifarious author, and is supposed to be spoken in the character of one of his Glendoveers. The imitation of the diction and measure, we think, is nearly almost perfect; and the descriptions as good as the original. It opens with an account of the burning of the old theatre, formed upon the pattern of the Funeral of Arvalan."—JEFFREY, *Edinburgh Review.*

1. For the Glendoveer, and the rest of the *dramatis personæ* of this imitation, the reader is referred to the " Curse of Kehama."

2. This couplet was introduced by the Authors by way of bravado, in answer to one who alleged that the English language contained no rhyme to chimney.

3. Apollo. A gigantic wooden figure of this deity was erected on the roof. The writer (*horrescit referens!*) is old enough to recollect the time when it was first placed there. Old Bishop, then one of the masters of Merchant Tailors' School, wrote an epigram upon the occasion, which, referring to the aforesaid figure, concluded thus :

> " Above he fills up Shakespeare's place,
> And Shakespeare fills up his below."

Very antithetical; but quære as to the meaning ? The writer, like Pluto, " long puzzled his brain" to find it out, till he was immersed " in a lower deep" by hearing Madame de Staël say, at the table of the late Lord Dillon, " Buonaparte is not a man, but a system." Inquiry was made in the course of the evening of Sir James Mackintosh as to what the lady meant. He answered, " Mass! I cannot tell." Madame de Staël repeats this apopthegm in her work on Germany. It is probably understood *there.*

4. O. P. This personage, who is alleged to have growled like a bull-dog, requires rather a lengthened note, for the edification of the rising generation. The " horns, rattles, drums," with which he is accompanied, are no inventions of the poet. The

new Covent Garden Theatre opened on the 18th September, 1809, when a cry of " Old Prices" (afterwards diminished to O. P.) burst out from every part of the house. This continued and increased in violence until the 23rd, when rattles, drums, whistles, and cat-calls, having completely drowned the voices of the actors, Mr. Kemble, the stage-manager, came forward, and said, that a committee of gentlemen had undertaken to examine the finances of the concern, and that until they were prepared with their report, the theatre would continue closed. " Name them !" was shouted from all sides. The names were declared, viz., Sir Charles Price, the Solicitor-General, the Recorder of London, the Governor of the Bank, and Mr. Angerstein. " All shareholders !" bawled a wag from the gallery. In a few days the theatre reopened : the public paid no attention to the report of the referees, and the tumult was renewed for several weeks with increased violence. The proprietors now sent in hired bruisers to *mill* the refractory into subjection. This irritated most of their former friends, and, amongst the rest, the annotator, who accordingly wrote the song of " Heigh-ho, says Kemble," which was caught up by the ballad-singers, and sung under Mr. Kemble's house-windows in Great Russell-street. A dinner was given at the Crown and Anchor Tavern in the Strand, to celebrate the victory obtained by W. Clifford in his action against Brandon the box-keeper, for assaulting him for wearing the letters O. P. in his hat. At this dinner Mr. Kemble attended, and matters were compromised by allowing the advanced price (seven shillings) to the boxes. The writer remembers a former riot of a similar sort at the same theatre (in the year 1782), when the price to the boxes was raised from five shillings to six. That tumult, however, only lasted three nights.

5. " From the knobb'd bludgeon to the taper switch." This image is not the creation of the poets : it sprang from reality. The Authors happened to be at the Royal Circus when " God save the King" was called for, accompanied by a cry of " Stand up !" and " Hats off !" An inebriated naval lieutenant, perceiving a gentleman in an adjoining box slow to obey the call, struck his hat off with his stick, exclaiming, " Take off your hat, sir !" The other thus assaulted proved to be, unluckily for the lieutenant, Lord Camelford, the celebrated bruiser and duellist. A set-to in the lobby was the consequence, where his lordship

quickly proved victorious. "The devil is not so black as he is painted," said one of the Authors to the other; "let us call upon Lord Camelford, and tell him that we were witnesses of his being first assaulted." The visit was paid on the ensuing morning at Lord Camelford's lodgings, in Bond-street. Over the fire-place in the drawing-room were ornaments strongly expressive of the pugnacity of the peer. A long thick bludgeon lay horizontally supported by two brass hooks. Above this was placed parallel ones of lesser dimensions, until a pyramid of weapons gradually arose, tapering to a horsewhip:

> "Thus all below was strength, and all above was grace."

Lord Camelford received his visitants with great civility, and thanked them warmly for the call; adding, that their evidence would be material, it being his intention to indict the lieutenant for an assault. "All I can say in return is this," exclaimed the peer with great cordiality, "if ever I see you engaged in a row, upon my soul, I'll stand by you." The Authors expressed themselves thankful for so potent an ally, and departed. In about a fortnight afterwards [March 7, 1804] Lord Camelford was shot in a duel with Mr. Best.

6. *Veeshnoo.* The late Mr. Whitbread.

7. *Levy.* An insolvent Israelite who [18th January, 1810] threw himself from the top of the Monument a short time before. An inhabitant of Monument-yard informed the writer, that he happened to be standing at his door talking to a neighbour; and looking up at the top of the pillar, exclaimed, "Why, here's the flag coming down." "Flag!" answered the other, "it's a man!" The words were hardly uttered when the suicide fell within ten feet of the speakers.

VIII.—DRURY'S DIRGE.

BY LAURA MATILDA.

"'Drury's Dirge,' by Laura Matilda, is not of the first quality. The verses, to be sure, are very smooth and very nonsensical— as was intended; but they are not so good as Swift's celebrated Song by a Person of Quality; and are so exactly in the same measure, and on the same plan, that it is impossible to avoid making the comparison."—JEFFREY, *Edinburgh Review.*

1. The Authors, as in gallantry bound, wish this lady to continue anonymous.

IX.—A TALE OF DRURY LANE.
BY W. S.   [SIR WALTER SCOTT.]
[Sir Walter Scott died 21st September, 1832, in his sixty-second year.]

"From the parody of Walter Scott we know not what to select —it is all good. The effect of the fire on the town, and the description of a fireman in his official apparel, may be quoted as amusing specimens of the *misapplication* of the style and metre of Mr. Scott's admirable romances."— *Quarterly Review.*

" ' A Tale of Drury,' by Walter Scott, is, upon the whole, admirably executed ; though the introduction is rather tame. The burning is described with the mighty minstrel's characteristic love of localities . . . The catastrophe is described with a spirit not unworthy of the name so venturously assumed by the describer." —JEFFREY, *Edinburgh Review.*

1. Sir Walter Scott informed the annotator, that at one time he intended to print his collected works, and had pitched upon this identical quotation as a motto ;—a proof that sometimes great wits jump with little ones.

2. Alluding to the then great distance between the picture-frame, in which the green curtain was set, and the band. For a justification of this, see below—" DR. JOHNSON."

3. [The old name for London :

> For poets you can never want 'em
> Spread through Augusta Trinobantum.—SWIFT.

Thomson in his " Seasons" calls it " huge Augusta."]

4. Old Bedlam, at that time, stood " close by London Wall." It was built after the model of the Tuileries, which is said to have given the French king great offence. In front of it Moorfields extended, with broad gravel walks crossing each other at right angles. These the writer well recollects ; and

Rivaz, an underwriter at Lloyd's, has told him, that he remembered when the merchants of London would parade these walks on a summer evening with their wives and daughters, but now, as a punning brother bard sings,

" **Moorfields are fields no more.**"

5. [A narrow passage immediately adjoining Drury Lane Theatre, and so called from the Vineyard attached to Covent or Convent Garden.]

6. [The Hand-in-hand Insurance Office was one of the very first insurance offices established in London. To make the engineer of the office thus early in the race, is a piece of historical accuracy intended, it is said, on the part of the writer.]

7. Whitbread's shears. An economical experiment of that gentleman. The present portico, towards Bridges Street, was afterwards erected under the lesseeship of Elliston, whose portrait in the Exhibition was thus noticed in the Examiner: " Portrait of the great Lessee, in his favourite character of Mr. Elliston."

X.—JOHNSON'S GHOST.

" Samuel Johnson is not so good: the measure and solemnity of his sentences, in all the limited variety of their structure, are indeed imitated with singular skill: but the diction is caricatured in a vulgar and unpleasing degree. To make Johnson call a door ' a ligneous barricado,' and its knocker and bell its ' frappant and tintinnabulant appendages,' is neither just nor humorous; and we are surprised that a writer who has given such extraordinary proofs of his talent for finer ridicule and fairer imitation, should have stooped to a vein of pleasantry so low, and so long ago exhausted; especially as, in other passages of the same piece, he has shown how well qualified he was both to catch and render the true characteristics of his original. The beginning, for example, we think excellent."—JEFFREY, *Edinburgh Review*.

1. The celebrated Lord Chesterfield, whose letters to his Son, according to Dr. Johnson, inculcate " the manners of a dancing master and the morals of a —," &c.

2. Lord Mayor of the theatric sky. This alludes to Leigh Hunt, who, in *The Examiner*, at this time kept the actors in hot water.

Dr. Johnson's argument is, like many of his other arguments, specious, but untenable; that which it defends has since been abandoned as impracticable. Mr. Whitbread contended that the actor was like a portrait in a picture, and accordingly placed the green curtain in a gilded frame remote from the foot-lights; alleging that no performer should mar the illusion by stepping out of the frame. Dowton was the first actor who, like Manfred's ancestor in the *Castle of Otranto*, took the liberty of abandoning the canon. "Don't tell me of frames and pictures," ejaculated the testy comedian; "if I can't be heard by the audience in the frame, I 'll walk out of it!" The proscenium has since been new-modelled, and the actors thereby brought nearer to the audience.

XI.—THE BEAUTIFUL INCENDIARY.

BY THE HON. W. S.

[WILLIAM ROBERT SPENCER. The best writer of *vers de société* in our time. He died at Paris in October, 1834, aged 65; and his poems were published in London the next year in one volume, 12mo.]

"'The Beautiful Incendiary,' by the Honourable W. Spencer, is also an imitation of great merit. The flashy, fashionable, artificial style of this writer, with his confident and extravagant compliments, can scarcely be said to be parodied in such lines."—JEFFREY, *Edinburgh Review.*

1. Sobriety, &c. The good humour of the poet upon occasion of this parody has been noticed in the Preface. "It's all very well for once," said he afterwards, in comic confidence, at his villa at Petersham, "but do n't do it again. I had been almost forgotten when you revived me; and now all the newspapers and reviews ring with "this fashionable, trashy author.'" The sand and "filings of glass," mentioned in the last stanza, are referable to the well-known verses of the poet apologising to a lady for having paid an unconscionably long morning visit; and where, alluding to Time, he says,

> "All his sands are diamond sparks,
> That glitter as they pass."

Few men in society have more " gladdened life" than this poet.
He now [1833] resides in Paris, and may thence make the grand
tour without the aid of an interpreter—speaking, as he does,
French, Italian, and German, as fluently as English.

2. [10th of October, 1812, the day of opening.]

3. Congreve's plug.   The late Sir William Congreve had made
a model of Drury Lane Theatre, to which was affixed an engine
that, in the event of fire, was made to play from the stage into
every box in the house.   The writer, accompanied by Theodore
Hook, went to see the model at Sir William's house in Cecil
Street.   "Now I'll duck Whitbread!" said Hook, seizing the
water-pipe whilst he spoke, and sending a torrent of water into
the brewer's box.

4. See Byron, *afterwards*, in *Don Juan* :—

" For flesh is grass, which Time mows down to hay."

But as Johnson says of Dryden, "His known wealth was so
great, he might borrow without any impeachment of his credit."

XII.—FIRE AND ALE.

BY M. G. L. [MATTHEW GREGORY LEWIS.]

[Mr. Lewis died 14th May, 1818, in his forty-third year.]

" ' Fire and Ale,' by M. G. Lewis, exhibits not only a faithful
copy of the spirited, loose, and flowing versification of that singu-
lar author, but a very just representation of that mixture of
extravagance and jocularity which has impressed most of his
writings with the character of a sort of farcical horror."—JEFFREY,
Edinburgh Review.

MATTHEW GREGORY LEWIS, commonly called *Monk* Lewis, from
his once popular romance of that name, was a good-hearted man,
and, like too many of that fraternity, a disagreeable one—verbose,
disputatious, and paradoxical.   His *Monk* and *Castle Spectre* ele-
vated him into fame ; and he continued to write ghost-stories till,
following as he did in the wake of Mrs. Radcliffe, he quite over-
stocked the market.   Lewis visited his estates in Jamaica, and
came back perfectly negro-bitten.   He promulgated a new code of
laws in the island, for the government of his sable subjects: one

may serve as a specimen : " Any slave who commits murder shall have his head shaved, and be confined three days and nights in a dark room."   Upon occasion of printing these parodies, *Monk* Lewis said to Lady H[olland], " Many of them are very fair, but mine is not at all like ; they have made me write burlesque, which I never do."   " You don't know your own talent," answered the lady.

Lewis aptly described himself, as to externals, in the verses affixed to his *Monk*, as having

" A graceless form and dwarfish stature."

He had, moreover, large grey eyes, thick features, and an inexpressive countenance.   In talking, he had a disagreeable habit of drawing the fore-finger of his right hand across his right eye-lid. He affected, in conversation, a sort of dandified, drawling tone ; young Harlowe, the artist, did the same.   A foreigner who had but a slight knowledge of the English language might have concluded, from their cadences, that they were little better than fools—"just a born goose," as Terry the actor used to say. Lewis died on his passage homeward from Jamaica, owing to a dose of James's powders injudiciously administered by " his own mere motion."   He wrote various plays, with various success : he had admirable notion of dramatic construction, but the goodness of his scenes and incidents was marred by the badness of his dialogue.

XIII.—PLAYHOUSE MUSINGS.

BY S. T. C.   [S. T. COLERIDGE.]

[Mr. Coleridge died 25th July, 1834, in his sixty-second year.]

" Mr. Coleridge will not, we fear, be as much entertained as we were with his ' Playhouse Musings,' which begin with characteristic pathos and simplicity, and put us much in mind of the affecting story of old Poulterer's mare."   *Quarterly Review.*

" ' Playhouse Musings,' by Mr. Coleridge, a piece which is unquestionably Lakish, though we cannot say that we recognise in it any of the peculiar traits of that powerful and misdirected genius whose name it has borrowed.   We rather think, however, that the tuneful brotherhood will consider it as a respectable eclogue."—JEFFREY, *Edinburgh Review.*

1. " He of Blackfriars' Road," viz., the late Rev. Rowland Hill, who is said to have preached a sermon congratulating his congregation on the catastrophe.

2. " Oh, Mr. Whitbread!"   Sir William Grant, then Master of the Rolls, repeated this passage aloud at a Lord Mayor's dinner, to the no small astonishment of the writer, who happened to sit within ear-shot.

3. " Padmanaba," viz., in a pantomime called *Harlequin in Padmanaba.* This elephant [Chunee], some years afterwards, was exhibited over Exeter 'Change, where, the reader will remember, it was found necessary [March, 1826] to destroy the poor animal by discharges of musketry.   When he made his entrance in the pantomime above mentioned, Johnson, the machinist of the rival house, exclaimed, " I should be very sorry if I could not make a better elephant than that !"   Johnson was right: we go to the theatre to be pleased with the skill of the imitator, and not to look at the reality.

XIV.—DRURY LANE HUSTINGS.

A NEW HALFPENNY BALLAD.

BY A PIC-NIC POET.

" ' A New Halfpenny Ballad,' by a Pic-Nic Poet, is a good imitation of what was not worth imitating—that tremendous mixture of vulgarity, nonsense, impudence, and miserable puns, which, under the name of humorous songs, rouses our polite audiences to a far higher pitch of rapture than Garrick or Siddons ever was able to inspire."—JEFFREY, *Edinburgh Review.*

1. [Mr. Whitbread—it need hardly be added for the present generation of Londoners—was a celebrated brewer.   Fifty years hence, and the allusion in the text may require a note which, perhaps, even now (1851), is scarcely out of place.]

18

XV.—ARCHITECTURAL ATOMS.

TRANSLATED BY DR. B.   [DR. THOMAS BUSBY, MUS. DOC.]

Dr. Busby gave living recitations of his translations of *Lucretius*, with tea and bread-and-butter. He sent in a real Address to the Drury Lane Committee, which was really rejected. The present imitation professes to be recited by the translator's son. The poet here, again, was a prophet. A few evenings after the opening of the Theatre, Dr. Busby sat with his son in one of the stage-boxes. The latter, to the astonishment of the audience, at the end of the play, stepped from the box upon the stage, with his father's real rejected address in his hand, and began to recite it as follows:—

> " When energizing objects men pursue,
> What are the prodigies they cannot do?"

Raymond, the stage-manager, accompanied by a constable, at this moment walked upon the stage, and handed away the juvenile *dilettante* performer.

The doctor's classical translation was thus noticed in one of the newspapers of the day, in the column of births:—" Yesterday at his house in Queen Anne Street, Dr. Busby of a stillborn *Lucretius.*"

" In one single point the parodist has failed—there is a certain Dr. Busby, whose supposed address is a translation called 'Architectural Atoms, intended to be recited by the translator's son.' Unluckily, however, for the wag who had prepared this fun, the *genuine serious absurdity* of Dr. Busby and his son has cast all the humour into the shade. The doctor from the boxes, and the son from the stage, have actually endeavoured, it seems, to recite addresses, which they call *monologues* and *unalogues;* and which, for extravagant folly, tumid meanness, and vulgar affectation, set all the powers of parody at utter defiance."— *Quarterly Review.*

" Of 'Architectural Atoms,' translated by Dr. Busby, we can say very little more than that they appear to us to be far more capable of combining into good poetry than the few lines we were able to read of the learned doctor's genuine address in the newspapers. They might pass, indeed, for a very tolerable imitation of Darwin."—JEFFREY, *Edinburgh Review.*

" 1. Winsor's patent gas"—at that time in its infancy. The first place illumined by it was [Jan. 28th, 1807] the Carlton-house side of Pall Mall; the second, Bishopsgate Street. The writer attended a lecture given by the inventor: the charge of admittance was three shillings, but, as the inventor was about to apply to parliament, members of both houses were admitted gratis. The writer and a fellow-jester assumed the parts of senators at a short notice. " Members of parliament!" was their important ejaculation at the door of entrance. " What places, gentlemen?" "Old Sarum and Bridgewater." " Walk in, gentlemen." Luckily, the real Simon Pures did not attend. This Pall Mall illumination was further noticed in *Horace in London :*

> " And Winsor lights, with flame of gas,
> Home, to King's Place, his mother."

2. " Ticket-nights." This phrase is probably unintelligible to the untheatrical portion of the community, which may now be said to be all the world except the actors. Ticket-nights are those whereon the inferior actors club for a benefit : each distributes as many tickets of admission as he is able among his friends. A motley assemblage is the consequence ; and as each actor is encouraged by his own set, who are not in general playgoing people, the applause comes (as Chesterfield says of Pope's attempts at wit) " generally unseasonably, and too often unsuccessfully."

3. [*Originally :*—" Back to the *bottom leaping with a bound,*" altered in 1833.]

XVI.—THEATRICAL ALARM-BELL.
BY THE EDITOR OF THE M. P.
[MORNING POST.]

This journal was, at the period in question, rather remarkable for the use of the figure called by the rhetoricians *catachresis.* The Bard of Avon may be quoted in justification of its adoption, when he writes of taking arms against a sea, and seeking a bubble in the mouth of a cannon. *The Morning Post,* in the year 1812, congratulated its readers on having stripped off Cobbett's mask and discovered his cloven foot; adding, that it was high time to give the hydra-head of Faction a rap on the knuckles !

XVII.—THE THEATRE.

BY THE REV. G. C. [THE REV. GEORGE CRABBE.]

[Mr. Crabbe died 3rd February, 1832, in his seventy-eighth year.]

"'The Theatre,' by the Rev. G. Crabbe, we rather think, is the best piece in the collection. It is an exquisite and most masterly imitation, not only of the peculiar style, but of the taste, temper, and manner of description of that most original author ; and can hardly be said to be in any respect a caricature of that style or manner—except in the excessive profusion of puns and verbal jingles—which, though undoubtedly to be ranked among his characteristics, are never so thick sown in his original works as in this admirable imitation. It does not aim, of course, at any shadow of his pathos or moral sublimity, but seems to us to be a singularly faithful copy of his passages of mere description."— JEFFREY, *Edinburgh Review*.

The Rev. GEORGE CRABBE. The writer's first interview with this poet, who may be designated Pope in worsted stockings, took place at William Spencer's villa at Petersham, close to what that gentleman called his gold-fish pond, though it was scarcely three feet in diameter, throwing up a *jet d'eau* like a thread. The venerable bard, seizing both the hands of his satirist, exclaimed, with a good-humoured laugh, " Ah ! my old enemy, how do you do ?" In the course of conversation, he expressed great astonishment at his popularity in London ; adding, " In my own village they think nothing of me." The subject happening to be the inroads of time upon beauty, the writer quoted the following lines :—

> " Six years had pass'd, and forty ere the six,
> When Time began to play his usual tricks:
> My locks, once comely in a virgin's sight,
> Locks of pure brown, now felt th' encroaching white:
> Gradual each day I liked my horses less,
> My dinner more—I learnt to play at chess."

" That 's very good !" cried the bard ;—" whose is it ?" " Your own." " Indeed ! hah ! well, I had quite forgotten it." Was this affectation, or was it not ? In sooth, he seemed to push simplicity to puerility. This imitation contained in manuscript the following lines, after describing certain Sunday newspaper critics

who were supposed to be present at a new play, and who were
rather heated in their politics :——

> " Hard is the task who edits—thankless job !
> A Sunday journal for the factious mob :
> With bitter paragraph and caustic jest,
> He gives to turbulence the day of rest :
> Condemn'd, this week, rash rancour to instil,
> Or thrown aside, the next, for one who will :
> Alike undone or if he praise or rail
> (For this affects his safety, that his sale),
> He sinks at last, in luckless limbo set,
> If loud for libel, and if dumb for debt."

They were, however, never printed ; being, on reflection, con-
sidered too serious for the occasion.

It is not a little extraordinary that Crabbe, who could write
with such vigour, should descend to such lines as the following :

> " Something had happen'd wrong about a bill
> Which was not drawn with true mercantile skill,
> So, to amend it, I was told to go
> And seek the firm of Clutterbuck and Co."   .

Surely "Emanuel Jennings," compared with the above, rises
to sublimity.

1. [You were more feeling than I was, when you read the ex-
cellent parodies of the young men who wrote the "Rejected
Addresses." There is a little ill-nature—and I take the liberty
of adding, undeserved ill-nature—in their prefatory address ; but
in their versification they have done me admirably. They are
extraordinary men ; but it is easier to imitate style than to fur-
nish matter.—CRABBE (*Works*, i. vol. Ed., p. 81.)]

2. [A street and parish in Lime Street Ward, London—chiefly
inhabited by Jews.]

XVIII., XIX., XX.—TO THE MANAGING COMMITTEE OF THE NEW DRURY LANE THEATRE.

"We come next to three ludicrous parodies—of the story of
The Stranger, of *George Barnwell*, and of the dagger-scene in
Macbeth, under the signature of Momus Medlar. They are as
good, we think, as that sort of thing can be, and remind us of the

happier efforts of Colman, whose less successful fooleries are pro-
fessedly copied in the last piece in the volume."—JEFFREY, *Edin-
burgh Review.*

1. [A translation from Kotzebue by Thompson, and first acted
at Drury Lane, 24 March, 1798.   Mrs. Siddons was famous in
the part of Mrs. Haller.]

2. [See Percy's Reliques of Ancient English Poetry, vol. iii.;
and Lillo's tragedy, "The London Merchant; or, the History of
George Barnwell." 8vo.   1731.]

XXI.—PUNCH'S APOTHEOSIS.

BY T. H.

[Mr. Hook died 24th August, 1841, in his fifty-third year.]

THEODORE HOOK, at that time a very young man, and the com-
panion of the annotator in many wild frolics.   The cleverness of
his subsequent prose compositions has cast his early stage songs
into oblivion.   This parody was, in the second edition, transferred
from Colman to Hook.

1. Then Director of the Opera House.
2. At that time the chief dancer at this establishment.
3. Vauxhall Bridge then, like the Thames Tunnel at present
[1833] stood suspended in the middle of that river.

THE END.

THE HUMOROUS POETRY OF
THE ENGLISH LANGUAGE,
From Chaucer to Saxe.

Narratives, Satires, Enigmas, Burlesques, Parodies, Travesties, Epigrams, Epitaphs, Translations, including all the most celebrated Comic Poems from the Anti-Jacobin, Rejected Addresses, Ingoldsby Legends, Cruikshank's Omnibus, Bentley, Blackwood, and Punch. With a collection of more than two hundred Epigrams, and the choicest humorous poetry of Peter Pindar, Cowper, Thackeray, Praed, Swift, Scott, Holmes, "Anon," Gay, Burns, Southey, Saxe, Hood, Prior, Coleridge, Byron, Moore, Lowell, etc. With notes explanatory and biographical,

By Jas. Parton,

Author of " Life of Horace Greeley."

1 Vol. 12mo. 689 pp. Price $1.50.

THE LETTERS OF

MADAME DE SÉVIGNE

TO HER DAUGHTER AND FRIENDS.

EDITED BY MRS. SARAH J. HALE,

Author of " Northwood," " Woman's Record," etc.
Being Vol. I. of the Library of Standard Letters.

1 Vol., 12mo.   438 pp.   Price $1.25.

" Madame de Sévigné, whose letters are here published, was one of those gifted ladies whose polished manners and brilliant intellectual accomplishments imparted such luster to the Court of Louis the Fourteenth ; and her letters—most of which were addressed to her daughter—not only give particulars which afford a perfect picture of the times, but are also distinguished by the easy gracefulness of their style, and the charming maternal tenderness which shines through all."—*Boston Traveler.*

" As a model of epistolary correspondence, these letters stand unsurpassed."—*New York Dispatch.*

" Apart from the personal interest in Madame de Sévigné which the work naturally excites, the volume affords a good insight into the manners and customs of the age in which she lived, and is also valuable to the historical student who desires to peruse a pleasant picture of social life in France two centuries ago."—*Boston Transcript.*

" Her letters are instructing and entertaining, embracing nearly every variety of subject."—*Phila. Sat. Evening Mail.*

" Her letters to her daughter and friends have ever been regarded as models of this, one of the most difficult and delightful species of composition."—*N. Y. Observer.*

" These letters are written in simple, easy periods, and are remarkable for that combination of wit, wisdom, and charity, which is so rare and so attractive."—*N. Y. Mirror.*

" Their lively pictures of French manners, and their trustworthy accounts of historical events, will always secure to them a large circle of intelligent readers."—*New York Tribune.*

" As a family book, this volume can not but be welcome."—*Boston Post.*

" While her letters are written with such almost unparalleled grace and beauty, they are highly characteristic of the period in which they were written, and reveal many curious facts illustrative of French society."—*Boston Puritan Recorder.*

" Nothing can exceed the grace, the liveliness, the simple beauty of these letters."—*Chicago Christian Times.*

" The irresistible charms of their easy, flowing diction, not only reflect the chameleon hues of an acute and versatile intellect, but are the vehicles of high moral and religious sentiments."—*Detroit Free Press.*

" There is a point and piquancy about these letters ; a ready, graceful, off-hand style, that is truly captivating."—*Phila. Dollar Newspaper.*

" No praise can be too extravagant when applied to the letters and genius of Madame de Sévigné."—*Boston Christian Freeman.*

" Her letters admit the reader into the inner recesses of French chateaux and salons, and make him acquainted with the ' very age and body of the time, its form and pressure.' "—*N. Y. Life Illustrated.*

" They afford a glimpse of French society at a period when great men and distinguished women were upon the stage, and abound in thoughts which are suggestive."—*Buffalo Courier.*

" They are delightful specimens of epistolary correspondence."—*Boston Journal.*

THE LETTERS OF
LADY MARY W. MONTAGUE.

Edited by Mrs. Sarah J. Hale,

Author of "Woman's Record," "Northwood," "Vigil of Love," etc., being Volume II. of the "Library of Standard Letters."

1 Vol. 12mo. 408 pp. Price $1.25.

"The work can hardly fail of interesting deeply the American reader. Lady Mary lived and wrote in the first half of the eighteenth century, when our land was a component part of the British Empire, and consequently her genius and her fame are ours by inheritance. Her letters will be found valuable, as well as amusing, aiding the student of history to catch the manners and opinions of English society in high life, then the dominant power of the realm, at the time Benjamin Franklin and his co-patriots in this western world were working out the problem of American independence and popular sovereignty."

"They are the utterances of a cultivated lady of the close of the last century; they were addressed to members of her own family, to distinguished ladies, and to literary characters, among whom Pope is conspicuous, and they will thus afford considerable insight into the various phases of English society half a century ago."—*Utica (N. Y.) Observer.*

"The letters of Lady Montague are singular productions—at times womanly, then masculine, then possessing an element which goes beyond and outside of each. They have intellect, soul and passion; now love, now hatred, now poetry, now fire—again sad, then gay, show ring with the sweets of roses, or, as the mood changes, with the bitter of gall. So much diversity of mood, intellect, feeling, we rarely find combined in one mind."—*Boston Bee.*

"The letters are valuable and amusing, and afford a curious and instructive insight into English manners and opinions."—*Boston Transcript.*

"They are full of a beautiful simplicity, which charms us no less than their genius and wit."—*N. Y. Eve. Mirror.*

"The most admirable letters written in our language."—*Boston Intelligencer.*

"They are, indeed, models of epistolary communications."—*Newark Advertiser.*

"Everybody ought to study these letters for their style."—*Peterson's Magazine.*

"They are written in a style surpassingly elegant, yet free from all affectation or pretension."—*N. Y. Family Visitor.*

"She portrays character and scenery with admirable effect."—*Concord (N. H.) Statesman.*

"Her letters are written with grace and spirit, and often with positive beauty."—*N. Y. Examiner.*

"The biographical sketch of the authoress (by Mrs. Hale), invests her writings with a peculiar interest from the sympathy it can not but awaken for one so gifted and beautiful, and each succeeding page deepens the interest, and leads the reader on from letter to letter."—*Detroit Advertiser.*

"They will be found valuable as well as amusing—instructive as well as entertaining."—*Phila. Inquirer.*

MR. HERBERT'S NEW WORK.

WAGER OF BATTLE,

A TALE OF SAXON SLAVERY IN SHERWOOD FOREST.

BY HENRY W. HERBERT, ESQ.,

Author of "Marmaduke Wyvil," "Henry VIII. and his Six Wives," etc., etc.

1 Vol., 12mo. Price $1.

" The story transports us back to the English forests, before the Norman and Saxon races had melted into one, and brings up a succession of domestic and rural pictures that are bright with the freshness of that primeval time. The present work is even richer in the elements of popular interest than Mr. Herbert's previous fictitious compositions, and will deservedly increase his reputation as a brilliant and vigorous novelist."—*New York Tribune.*

" 'The Wager of Battle' is the best of Herbert's works."—*N. Y. Sunday Dispatch.*

" The story is one of intense interest."—*N. Y. Daily News.*

" The condition of the serf—the born thrall of that period, is accurately delineated, and the life, daily occupations, and language of the twelfth century placed vividly before the reader. There is no incident in the book that is tame and lifeless."—*N. Y. Picayune.*

" Herbert is the best living historical novelist."—*Cor. Boston Transcript.*

" It is a very beautiful tale—in its descriptive scenes, and in much of its coloring, reminding us more than once of Ivanhoe."—*Boston Traveler.*

" In this work, Mr. Herbert has bent his acknowledged genius to the agreeable task of creating a succession of highly attractive and interesting scenes, which completely transfer us, for the time, to the wild age to which they relate."—*Portland Eastern Argus.*

" This is an exceedingly able story, one which is sure to find favor with all classes of readers."—*Phila. Sunday Dispatch.*

" We like a good historical novel, and we know of no living writer better qualified to write one than Henry W. Herbert. In the present volume he gives a fresh, bold picture of Saxon serfdom in England before yet the two races of Norman and Saxon were mingled into one. The delineation of outward habits, and the customs of the time, are admirably done, and the story is one that can not fail to interest all who read it."—*Gospel Banner, Augusta.*

" A story of great interest. * * * Written in an attractive style. * * * Built upon a well-arranged plot. * * * The best of Herbert's works."—*Dayton (O.) Empire.*

" Herbert is a pleasing, busy, instructive, successful novelist historian."—*Boston Christian Times.*

" It displays much dramatic skill and felicity of description, and accurately depicts the manners, customs, and institutions of the Saxons and the Normans, at the time of their fusion into the great English race."—*N. Y. Chronicle.*

" Mr. Herbert's style is clear and fine, and the plot of his story well constructed."—*State of Maine.*

" One of the best stories of the author."—*Cor. Boston Traveler.*

NAPOLEON AS LOVER AND HUSBAND.

THE CONFIDENTIAL CORRESPONDENCE

OF THE

EMPEROR NAPOLEON AND EMPRESS JOSEPHINE,

Including Letters from the time of their Marriage until the
Death of Josephine, and also several Private Letters
from the Emperor to his brother Joseph, and
other important personages. With numerous
illustrative notes and anecdotes.

By John S. C. Abbott,

Author of " The History of Napoleon," etc.

404 pp. 12mo. Price $1.25.

LANMERE.

By Mrs. Julia C. R. Dorr,

Author of "Farmingdale."

1 Vol., 12mo. Price $1.25.

"In the delineation of character Mrs. Dorr is almost equal to Currer Bell, and nothing can be more true to nature than her drawing of Mrs. Allison, Margaret, and the bewitching Jessie."—*Buffalo Republic.*

"The style of the work is certainly beautiful—at times it almost melts the reader to tears by its pathetic descriptions, and captivates by its truthfulness to nature."—*Hudson Star.*

"We know of no child heroines, even among those of Dickens, more delicately drawn than Bessie."—*N. Y. Eve. Mirror.*

"'Lanmere' is no ordinary production; aside from the intense interest the story must create in the mind of every reader—aside from the natural and ingenious manner in which the plot is developed, and the faithful portrayal of characters, whose exact counterparts exist in our very midst, there is a deep moral which will find an abiding place in every heart."—*Boston Yankee Privateer.*

"It is eminently a home book—a book for the fireside, for mothers and daughters."—*Albion American.*

"A splendid domestic romance, illustrating the offices of natural government, and giving us a greater feast than in her former essay."—*Boston Intelligencer.*

"One can not rise from its perusal without feeling that the heart has been put in closer and happier community with humanity and heaven."—*Boston Family Visitor.*

"Mrs. Dorr excels in her illustrations of Yankee character, and 'Dibby,' the faithful, tidy, and industrious housekeeper, will be instantly recognized as a genuine study from nature."—*New York Eve. Post.*

"It is written in a style of calm beauty, and yet abounds in vigorous thought, and in excellent lessons which are fitted at once to impress and improve the heart."—*Boston Puritan Recorder.*

"It is a story of New England domestic life, told without exaggeration, full of gentleness and sweetness, and all manner of delicate refinements."—*Phila. Inquirer.*

"A delightful book—one that may be read with pleasure and profit around the home fireside."—*Hallowell (Me.) Gazette.*

"A truthful village tale well told."—*Boston Daily Courier.*

"A quiet, cosy, comfortable tale of every-day life, worked up artfully and naturally, and abounding with passages full of attractive spirit and remarkable beauty."—*N. Y. Sunday Times.*

"Written in a simple, easy, natural style, abounding in beautiful and life-like delineations of character, governed always by a nice and appreciative sense of the true, the pure, and the healthful, in intellectual entertainment."—*Fulton Gazette.*

Check Out More Titles From HardPress Classics Series In this collection we are offering thousands of classic and hard to find books. This series spans a vast array of subjects — so you are bound to find something of interest to enjoy reading and learning about.

Subjects:
Architecture
Art
Biography & Autobiography
Body, Mind &Spirit
Children & Young Adult
Dramas
Education
Fiction
History
Language Arts & Disciplines
Law
Literary Collections
Music
Poetry
Psychology
Science
…and many more.

Visit us at www.hardpress.net

CPSIA information can be obtained
at www.ICGtesting.com
Printed in the USA
BVHW071051120819
555627BV00004B/356/P